Finding
LALLA'S ANNA

ANNA DAO

where words connect

Finding

LALLA'S ANNA

ISBN: 978-1-959811-40-4 (Paperback)
ISBN: 978-1-959811-41-1 (e-book)
Library of Congress Control Number: 2024903820

Cover Design: Christina Panagiotis
Interior Design: Amit Dey
Illustrations and Photographs: Anna Dao
Author Cover Photo and Makeup: Christopher Michael

Published by Wordeee in the United States, Beacon, New York 2024
Website: www.wordeee.com
X Formerly Twitter: wordeeeupdates
Facebook: facebook.com/wordeee/
e-mail: contact@wordeee.com

ADVANCE PRAISE
FOR FINDING LALLA'S ANNA

Finding Lalla's Anna is such a heartwarming and honest story. A journey about finding one's true self, and trust in a loving Creator. It's filled with gems of wisdom, hope, perseverance, and unwavering faith. From beginning to end, it offers an homage to the knowledge of our ancestors and grandmothers. This deeply personal yet profoundly universal story touched my heart, moving me to both tears and laughter. It made me feel seen and understood…reminding me to "be more kind to myself." A story about trials and triumphs. It exemplifies growth, both spiritually and in the physical world, reflecting the true meaning of healing and happiness. I feel incredibly moved and inspired.

—Maria Owens-Fajardo
Creative Producer - NYC

"This is the beautiful love story between a grandmother and grandchild. Filled with lessons of love, laughter and tears, *Finding Lalla's Anna* is a heart tugging story that really shines a light on intergenerational relationships and the beautiful wisdom that is lovingly passed from grandparent to grandchild."

—Tamyra Alicia
Multidisciplinary Artist

"*Finding Lalla's Anna* is perfectly authentic yet relatable antiquated wisdom pleasantly curated for modern day troubles and certainly a remedy for the everyday scenarios each soul confronts within the existence and experience of life. Whether be it woes of self-discovery, reclaiming inner happiness or instilling self confidence in a dark period of life and tribulation, the well-packaged quotes from Lalla blended with the veritable story of author Anna Dao provide an intimate experience leaving the reader refreshed and renewed to continue their own personal journey called life."

—*Marcus G. Monroe, Author*
Deranged Book Series 1-5
Co-host, Spiritual Advisory Podcast

"An incredible journey of a little girl growing up with lots of pain and heartache, finding her way through life by investigating and absorbing religious and ancient wisdom and using it to confront and overcome life's and relationships difficulties. This story is filled with knowledge, wisdom, turns and twists you don't expect. A must read!!"

—*Behzad D. Panah*
Author, Actor

And Daba created nothing that can
be compared to love

—*Malian Wisdom*

TABLE OF CONTENTS

DEDICATION

Lalla

Her face when she was serious or laughing always looked beautiful to me.

Her rough hands were careful and loving when touching me.

Her voice, reassuring, told me I could do no wrong.

She poured herself into me.

Her love was possessive, comforting, sweet, and always present.

She flattered and spoiled me. She also annoyed me and made me feel guilty.

She poured herself into me.

She told me about herself and about life, so I would know she didn't hide herself from me. I could ask her anything.

She promised to always be present in my life, in person or in spirit.

She poured herself into me.

Lalla—my shining star—the *Lioness* as the family liked to call her, for she had always been a force of nature. She stood in her truth, and forged her own path fearlessly, and unapologetically.

And she poured herself into me.

Lalla—Daba's gift to me. She walked me to the gate then dared me to go in and take the mysterious, perplexing, and at times incomprehensible journey to finding, and becoming, the Anna only she saw in me.

She poured herself into me.

And I hope I turned out to be a lot like her.

I WILL STAY UNTIL YOU FIND YOUR WAY

All arrivals lead to departures.
The world is not a place where we come to stay.
All things built are bound to crumble.
The world is a place we come to taste.
But being used to someone makes parting so hard.
The world is not a place where we come to stay.[1]

*M*y life was too blue. My eyes too red. The world too unforgiving. People too disappointing. Denial too comforting. Who needs to turn inward when outward feeds the square peg inside me, while everyone wants me to be a round hole? Memory serves no good purpose, but there is no denying its force. 7:00 a.m. the alarm goes off. *Time to get up.* My hand finds the phone. I read: "Anna, your grandmother left us this morning."

I bolt upright, now understanding why for the past week I've had this unexplainable, relentless anguish and despair deep within. My being had sensed the huge loss coming. Tears fill my eyes as the words sink in. Lalla's transition to the other

---

[1] Words found in many traditional songs about the cycle of life.

side of life wasn't unexpected but no less heart-wrenching. For weeks now my grandmother and the universe had given warning signs to prepare me for this moment.

The previous month, my ninety-plus-years-old maternal grandmother had suffered a stroke and I'd dropped everything and flown home to Mali. I had been living outside of Mali since the age of thirty-one, in the United States, but home was no stranger to me. As long as Grandma Lalla was there, I would be tied to my homeland and I would make frequent trips to see her and the rest of my family who remained there. My roots, like Lalla's, are deeply embedded in the old country in West Africa that at one time was most powerful in all of Africa. With indelible traditions and culture, no matter where we find ourselves, Mali lives in the marrow of our bones.

When I arrived at Grandma's home, her caretaker, Mariam, the young lady who had long become part of our family, ran to greet me. She held my hand as if she knew I needed comforting. We walk together into Lalla's room. My heart sinks. My grandmother looks so frail. Her eyes are closed.

"Come closer, she's not sleeping. Just resting," Mariam says. She walks to the bed and says softly, "Mama Lalla, Anna is here."

My grandmother smiles and opens her eyes. I take off my shoes and climb into bed, beside her. I wrap my arms around her chest and hold her tight.

"Did you really think, old lady, that you could get sick and I would not rush to come see you?"

Lalla giggles. I kiss her cheek. She presses her cheek over and over to my lips, asking for more. Mariam leaves the room, and for the next two hours, I lie quietly next to Lalla. We don't talk. We just hold on to each other until I know she is asleep.

Mariam was in the living room watching TV. She smiled when I came in.

"She's sleeping." I say.

"She does a lot of that."

"Mariam, what happened?"

She sighs. "Oh, my manners. Do you want some water, or maybe some juice?"

"No, I'm good."

I smile at Mariam and my heart fills with love and gratitude for the young lady I called my first daughter. She loves Lalla as much as I do. For more than a decade now, Mariam has been part of the family. First as a helper to the maid, and then as the person I entrusted with Lalla's well-being. She and I speak at least once a week.

"What happened?"

Mariam sits close to me. "Anna, I didn't want to tell you. This is not something you say over the phone." She pauses. "A few days before her illness, Mama Lalla woke up in the middle of the night frantic. She went to the door and told me to let her out."

"What?"

"It was a scary night. I tried to calm her down. But she wouldn't listen. She said she had a dream, and she needed to get out of the house. She took a spoon, pulled a chair, and started banging on the door. For hours I pleaded with her to go back to bed. I told her I would call you as soon as the sun came up, and that I was sure you would find a place for us to stay. But she didn't want to wait that long. She said there were forces in her room that had come for her. She needed to move out. She kept hitting the door, asking, then begging me to let her out.

"I didn't know what to say or do to calm her down, so I stayed with her, and I just kept repeating that I would call you in the morning. Slowly she got tired and by the time she stopped, it was dawn. We were both exhausted. I walked her back to bed, told her to get some sleep while I tried to reach you. She nodded 'yes.'"

"Mariam, you should have called me."

"I know, and I wanted to, but I was afraid because I know you worry too much; and you are so far away. Besides, when she woke up around noon, she didn't talk about the dream, but she refused to take her medication. So, I called Mohammed. When he arrived, she kicked him out."

Mohammed was my cousin and my Uncle Layes' only child. We both burst out laughing. The lioness will never change. You cannot make her do what she doesn't want to do. Period.

"I pleaded with her, but she wouldn't budge—she was tired of taking pills. A few days later, she fell ill. We had to call you... I'm so glad you are here."

"Me, too."

Lalla had a stroke because she'd stopped taking her high blood pressure medicine. Later that afternoon, I'm in Lalla's room. My grandmother pulls my head until my ear is close enough to hear her whisper. "Anna, they came for me."

"Who?" Fear appeared and tightened my throat and my gut.

"My big brothers." She names them. I vaguely remember some of them because Lalla had sixty-five siblings.

"They came for me, but I told them I couldn't leave...not until I saw you."

Silence. We have nothing to say after that. Lalla rests her head on my breast and I rock her the same way she used to do to comfort me when I was a little girl. As I cradle the woman whose love had brought me home, in that moment, I knew our roles had changed. It was *my* turn now to reassure her she had nothing to worry about; I had found my way; I would be alright.

I hold my elder adoringly.

I hold her, my entire being aching.

She doesn't want me to see her like this.

Yet we are both grateful for the time together.

I stayed near so she could pull me to her and rest her head on my chest whenever she needed or wanted to. I stayed close so I could hold her and rock her. Lalla's voice is a whisper, but we don't need to talk. Our love story is beyond words. Our story is the story within the story.

I stayed ten days. And for ten days I hugged and kissed my grandmother again and again until she said, "Enough." For those ten days I watched my grandmother mutter pleas to the Creator to look after and protect me. The days pass too quickly. I had just arrived and it was already time to leave; time to go back to my life in New York City. We don't say goodbye. I can't. Instead, I wait until she is asleep. I kiss her gently on the forehead, and holding back my sob, say, "I love you, Lalla."

I lean on the creator asking for a good transition for Lalla. Because my religion is Islam as is 95% of people in Mali, the other 5% being Dogon, traditional African religion, or Christian, I beseech Allah. "Allah, I give you my Angel. Please watch over her. Take good care of my grandmother." My grandmother's circle was closing, I knew that. Still, my life needed to move on to meet the obligations I had left in New York.

I am gripping the phone as salty tears wet my cheeks and my runny nose bring me back to the reality of the moment. my grand mother has crossed over. Mariam is on the line and I am processing what she is saying. My grandmother has crossed over. Though I'd just left Mali I must go home again to Lalla. I hang up the phone and head straight to my computer. My laptop screen is now open, I check the flights to Mali for the day. I buy my ticket and call my cousin Mohammed to let him know I'll be on my way to Lalla. The twelve-hour journey— seven hours from JFK to Paris, a two-hour layover, followed by another five-hour flight to Mali—was about to begin. I know I would miss the funeral because our Islamic tradition requires burial as soon after death as possible. Still, I would be there to see my Lalla's resting place.

I sat waiting to board the flight to Paris. It struck me, *Here I am again at the airport. A Saturday! I knew it.* Coincidence? No, in life there are no coincidences. Superstition? Maybe, but can you really call something an irrational belief when it happens to you? Or is it truth? In Malian tradition, there are no ordinary days. The days of the week have meanings, each shaped by and containing the energies of the star, the comet, and the planet they aligned with when they were created. These mysterious forces and energies have an effect on all our endeavors and must be considered as part of the rhythm of life. Hence, in Malian tradition all major events in the community—the beginning of the agricultural season, harvesting, weddings, and travels—require our elders to get together and carefully choose the day considered most auspicious for the occasion.

For reasons I do not know, Mondays are considered good days for travel. Tuesdays and Wednesdays are called slow and stubborn days. You do not want to start new projects on either of these days because it's asking for laborious and exhausting beginnings with very slow-to-come success. Thursdays and Sundays are considered fortunate and are good days for people who want to move into a new house or get married. And finally, there is Saturday—the heavy, troubled day. It's called the "twin" day because whatever good, bad, or sad events occur on a Saturday will reoccur soon after. When I left Mali the month before, it was on a Saturday morning, and something told me I would be back. I brushed it off because I'd said my goodbye to Lalla. Yet, true to our traditional Saturday meaning, here I was, returning to the country for a heavily, burdened reason. There was no way I could not have gone home to Lalla. I have a window seat and an empty seat next to me.

My hands clutch the armrests. The plane taxies down the runway and the wheels leave the ground. In seven hours, we would reach Paris.

"Lalla." My head keeps repeating her name. But nothing follows. No images. No memories. I close my eyes and breathe slowly, in and out. My body begins to relax.

"Lalla." Pain, love, and gratitude wash over me. *You kept your promise.*

"I will not leave you," she'd said to me years ago.

"Anna, I will not leave you I will stay until I know you have found your way."

My father was a career diplomat and I was born May 1st, 1962, in Paris where I lived until I was two years old. From two to nine I lived in Bamako, Mali and then my father was re-stationed in New York, then Germany. While he was in Germany my sister and I were sent to a Catholic boarding school in Brussels. In 1974 my family once again returned to Mali. I was twelve.

So, long, long ago, when I was a child and during my tumultuous teenage and young adult years—the years I was labeled a lone peculiar straw because I was the oddity who didn't find her place in the family or our community, I'd come to know and adore my grandmother. Lalla refused to give up on me, ever. My grandmother was always in my corner with unconditional love and unwavering support. She stood by me and defended me even when she didn't understand or agree with my words and actions. I was so used to finding her every time I needed her that I didn't want to accept that there could be a day when she would no longer be here.

"Excuse me, ma'am…ma'am."

"Yes"

The flight attendant is asking me to choose between the meat or vegetarian dinner. Chicken, mashed potatoes, and some boiled pitiful-looking vegetables would be just fine. I force myself to take a few bites. I stop. I have a lump in my throat. Pushing away the tray, I exhale. I am going home to Lalla. I am going home to tell Lalla and myself that I will be alright. My Lalla who kept her promise. Who stayed with me and guided me until I found my way. Who stayed with me until she knew I could go on without leaning on her. No, this is not goodbye. This is eternal love and gratitude.

No matter how we came and went, even when my family once again moved to Canada, when Papa was nominated as Ambassador of Mali in Ottawa, for five years, Lalla never left my life. After I returned to Bamako at age twenty-one our love affair became a solid beacon in my life and at thirty-one when I stepped out to find my way in New York, Lalla's love sustained me.

Lalla was also the one who started me on my journey into self. I remember on one of our calls when she said to me: "You are fine, and you'll continue to be fine. If I know nothing else, I know that."

At that time, I wasn't fine. I wasn't where I wanted to be. I wasn't who I wanted to be. I was physically and emotionally wiped out. My mind and my spirit were burned out. It was my grandmother's guiding hand and comforting voice that got me through. Lalla and the elders often said a situation can only begin to cool down once it's reached its boiling point. I had reached that level then—my boiling, my turning point. My life left me confounded, it had me wonder:

Dreams and aspirations,

Where were you?

I built my life around you.

My worth, and my happiness depended on you.

I lived and breathed you.

No efforts were too much to conquer you.

I pursued you

Year after year

I stayed the course

Refusing to give up.

Through all of life's delays—all the things that didn't happen that made me at times wonder if these dreams of mine would ever materialize.

I stayed the course.

Through sleepless nights, panic attacks, fears, and doubts.

I stayed the course.

Through jobs lost, economic crisis, and missed opportunities.

I stayed the course.

Through tough times when all I could afford for my daily meal was a cup of coffee and a bagel.

I stayed the course.

Through all that I dreamed that coming to America would be but wasn't. Even when I was no longer certain of my own ability to stay the course, in the end, I stayed the course. I was no quitter. I was no failure.

But patience cannot win over what seems to drag on forever. And so I was at a crossroads, a place of unknowns where the way things should be, clashed with the reality of what they were. I lost my dreams and all my certainties. Why was everything in my life so difficult? Why was everything such a struggle? And it was in this turmoil—this collapsing of all the Anna I knew how to be—that Lalla had said, "Anna, you are fine, and you'll continue to be fine. There is nothing wrong with you. You are struggling because you are fighting against your own self."

What? What was that supposed to mean?

"Anna, life is not hard on you, you are hard on life. But now that you are tired and no longer have the strength or the will to be hard on yourself, I can remind you of *the good path*, my own experience of life, and what I have learned to be true."

I was grateful and annoyed at the same time. Grateful that Lalla, as always, would know what to do to help me fix my life; and annoyed that she felt she had to lecture me first. As if she knew what I was thinking and feeling, my grandmother added mischievously: "Young people run faster, but we the elders know the way. If you listen to what I have to say and walk in our footsteps and follow *the good path*—the ancestral teachings and philosophy of life left by those who came before us—I promise you that your world will change for the better. You will make sense of all that you have been through, and realize that *nothing*, not even the confusion you're in right now, is in vain. After that, you won't be shaken when things don't work out as planned. You will remain grounded and settled within. And you will never again go to battle against yourself."

I had no idea back then what Lalla was talking about. And that was good because I don't know if I would have willingly gone on such a long, unpredictable, and painful journey. Yet, it was the path I needed to take to find answers to the whys of my unhappy life, and in the process become the Anna my grandmother saw in me, but I didn't know existed. In retrospect, I came to appreciate that: *It's the one who gets lost who discovers new paths.*

Lalla and I had many conversations and so, the road to finding Lalla's Anna, while mending and understanding the scattered pieces of my turbulent life began with that one exceptionally long phone call.

Chapter Two

UNBURDEN YOURSELF

*The world may be old, but the future still comes
from the past. And from yesterday to today,
every generation has stood on the shoulders of the elders
to see and guide its future.*

That call came on a Sunday. Sundays are supposed to be good days! After my morning coffee, I returned to bed, unable to muster the will to think or do anything for the rest of the day. It didn't matter what time of the day it was—early morning, middle, or late afternoon—the past few weeks had been physically and emotionally draining. Is it possible that I could spend another day in bed like I had done the day before? I didn't want to go through another entire day feeling grim, carrying the dreadful numbness inside of me that rendered me prostrate. So, I stayed still, trying to pull my will together. I stayed still until my impatience flared up and I became exasperated with myself. What was the matter with me? Why couldn't I bounce back the way I always had when faced with setbacks? A knot in my throat formed, tears filling my eyes. *No, I will not cry*! I breathed deeply until I calmed down. I could no longer keep things bottled up inside of me. I was embarrassed about the state of my life, but the need to talk was more pressing than my shame. I had to find relief. I picked up the phone and dialed the number. I waited. The phone rang once, twice, then:

"*Allo?*"

I sighed, relieved. It was the voice of my indefatigable champion—the one person who, though oceans away, would tell me how to pick myself up, and make me feel better.

"Lalla, it's me."

"Anna," my grandmother said—and she laughed, happy. "How are you? Are you in good health?"

"Yes, I'm okay, and you?"

"What is bothering you?"

And before I could answer, my grandmother said, "*Do di*" which in our language means unburden yourself.

I tried to speak but a wave of emotions choked me. There was silence as I struggled to find my composure.

"Calm down, there are no pots without covers," Lalla said, pronouncing the exact words I needed to hear. "Seat your mind," she repeated softly.

We remained silent as I wiped away my tears and regained some self-control.

"What happened? Tell me."

"Life...nothing good is happening, nothing is working for me...I don't understand...."

My life in the U.S. had hit another wall. I had to let go of the job I loved at an organization working for the prevention of HIV/AIDS in faith-based communities in the U.S. and parts of Africa. And I hadn't been able to find similar work. Forced to confront my reality, paying rent, and covering my basic needs, I settled for what I could find: a position as an entry-level salesperson. And soon after, before I could learn to bear the pain and sourness of my new life, I faced another debacle: the demise of what I wanted to believe was a love story. How could I fall and fail so miserably? "It's all over, everything," I said. "Even him."

"Finally! It's over," my grandmother said.

"Lalla!"

"Anna, you were not happy. You complained about you two constantly arguing about nothing. You said you were two very different people. I couldn't understand why you stayed for so long in a relationship where every day was, "Hey, you walked on my head… and ouch, you stepped on my toe."

"Don't make me laugh."

"I don't like it when you're sad. *Do di.*"

The word, the soothing tone of her voice took me to the place—a place only known to her and me. A place where I could unload my worries and sadness without fear or guilt—a place where there was no judgment. Only Lalla always knew how to make any situation better.

"Lalla, I am not where I thought I would be."

"I know. I've been hearing anxiety in your voice for a while now. It sounds like your gut is boiling with worry and you can't find sleep—even if you pretend that everything is fine when we speak so I wouldn't worry. But I do. I didn't say anything because I was waiting for you to come to me."

Indeed, my gut was boiling with fear. This was not where I imagined I would be at this stage of my life. I was in my forties, and I still didn't have the wealth, the professional success, or the love I desired to be happy. Instead, my days were spent in a boutique, competing with young people half my age to be the best salesperson of the week. No, this was not where I wanted to be. I couldn't repress the anxiety I felt inside. Maybe the thoughts in my head that I might be a failure, were the truth.

"Lalla, my whole life, I have never been in a situation like this. I've tried everything. I don't know what else to do. After all these years, why am I struggling again? I worked so hard for so long. And for what? So little…. It's like sweating in the rain. I'm exhausted. I don't want to run after anything anymore."

"It's time you stop running then. Stay still until you figure out what it is that you want to do next."

Silence. What do you say to such a simple and almost inconceivable solution? Life is more complicated though. "Yes, but you and the elders assured us many times that if we showed patience and endured, we would overcome our challenges."

"So, we lied to you?"

"No, no, that's not what I'm saying at all. It's just that what you told us may be true for others but it didn't turn out to be true for me. I am starting over…again."

"You are not starting over."

"Lalla, I have the same salary I had when I first started working in the U.S. almost fifteen years ago. What am I doing wrong?"

"Only you have the answer to that."

But you're supposed to help me fix this! Why did I call?

"*Lagaré*," which means the baby of the family, "Don't be mad. Just listen to me. Did you work hard and try everything that you could do to reach your goals?"

"Yes."

"Did you pray the way we taught you to?"

"Yes, I did." I wanted to add "and then some" but didn't.

Silence.

"Lalla."

"I'm here."

"Tell me, what are you thinking? What am I doing wrong?"

Lalla sighed. "The reason I waited for you to tell me about your unhappiness is because if you ask for my advice, then I'm sure you are not looking for me to tell you what you want to hear. You know me. My words may taste bitter, but they are my truth. They are what I know."

This was not what I expected. I wanted Lalla to reassure me and tell me that everything was going to be alright. I didn't know where the conversation was going, and it looked like this would be a long and expensive call. Indeed, once Lalla started talking, I couldn't interrupt or tell her to hurry up. If you did any one of these things to Lalla, or any elder in our community, they would stop talking, and no amount of pleading would get them to share their knowledge with you. I couldn't go on not knowing what to think or do with myself, and with my life. I desperately needed a plan, or at least some direction.

"Do you want to hear what I think?"

"Yes, I'm listening."

"Anna, pursuit has two purposes: Either you find wealth or you find yourself. What have you found?"

Shame drowned me as I stared at the bitter truth of my situation—I didn't have wealth and I wasn't happy. Finally, I said, "Nothing."

"You have done everything you could think of to get what you wanted out of life. What has your struggle shown you?"

"That I obviously still didn't know how to get ahead in life; that I am powerless, that I have no control." That this call was a bad idea. I should have just stayed in bed.

"No, Anna. Your struggle shows two things: One, when you are tough on life, life is hard on you in return. As our elders used to say: Once someone gets used to eating hot pepper all the time they think that all food should be piquant and fiery. But that shouldn't be the case. You've been hard on yourself for so long that it has become the only way you know how to be. And, two, you are persistent, you don't give up easily. You deserve to be happy. Still, you have to remember that nothing happens without a reason. Therefore, if in spite of everything you have done, Allah still didn't allow you to achieve your pursuit, it could be that what you are pursuing is not for you, or that you are not pursuing properly the things you want. Something is missing—so what is it that you are not seeing? What is it that you are not doing? The time has come for you to sit still, calm your mind, and then ask yourself questions."

I was annoyed.

"Anna, if I don't tell you the truth, who will? If you were happy, I would be the happiest person in the world. I love you more than my own children, *lagaré*, but that shouldn't prevent me from telling you the truth."

I felt her compassion in her voice, and in the words she spoke. "My *lagaré*, I want you to stop worrying, you hear me?"

"Yes," I answered, relieved to have finally found the reassuring voice that always melted my troubles away.

"I'll say it again. When it comes time to ask questions, don't ask the world. Ask yourself. You have worked hard. You have prayed, and you have never stopped seeking your good path. You have read books; and you have listened to people tell you what you should do to attain happiness. You've discovered and tried the things you found in others that you wanted to believe were good for you to emulate. Still, you didn't find your way. Anna, it's time to stop this pursuit for now. Stay still. Take time to gather yourself and quiet your mind."

She paused and then asked: "Tell me, do you remember the game we used to play when you were little?"

Game, what game?

"*N'tin, n'tin!*" Lalla said, starting the riddles in the traditional way.

"*N'tin massa.*" *Where are we going with this?*

"I'm taller when I sit down than when I'm up. Who am I?"

"A dog," I replied.

"You are right."

"*N'tin, n'tin!*"

"*N'tin massa.*" *This phone bill is going to be heavy.*

"This henhouse is filled with small white hens. What is it?"

"Your mouth with teeth."

"*N'tin, n'tin!*"

"*N'tin massa.*" *This is ridiculous. I'm too old for this.*

"There are fruits in the sky, but no one can pick them up. What are they?"

"The stars."

"You're right again. Very good. You remember. Now, like the riddles, I am going to give you some old words my elders gave me when I too was young. I'm going to ask that you do the same thing they had asked of me—listen, hear the words, and then let them settle in you. Meditate on them, wait, and see what they bring out of you. I don't want you to call me back tomorrow or the day after with what your head told you to say. I want you to let the answers come from your gut. Don't ask anybody's opinion or advice. You've already done that. The solutions the world gave you haven't worked for you. It is time to find out what's in your belly. You might not believe me, but your gut is not empty. It holds all the truths, all the knowledge, and wisdom we taught you long ago that you were supposed to call upon and lean on so you can find your seat. But you and many of your contemporaries have disregarded our teachings as knowledge from an era that has no relevance to the world you live in today."

"*Lagaré*," Lalla said softly as if she regretted being so blunt, "if you hear me and follow the good path, I promise your life will change. You will finally see and get to know who you truly are, and that in turn will reshape how you receive and respond to life's events."

"That said, let me give you the three ancestral truths I want you to think about: The first is when you don't know where you are going, go back to where you came from. If you don't understand where you came from, you will not know where you're going. For who you are...."

I completed the sentence, "Began where you were, I know."

Lalla continued, undeterred by my interruption. "Then, you also know that it's good to want to learn how to swim or how to ride a horse. It is good to want to learn new things. But the first and best knowledge of all is knowledge of self. Why? Because every human being is an unfathomable seed of the world. A miniature universe within the universe. Know yourself—learn to understand and contain all the beings and things that are in you. As long as you do not recognize the powers within, your life will remain incomprehensible to you. You'll continue to struggle and sweat in the rain.

"The two remaining truths actually complete each other. You can choose to answer the one that seems easiest to you. In the end, whatever you find will lead you to the last adage.

"The second is a question: Why do you want so much the things that you want? What is the purpose of your pursuit? What do you believe your quest will bring you?

"Finally, remember this: The thorns can only be pulled from where they penetrated. Uncover yours, and pull them out so you can free yourself, and be you. What I see in you, you cannot see in yourself because you are too scattered. You don't know all that you are yet."

So much love in her last words! I was a treasure to her only. I brushed off and took for granted her unconditional love that saw the good in me.

"Reflect on these words," Lalla insisted. "Understand the truths behind the wisdom and find how they apply to your life. Don't rush, don't force, and don't rationalize. Let your gut give you the answers. Once you do that, you'll begin to comprehend the things that now make no sense—the whys of all these years of struggle. Afterward, your dreams and ambitions might be different because they will finally be in alignment with who you are and the things you were sent into this world to do.

"And you'll become your own compass when you understand why you believe in Allah when you trust your faith enough to lean on it and let it anchor you to the Creator. Promise me that you will let the words settle in you and listen to whatever comes out of your gut. Promise."

I thought my grandmother's request was odd—when did I stop listening to myself? I always heard my thoughts. But I promised to follow her direction.

"*Lagaré*," Lalla said tenderly, "our elders said that if you cry Help! Help! And no one comes, in the end, you will show up and help yourself out. I am telling you to do what you have not done before—look and work with what you have inside of you. Other than that, you are fine, and you'll continue to be fine. If I know nothing else, I know that."

"But what if I don't find anything in my gut to work with?" I asked, secretly hoping that she would tell me something to offer me the quick comfort I had been craving.

"You will."

"How do you know?"

"First, you are my granddaughter. Second, we always understand the things we commit ourselves to."

I was oceans away, but I still knew how to read between the lines. Lalla was challenging me, questioning my commitment—was I serious about finding the reasons for my unhappiness? Did I really want to understand my life or was I still looking for a quick fix?

"And that is all I will say today."

It was the end of our phone call. Though a little worried about my next telephone bill, the long and honest conversation with my grandmother made my sadness disappear. Lalla didn't lift my spirit the way she had done many times in the past, yet, I could take comfort in the fact that my elder had given me "homework" to focus on that would keep my mind from drifting to a place of restlessness.

My grandmother had given me everything she knew I needed for the next step—the beginning of what she and the elders describe as the battle you have to wage against your own self to find the true you. Lalla was reminding me of the wisdom of our people. I just had to remember.

Chapter Three

IF YOU DON'T SHAKE THE BUSH

*When you don't know where you are going,
go back to where you came from.
For if you don't understand where you came from,
you will not know where you are going.*

For several days, I thought about this old truth my grandmother had given me. It was not just a truth she made up but one that had been passed down in Malian tradition from time immemorial by the *griots*, the wise men, and women of our culture. *Griots* which is the French rendition of the Malian word *Jali*, were far more than storytellers. They were thought leaders who for ten to twenty years studied the art of becoming cultural and social historians, advisors to the kings, anthropologists, rites of passage mediators, as well as, keepers of Malian history and so much more. The good path for all descendants of Mali had already been trotted. Why would I reinvent the wheel?

I made a conscious effort to bring Lalla's words of wisdom into my mind every chance I had; in the morning, on the train, throughout the day, during my lunch hour, and at night before I fell asleep.

"Don't rush, don't force, and don't rationalize," Lalla had said, "let the answers come from your gut."

After days of trying, I grew tired of repeating a sentence that drew nothing to mind. I didn't want to admit it, but deep inside I resented the statement for what I believed it was asking me to do: Go back and relive a past I was not interested in revisiting. For what purpose? It was obvious that I didn't know where I was going, but going back to where I came from didn't seem to be the right answer either. The reason for my unhappiness wasn't in my past. It was something I kept on doing wrong. I just needed to find what it was so I could fix it.

Two weeks later, on the last day I unenthusiastically tried to make sense of the old words, I felt overwhelmed and wanted to cry. Then I remembered that everything speaks to those who know how to look and listen. I took a deep breath and as I exhaled, admitted to myself what was holding me back: I really didn't feel like revisiting more than forty years of my life. I decided to focus on the adage that resonated with me the most. It was the last wise saying Lalla asked me to think about: *The thorns can only be pulled from where they penetrated.*

I liked that old saying because, unlike the first puzzle, I had answers for this one. My main thorn was my disillusionment stemming from the fact that for years I attempted, but never succeeded, in bringing to life the image of the financially well-off and successful career woman that lived in my head. Lalla said that pursuit had two purposes: either to find wealth or to find yourself. I didn't have either—I wasn't rich, I wasn't a success, and I no longer knew who I was supposed to want to be. Then my elder pointed out that if in spite of all the hard work and sacrifices I had made through the years, I still hadn't achieved my goals, either I wasn't doing something right, or what I wanted was not for me. I had tried everything I could think of, everything I knew how to do to attain my ambitions, so if what Lalla said was true and my ambitions were not for me, why was I holding on to them?

If you don't shake the bush, you'll never know what it hides.

And so, the internal probing began. Why did I want the things that I wanted? What was the purpose of my relentless pursuit? Initially, the questions surprised me because I had never questioned my motives—the real reason behind my quest. My head went to work and produced a first response: "Because I wanted a good life for myself and all the people I loved."

This was a logical and sensible answer, but it wasn't enough. Something was missing. It was a half-truth that couldn't conceal what I felt deep within—a repressed, muddy mix of pain and anger. Where did these feelings come from? And so, I kept asking myself over and over why did I want the things that I wanted?

The problem-solver in me shows up and provides some good and logical answers. I believe in myself and I could do anything that I wanted to do. I am a hard worker who deserves to reap the benefits of my labor and sacrifices. I am a good person whose family and friends all agree deserve to be happy. I am a fighter. I am a person who never gives up, never quits.

All of my self-assessments were true, but they weren't enough; they didn't tell me why I wanted the things I wanted. I couldn't answer that question, and I couldn't let it go. The question became a lingering fixation.

Words are energy. Words are power. Words travel through the body and emerge filled with the strength and intention of their owner. They set off emotions that shape the response, and sometimes alter their recipient. Words can start or end everything; and sometimes, words can kill.

I was resting, surrounded by total silence in my room. It was cold outside, but sunny. I didn't turn on the TV that day. I could hear myself breathe, drawing in a feeling of peace, but as I exhaled, words tore out of my gut like a thorn that had been stuck there, festering: "You are nothing. You will never amount to anything."

A bolt of lightning! That's why—because I wanted to prove they were wrong.

I was stunned. For a moment I became the teenager who silently, with my head cast down, received those words. I was stung and deeply shocked at the time because they came from Lalla—my beloved grandmother, who I revered, and who I knew adored me. But I didn't know that they had traveled beyond the immediate hurt and humiliation to a place deep within. And that from that hidden space, they would influence and shape my perception of myself, my family, my community, and the world surrounding me. When the only person in the world who you believe loves you unconditionally says those words, they don't bounce off like water on a duck's back, they penetrate deep, like a thorn embedded so deep and bent on destroying one's very soul. I had heard those words before, but coming from Lalla, the only one who believed in me they were poison.

Those words created in me the fear of failure, and the fear of never finding a place or a space where I would fit in.

I am dumbfounded to realize that an event I had brushed off as "nothing" had such an impact on my adult life. I feel raw and tender inside. But I also experienced relief: This painful memory, so long held within me, festering, and rendering me fearful, had been freed. Strangely enough, I wasn't angry at Lalla; instead, I felt a wave of empathy for my elder. Where did this outburst of love and compassion for Lalla come from? Did I want to excuse or justify the harsh words or the pain they caused? No, I didn't. I just knew my grandmother too well—a woman who only knew how to be absolute in every aspect of her life. Lalla didn't know how to love a little, give a little, say a little, or be a little more of this and a little less of that. To her, everything in life demanded either her all or her nothing. She loved too much, protected too much, did too much, and on many occasions, said too much.

I understood my grandmother. Too many hardships in her youth had forced her to become fierce and make her razor-sharp tongue her best weapon. She had spoken those words on a very ordinary day, but now I was able to sense what the fourteen-year-old girl decades earlier couldn't see, that beyond the biting, angry words and the demonstration of outrage that made me bleed inside, my grandmother's words were most of all fueled and propelled by her own fear. My perceived failures were not mine alone. They were also her disappointment, and her shame to bear. I wanted the things that I wanted to prove her wrong and make her proud all at once.

I took a deep breath and as I exhaled and began to relax, I noticed that my neck and shoulders were sore from being tense. A stiff neck is a sign of rigidity. A person with a stiff neck and shoulders is said to be inflexible and set in their ways, and both tense and anxious inside. When and why had I become so hard, so stiff, inside, and out?

I smiled. I had solved two of the three enigmas my grandmother had given me. I couldn't help but think, would Lalla—the cause of my pain, and my greatest defender—ask me to let the truth come from my gut if she could have imagined what would come out? The answer came calm and certain, "Yes, she would have."

"Anna, I love you more than my own children," Lalla sometimes said. It was true. Our complex, boundless love story started when I was born. She loved me without doubt but she also feared that if I didn't find the good path, I could be lost for too long.

I still had one unsolved puzzle—the one I didn't really want or know how to tackle: *When you don't know where you're going, go back to where you came from.*

My gut is supposed to provide the answer to this last inquiry. But when and where would I hear from it again? And what part of my past would it bring back—my childhood, my adolescence, or maybe my early adulthood? My gut was still a mystery to me—an inexplicable, and bottomless space within, that contained all that I had been, all that I was, and all that I would become.

Lalla had asked me to stay still, and that's exactly what I'm going to do. As challenging as it might be at times, I will remain still and let the unknown forces within my gut spill and reveal what they hold deep inside, the way they inevitably do—when I least expect it, when I'm not actively searching for its answers.

For *that which is hidden is truer and more profound than that which is visible.*

I grin. Even for me, this new behavior is quite a departure from my usual take-charge attitude. I am embracing not knowing, and letting fate happen, when most of my life I have tried to control every aspect of my existence to avoid or hush my fear of the unknown.

Everything in life has a starting point which, like a seed, evolves to full realization.

Things didn't happen as I imagined they would. I thought the past would bring itself to me. Instead, I am taken to the door of my yesterday. I am lying on the couch looking at my iPad. I recognized the photo of one of my favorite cousins—Kady—who'd friended me on Facebook. We hadn't seen each other in more than twenty years. She hadn't changed much, except she now wore glasses—just like I did. When it comes to aging, the eyes are the first to go. I accepted her request. My cousin soon followed with a longer message that read:

Hi Anna, I hope you remember me—it's Kady—your cousin. I currently live in Côte d'Ivoire. I was surprised and happy when I saw your picture on Facebook. It would be so good to hear from you. It's been so long.

I enthusiastically reply: *Hi Kady, I can't believe this! Of course, I remember you dear beloved cousin. What a joy to reconnect like this on Facebook! I've been living in New York for almost 25 years now. How are you, how are the children? Hugs.*

She replies almost immediately: *Anna, the kids are all adults and have their own families. My dear, we have six young grandchildren. By the way, I don't know if you are aware, but our family group is also on Facebook. You should join.*

I ask her: *Family group—what family group?*

Kady explains that our Uncle Buba had for years traced and put together the history of our great-grandfather. Uncle Buba was Lalla's nephew. His father and Lalla were half-siblings who shared the same father. In our culture, your grandparents' siblings, cousins, and friends are all considered your elders. Parents' brothers, sisters, friends, and relatives are all uncles and aunts. My younger sisters and brothers consider all my contemporaries as their older siblings.

And so, the year before, they had a big family reunion at Duba, our family compound, and our uncle made a PowerPoint presentation of the family tree.

"It was so good to see everyone," Kady said. "We've all gotten older of course, but some of us still looked good. It was also wonderful to meet the younger generation—most of whom, I didn't know until they told me their parents' names. At the end of his presentation, Uncle Buba said that now we all knew where we came from. He was passing the baton, and it was up to the next generation—us and our children to continue the work. And that's when we decided to create a group that would be open only to all the direct descendants of the Patriarch."

The group had more than three hundred members from all over the world. I joined them, and soon after Kady forwarded me the home movie of the family reunion at Duba. I watched the event, my heart filled with nostalgia. I smiled when I saw Lalla's picture on the family tree. She was one of our great-grandfather's youngest children.

The movie ended, leaving me fondly reminiscing about the time when I too lived at Duba. I recalled the dirt paths we used to run on, the faces of chums I hung out with, cousins like Kady. Some I recognized, others I sadly learned had passed away. We were all children, who at some point had spent time in the family compound. It was there that I had lived the happiest first few years of a turbulent childhood. Yes, Lalla was right: *Who you are began where you were.*

Chapter Four

SHAPING THE CLAY

*All beings and things are first and foremost the product
of a past that created them.
First, you shape your fresh clay into a human being—
a small person whose behavior and words are expected
and accepted in the family and in the community.*

I was the firstborn—the first child of both my father and
my absent, yet irreplaceable, mother.

I was the firstborn—a status that would be attached to my
name for as long as I live.

I was the firstborn. I belonged to a large clan made of
Papa, Lalla, my elders, uncles, aunts, cousins, neighbors, and
close friends—people from different walks of life, skin color,
nationalities, and religions. Some were intellectuals, others
had never set foot in school and didn't know how to read or
write. Some were Catholics, some were Muslims; others had
managed to quietly practice one of these two "official" religions
in Mali, along with the *good path*, the ancestral teachings and
philosophy of life practiced by their elders. *The good path* was
their most profound spiritual allegiance.

Customs and traditions were the bedrock of my elders' world. Their foundation—the ancestral beliefs and irrefutable truths passed down through generations—imparted the knowledge that would alleviate in each of us our ignorance of ourselves, our families, our community, Mother Nature, and Daba. For as human beings, we were part of the universe: the seven skies; the seven Earths; the air and all that is contained within; the waters, underground and above the Earth; the inanimate objects; the flora, from the smallest bit of moss to the biggest tree; the fauna, from the tiniest insect to the largest animal; mankind, from the smallest imp to the biggest giant— all have their role in the good or bad running of the universe. Fate or chance plays no part in life. Nothing of what Daba has produced could be disregarded or neglected. And nothing of what humankind thinks or does is without consequence. In each of us is a whole universe.

It was essential that every newborn gradually learn this heritage passed on by their forefathers and mothers. They then needed to learn and earn how to hold their place in the family and the community. This diverse group of our nearest and dearest folks maintained that good rearing was the most important wealth you could give a child. And so, they poured their love, living principles, values, knowledge, expectations, and fear into us—me included. Gradually, I'd learned to see, talk, think, process, understand, and imagine the world the way they did. I'd learned to respect and follow the rules of living together, of respecting and living in harmony with nature which allowed me to become a little person who fit in my assigned place within family and community.

Papa told me that I was two years old when our family minus my mother had moved back from Paris to Bamako. He had a busy work schedule and was happy and grateful when Lalla offered to help him care for me. I went to live with my mother's mother, but my earliest memories of that time with Grandma Lalla was when I was about three or four. Life was bliss. There was no Papa, no Mother. No step-mama. No siblings. No expectations. No pressure. And no fear. My life revolved around Lalla, my guardian at the time. Lalla was my Lalla—the woman who didn't hide herself from me—who was and would forever be both mother and grandmother to me. I was the first grandchild of her two children, but she continually said that I was her *lagaré*. She didn't say, "I love you;" instead, she sang me lullabies:

> *Did you see Daba's gift*
>
> *The Creator's beautiful gift to me?*
>
> *And I pray that Daba gives you a long and healthy life*
>
> *So, everyone can see*
>
> *The Creator's beautiful gift to me.*

My grandmother would play a major role in shaping and molding, loving, and exasperating me. Her constant presence in person or in spirit would forever guide me. Her influence began in those early years when I was absorbing the lessons around me on how to be human. I was with Lalla and we lived together at Duba.

Duba was the family compound in Bamako. Lalla's father, my great-grandfather, was born around 1867, and he died in 1937 at 70. From age 20-21—which was considered then the appropriate age for men to start their family, to the time of his passing—great-grandfather fell in love many times and married the woman he was infatuated with every time. Hence, through the course of his life, he married fifteen times and had sixty-five accounted children.

Great-grandfather was in his sixties when he married Lalla's mother. Together they had four children: three girls and a boy. Lalla was their second child followed by Grandma Fanta, and Grandpa Sekou who died when he was a toddler.

Great-grandfather had acquired the land, which stretched through the equivalent of half a New York City block.. A rectangular rampart wall that was high enough to prevent even the tallest person from seeing what was going on in the household delineated the four corners of the estate.

Inside, my great-grandfather had built two- or three-bedroom homes for each of his fifteen wives and their children, sixty-five in total. Each had a covered veranda, a bathroom, and a small area that served as the kitchen. All the homes were connected by a large, open area that became a playground for the children and a meeting place for the adults. Connecting the homes were open paths, some large, others so narrow that two people could not cross them at the same time. Great-grandfather and his wives had all passed away decades before I came along, and the compound was now home to the next generation—his sons, his divorced or widowed daughters with their own offsprings.

It was into this mini world within a world, bustling with men going to work, young girls going to school and then coming home to help their mothers in the kitchen or doing household chores, children running from house to house, that I lived happily.

Lalla, her brothers, sisters, and sisters-in-law were our elders—grandfather and grandmother figures that watched over us as we spent our days playing and dashing from one household to the other.

Every morning I heard, "Anna, wake up, the sun is shining." My eyes opened to the happy smile on Lalla's face as she said, "Go wash your face and mouth while I make you breakfast."

Afterwards, I would sit with my grandmother and watch as she made my favorite breakfast, *fru-fru*. These were small fried pancakes made with sorghum flour that she mashed in a bowl, adding warm milk and sugar. Lalla watched me eat.

"Did you have enough?"

"Humm."

"You sure? Do you want more? You can have more."

"No, Lalla, I am full."

My grandmother would laugh and send me out to play with the other children of my age. The open spaces at Duba were our playgrounds. We spent the days racing through corridors or singing and dancing. We formed a circle, and as we sang and clapped our hands, we took turns entering the middle of the circle to perform our best moves. When tired, we walked to the closest home to rest and drink water.

I sometimes got lost, but never for long because all the adults knew I was Lalla's Anna. This simple statement told everyone who I belonged to and where I lived. I was also known as Lalla's Anna because every time I ran back home in tears after losing a fight, Lalla would march over and scold the mother of the child who made me cry. She comforted me, drying my tears while inventing cradlesongs that pleaded with me to stop crying because my tears made her sad—and did I want to see her sad? I vigorously shook my head "no." Lalla then gave me treats that helped me quickly forget my pain.

Another favorite game was to pretend to prepare a real meal. First, we decided on the meat. "Are we having beef or chicken?" Fish was never an option. No one liked fish. Then, "What sauce are we preparing to eat with the rice?" Usually, peanut butter or tomato sauce. We imitated our elders as our leader cousin, Kady, told us what to do. She was our natural and indisputable leader because she was taller and stronger than most of us. And the one or two girls who challenged her by disagreeing with her learned painfully that she could fight. I feared and admired her. I agreed with everything she said. Kady liked that and became my protector. No one could touch me when she was there.

Kady would sit in front of the imaginary pot atop the stove. She was in charge of two important things: cooking the meat, which were small pebbles we all helped pick, and stirring the sauce to make sure it didn't stick to the pan or burn. Another girl was in charge of crushing the black pepper in the mortar, while another pretended to peel onions. I still recall how seriously we all took our assignments as we busied ourselves with the preparation of our feast. Some of us asked:

"Kady, did you add salt? The last time there was not enough."

The question irritated her. We felt it in her answer: "I did. You want to taste the sauce to make sure?"

"No, that's fine."

Another girl rushed in with the imaginary mortar, "Kady, here's the pepper you asked me to mash, is it mush enough?"

"Yes. Give it to me."

She handed Kady the mortar. And as we all had witnessed our grandmothers do so many times, Kady scraped the pepper with a stick that was our spatula and threw it in the imaginary pot.

"Hmm, this smells good."

"I know, it's ready. Let's eat."

We sat in a circle around the invisible bowl of food. We chewed and commented, "Hmm, this is so good."

"Yes, it is."

When I came home from our luncheon with dirty hands full of mud and some on my clothes, Lalla would laugh: "Today was cooking day?"

"Yes."

"What did you prepare?"

"Peanut butter sauce."

"Was it good?"

"Yes, almost like yours."

"Keep doing it, one day it will be better than mine."

"No, that's impossible."

My grandmother would laugh, delighted. She'd wash me and we'd have a real meal together. Later in the afternoon, our elders shared with each other our cooking experience, amused and proud that we were already imitating them.

My days unfolded the same way. Every morning after breakfast, Lalla sent me out to play. A little before lunch, regardless of where we were, the adults would remind us that it was time to go home. After my nap, I would go back out again to play with my clan. Our afternoons were quieter. We spent most of them repeating what we remembered of the tales our elders recounted for us.

Late in the afternoon, the moment our grandfathers started coming back from work, our grandmothers would send all of us home for our daily bath. After Lalla washed me, I would sit beside her on the veranda and do the only chore she asked of me: clean the glass of our kerosene lamp.

Inside Duba, the families where the heads of households worked as schoolteachers, administrators, or government officials, were more well-off than my grandmother who was both a hair braider, and a self-taught couturiere. These, administrators, and government officials, had been able to improve their households with electricity. We didn't have electricity in our one-room bedroom with its queen-size bed where every night I fell asleep snuggled up and safe in my grandmother's arms. And so, every late afternoon, right before dusk, Lalla would check that the wick was long enough, and that there was enough kerosene to last another night. Afterwards, she would carefully remove the glass and I would clean it—wiping with a damp cloth, the dark spots left by the burning wick from the previous night.

After dinner, I would lie beside Lalla on the mat and listen to her and her sister talk about their days and share the latest news in the neighborhood or the country. Then my grandmother would tell me tales with a clear moral or sing children's songs until I fell asleep.

The stories were always about animals that could talk and highlighted the triumph of the lion (courageous), the rabbit (clever and mischievous, but always goodhearted), over the hyena (stupid/greedy and mean). There were also children—orphans and/or stepchildren—mistreated by the adults who were supposed to care for them. Children who patiently endured their misery, and whose silent suffering was, in the end, rewarded. The once-abused children got their revenge when, as adults, they conquered their villages and became reigning kings or wealthy queens whose success shamed those who had mistreated them. The lessons of the tales had the same themes: Good triumphed over bad; generosity over greed; kindness over meanness; right over wrong. Lalla used the moral of the tales to encourage me to always be a good, obedient girl because no good came from being disrespectful and disobedient. From those early years to the end of her time on Earth, my grandmother never stopped talking, singing, and teaching me what she knew of life.

My bliss—my happy and carefree life—ended abruptly. I was five, and without warning, without any explanation, my world was turned upside-down. It began with what seemed at the time like an inconsequential event. A car came to take me away. Lalla didn't tell me where I was going, or how long I would be gone. She put on a brave smile as she said goodbye and let me go with strangers to an unknown destination. I was an obedient child who knew better than to question the ways of my elders. For even in those early years, on the very rare occasions when I disobeyed Lalla, I had been the recipient of the painful spanking that always came.

An hour later, we were far from Lalla's house and driving in a neighborhood that was a foreign land to me. The car stopped in front of a big house full of people—mostly adults—I didn't know. The home had electricity, and the people were kind to me. They smiled, asked how I was doing, and how was my grandmother.

"Fine." Everything was fine.

Later, we ate, and I spent the night. The next morning, I'd had enough. I liked the visit, but I wanted to go home. I missed Lalla. I went to the one adult who intimidated me the least—I would later find out he was the youngest of my uncles—and asked when I could go home.

"Soon," he said in a reassuring tone, "as soon as I see a taxi."

I trusted his words. I waited patiently for as long as I could. Then, fearing that he might have forgotten, I asked, when would I go home? "Soon," he said again and again, as the hope to see Lalla rose and fell. "Soon," he said over and over as I grappled to accept that I didn't know how long I would have to stay in this house away from my grandmother.

I hadn't known that the adults had decided to have Lalla take care of me while my dad settled but now at five years old it was time to start school.

In the end, "soon" never materialized. I didn't dare cry in front of the people of the house. My new home was an assigned government house as Papa was working now as a high official in the Malian administration. For a long time, every morning when the adults went to work, and the maid was in the kitchen, alone in a room, I sobbed and sobbed. I ached. I missed Lalla. I missed Duba. And it seemed that I would never go back.

I didn't know it then, but moving to the new house marked the end of my happy and carefree years. This was the beginning of a new era—one where I would learn to see, experience, and accept things I did not understand. Soon, expectations, pressure, and fear would enter my being—and with the years—develop, blossom and become an operating system that would run my life. Still, in those early years, I was a little girl lost in a house full of strangers, family members as I would later come to know. The big house was a villa with four bedrooms, two bathrooms, a large living room, and a big open terrace that served as the family room. Unlike my maternal great-grandfather, my father didn't have communal wives but he would marry four times.

In the house was Papa, the distant authority who ruled the house; Mama Sweetness, my first stepmother; her daughter Tita, my baby sister, who was two years younger than me and Papa's four cousins who had left their village and were now working and living in the city. They didn't stay with us, but we took our meals together.

Papa. Where do I begin? Papa was kingly and true to form, Mali is known as the land of Kings from which Mansa Musa, to this day, is considered one of the richest men that ever lived. Papa was king of our household. Papa came from Tandio, a small village, in the center of Mali some distance from Bamako. He was the son of one of the notables of the community. My grandfather was a farmer who owned a lot of land and cattle. In the early 1930s when Mali and many west African countries were living under the French colonial rules, the French built schools and required that the sons of all the dignitaries be forced to attend them. The schools controlled what children were taught, and they were a persuasive deterrent to all rebellions from the locals. Locals who had no easy access to the schools their children had to attend were pliable. The French then used education as a way to demean and deride the elders' way of life--their beliefs, customs, and traditions--while boasting about the superiority of the French culture. The plan was to transform the children into acceptable adults who could be part of their world, but never fine enough to be their equals.

Papa liked to recall that when he was old enough to help his big brothers and cousins, he used to follow them into the field until they all realized that farming was too difficult a task for his frail body. Then, he tried being a shepherd, but that didn't last long because almost every day, he fell asleep after eating lunch and forgot about the flock of sheep and goats he was supposed to sentinel. And so, being physically useless he was drafted to go to school but with his failure rate at everything he tried before, his elders mocked him, saying it would be just a matter of time before he gave up, especially because of the miles he had to walk to get to school. This they said was too much for such a feeble child. He was determined to prove them wrong—and he did.

Not only did Papa stay in school, but he excelled and after finishing high school received a scholarship to attend one of the most prestigious schools in Paris—École Nationale de la Statistique et de l'Administration Economique (ENSAE)—where he graduated specializing in statistics and economics, with a minor in mathematics. From these humble beginnings in a small village, Papa had built a successful career, a family life, and a pedestal from which he wanted to be seen, obeyed, and adored. As long as we were under his roof, Papa, the husband, the father, the big brother, made it clear he was the head of the household and he ruled it with an iron hand. All those who lived under his roof loved and feared him at the same time. Papa was inflexible and moody with all without discrimination. He didn't smile often. I didn't hear him laugh much. Mama Sweetness, my uncles, their spouses, my baby sister, and our little cousins all seemed to live to please Papa. No one in our household questioned or disputed his rule.

My father terrified me because he was swift with his reprimand. If I broke a glass or a plate, the punishment was immediate and brutal. A slap in the face or a beating with his belt. I became afraid of even hearing Papa call my name. And looking back, it seemed that he only called me when I did something wrong. Living in the big house with Papa normalized my constant fear of what might be wrong every time someone said my name— an anxiety I carried with me for most of my adult life.

Papa was strict, no doubt yet, with time, I would discover other sides of my father. There was the loyal Papa, the man who never forgot where he came from. Even today, my father has a profound love for the village where he was born, and the family that still lives there. The generous Papa. Through the years, uncles, aunts, cousins came to visit or to seek medical attention for their health problems and Papa would take them to their appointments, buy the medicines, and make sure they followed the treatments. He looked after them until they were healthy again before letting them go back to the village. To this day, he continues to contribute financially to the affairs of the village.

Then there was Papa the social butterfly, perfect for his future diplomatic position, the affable charmer with a great sense of humor. This Papa, who people outside of our home respected, loved, and valued, came out mainly for the relatives, the friends, the colleagues, and supervisors he esteemed, appreciated, or needed. Among those he liked were our next-door neighbors—a young French couple, Babette, and Jean-Yves. It was their first expatriate assignment and their first travel abroad. Jean-Yves was a high school history and geography teacher, and she taught French grammar and vocabulary in a vocational school that trained office secretaries. For months, we only exchanged hellos. Then one day, Babette came running, hysterically crying because Jean-Yves had collapsed, and she didn't know what to do. Papa and Mama Sweetness, who was a nurse rushed them to the hospital where she worked, and Jean-Yves was treated for malaria.

After his release from the hospital, Babette and Jean-Yves became frequent visitors. They didn't have any children and took a liking to Tita, Mama Sweetness's first child, and me. Every time they came to visit, they played with us for a while and stayed to chat with our parents. Later, they would have a tremendous impact on me.

From time to time, Papa would let me go visit Lalla. My grandmother and I were overjoyed to be together. Lalla used these rare visits to recount for me the tales and songs of her childhood. At the end of every stay, when it came time to say goodbye, I didn't want to go. My grandmother would pull me close, and as she held me against her chest, she would whisper, "Don't cry." Her words helped me walk away with my head held high, but my heart was heavy as I swallowed tears.

Months after I moved into the big house I started going to school. Elementary school brought new demands. I was the firstborn, and so all eyes turned to me to be the example for my baby sister and my younger cousins to follow. I was also expected to do well because Papa would suffer great embarrassment if *his* child failed in school. I didn't disappoint that first year. And with my good grades, I discovered what it meant to be worthy. Papa's nod of approval, smile, compliments, and words of encouragement were special treats that thrilled me. I was as proud as my father when he casually mentioned what a good student I was in front of approving family and friends. But no one was surprised. The sympathetic listeners reminded my father that he had been a studious schoolboy in his time; of course, I would continue the tradition of excellence he set. This new Papa, the Papa of compliments even though strict, was a great Papa.

As my first year in school ended, I had finally settled in and was now used to life in the big house. I loved Mama Sweetness—she was the second mother figure in my life, and she loved and treated me like Tita, my baby sister. I had dubbed her Mama Sweetness because of her sweet and gentle personality. She never made a distinction between Tita and me and dressed us in identical dresses that were made by local tailors. We also wore the same color shoes. Though I missed Lalla, life was shaping up to be good.

One sunny morning, right after we'd had breakfast, I saw Mama Sweetness walk into a room that was our attic—a place where we stored all the things the family didn't use. I followed her.

"What are you doing?"

"I'm taking out our suitcases."

"Why?"

"Because me and Tita are leaving."

"What about me?"

"You are staying with Papa."

I burst into tears as my world once again came undone. Why was Mama Sweetness leaving without me? Mama Sweetness couldn't hold back her tears. We cried all day, as she packed their belongings. Papa, my uncles, their spouses, and children who ate with us every day were nowhere to be seen. Late in the afternoon, a truck came to pick up all her things. Mama Sweetness left with my little sister, and I was left alone. I spent the night in the big empty room I used to share with Tita, lonely and terrified of being without them.

The next day, Papa came back from where he'd gone; and so, did the uncles and their families. Life went on as if nothing had happened. A week after the divorce, I worked up the courage to ask Papa permission to go see Mama Sweetness. My father allowed me to visit her in her new home. For one day, my life was normal again as I played with Tita, and every time I turned there was Mama Sweetness smiling at me. It would be our last time together. After that, Papa said that I couldn't see Mama Sweetness anymore.

A cousin came to live with us and babysat me for a while. I got used to her presence as life went on as if Mama Sweetness and Tita had never been part of our lives. At the time, Papa worked as the CEO of the Government new Data Analysis Bureau. Eventually, he went on to become a diplomat. He was appointed as a representative of the Mali Mission to the United Nations in New York City, but his nomination posed the question of what to do with me. I was about to turn seven, and my father couldn't picture himself taking care of such a small child on his own, so he made a plan with Babette and Jean-Yves, and they agreed to take me in. I went to live with the couple, who became my guardians for the next two years.

Jean-Yves was like flowing water—always patient, always calm. He was Catholic and went to church every Sunday morning. Babette was thunder ready to roar at the smallest irritation. She was a free spirit who didn't practice any religion yet showed a profound respect for all belief systems.

In the beginning, Babette and Jean-Yves took me in as a favor to their dear friend Papa. Every Sunday, before going to church, Jean-Yves dropped me off at Duba, where I spent the day with Lalla. And just like that, life was good again.

To this day, I don't know the arrangements they made with Papa. But for two years, they poured their love into me. For two years, I was as if their own child. Every day, Babette sat with me and helped with my homework. She taught me how to read and write. Jean-Yves taught me his love of books, music, and orange jelly. Babette passed on to me her love of the outdoors—walking and swimming. And together we loved cats, going to the movies, French baguettes and cheese, salads, and homemade soup made with fresh legumes from Jean-Yves's garden.

On Saturday nights, we picnicked on the veranda, eating the crepes Babette made, and singing songs while Jean-Yves played the guitar. Every other week, Babette made her delicious, fresh apple pie. These are things that I still enjoy today.

Papa wrote letters that Babette read to me that always said the same things: Be good and do well in school. Babette made me write letters back that said I was doing well and sent him plenty of kisses. At the end of my first school year living with them, Babette, Jean-Yves, and I traveled to France for our summer vacation.

The voyage was a big deal. It was my first time ever flying that I was conscious of as I was born in Paris and lived there for two years before returning to Bamako. We wore special travel outfits that Babette had made for the three of us by local tailors. We arrived in Paris where we would stay a few days with Babette's mother.

I remember the paved street! The well-maintained building, we would stay at that I loved. The outside walls were thick and made with different sized cut stones. In the middle of its lobby was a majestic iron cube—I later learned was an elevator. When the elevator doors opened, Babette pushed our suitcases in and then told me to get in. I hadn't noticed when she pressed the button on the inside and screamed when the door closed and it suddenly lurched upward, "It's going up! It's going up!"

Babette smiled. "It's the elevator. It's taking us upstairs so we don't have to walk the stairs with all this luggage."

I was in awe of the box-shaped machine that was moving up. The ride ended too quickly. I followed Babette. She knocked on a door midway down a long corridor.

"Maman, it's me."

"Oh, Babette!"

The door flew open. A lady with white hair appeared. I watched as she and Babette kissed and laughed and touched each other's hair and face.

"Maman, this is Anna."

"Anna, this is my mommy. She's your Mammie-grandma of Paris."

Mammie of Paris hugged me. It seemed to me the three of us, with our baggage, were a bit much for her small studio with the large open window that let the sun and the summer breeze in.

During our stay in Paris, I spent my nights with Mammie of Paris while Babette and Jean-Yves stayed in a nearby hotel. She became my designated babysitter. Mammie of Paris took me everywhere she went—her office, the hospital to visit relatives, and every day we all had lunch together in an outside café.

After a week in Paris, we arrived at Jean-Yves's family home in a small village in the Loire Valley in France. There I met Jean-Yves's parents, his father, Pappy, and his mother, Mammie. His parents lived in a three-story house where Jean-Yves and his three siblings were raised. The mezzanine was the garage and the place for all of Pappy's gardening tools. On the first floor was Pappy's garden, where he grew all the vegetables—zucchini, cabbage, carrots—that Mammie used to make her delicious soups.

On that same floor was the large kitchen that served as the family room. Every night after dinner, we all gathered in the living room, and Jean-Yves and his siblings played songs on their guitars.

Babette and Jean-Yves were the first couple who showed me what living a "colorblind" life looked and felt like. They took me in. Everywhere we went, restaurants, movies, and even to their families in France, I was part of their clan. I don't believe they could have loved me more or treated me better if I had been their own child. We were family. Life was simple. They knew my stay with them was temporary, but they believed they could persuade Papa to let them keep me.

After two years of a contented and stable life with Babette and Jean-Yves, Papa came back for his first vacation. I was a happy nine-year-old girl, unaware that this was the beginning of the end of my life with Babette and Jean-Yves. One afternoon, a car stopped in front of our home. A carefree, bubbly little girl came out. It was Tita. She had spent the last two years with her maternal grandparents, but now that Papa was back, so was my little sister. I was happy and jealous of Tita. I was afraid that her presence would mean that Babette and Jean-Yves would love me less. Babette sensed my fear and reassured me—I had nothing to worry about. No one could replace me in their hearts.

While Tita and I stayed with Babette and Jean-Yves, Papa went away and married his third wife—Mama Fire—in their hometown. She was young, impetuous, good-hearted, and full of fire, so I dubbed her Mama Fire. A few weeks later, the newlyweds came back to Bamako. Tita and I moved from Babette and Jean-Yves's house to the villa Papa had rented for his new family. Babette and Jean-Yves couldn't convince Papa to let me stay with them. He wanted his children together under the same roof as him.

I can't imagine the pain Babette and Jean-Yves must have felt as they packed my belongings—my clothes, my books, my toys, my favorite teddy bear—the sum of two years of my life with them—and watched me leave for a new chapter that didn't include them. We cried as we said goodbye, and Papa in a moment of compassion, promised that we would spend our next vacation with them. Babette and Jean-Yves left for France soon after. I was learning about the impermanence of life.

As it turned out, Tita and I were going to live with Papa in New York City where he would continue to serve as a diplomat. Mama Fire stayed behind, but she would soon join us. Lalla came to the airport, and as she was ready to bid me farewell, whispered, as she always did, "Please don't cry." It was hard, but I managed to swallow my tears. The pain of my separation from Babette and Jean-Yves and Lalla was lessened when we arrived in the U.S. and I began to love everything in my new life. The house in Bronxville was a mansion. We lived in the main house, which had two dining rooms—one for our family and the other one for official dinners with dignitaries. There was a spacious living room, where the Malian delegation would come together almost every night to dine after meetings at the UN General Assembly sessions. Tita and I would peek in at all our "aunties" and "uncles" from the stairways—admiring or making fun of their height, their faces, their bellies, the way they walked or danced.

I loved the house. My sister and I shared a large bedroom with twin beds and desks side by side. The staff—a cook, a housekeeper, and the chauffeur—had their lodgings on one side of the property. The home was bought early in the sixties, when Mali opened its representation to the United Nations, shortly after gaining its independence from France. It sat in the middle of a large, manicured block with trees, allowing for barbecues and parties during the summer.

I loved Mam Agnes, our cook, and her daughter, Lucille, who was the housekeeper. She braided our hair and readied us for school every morning. They were kind to Tita and me. I believed they sympathized with us because we were so young and without the presence of a mother to care for us. I had long been without a mother as she'd left my father shortly after I was born.

I loved our new school, the Lycée Français of New York—an international private French school that many diplomats' children attended. I was a social butterfly who made friends easily and quickly. Tita was shy. Decades later, as we were having brunch in one of my favorite cafés in Harlem and talking about our childhood, Tita confided that she felt invisible, tired of being called Anna's little sister.

During the New York years, it was just Papa, Tita, and I in our new home. Mama Fire came to visit, then went to France to pursue her studies. Tita was eight and I was ten. It was there that Papa imposed on himself the role of being both a father and mother figure to us. Papa was intent on raising us his way—and his way meant there was room for no one else. We belonged to him. Maybe our respective mothers didn't realize it at the time, but the dissolution of their unions to Papa meant they were also terminated from us. Papa completely blocked out our mothers, even though they were both alive and well. It was almost as if they didn't exist. Still, because he was the only parent in our lives, the one cheering us on at every school event, Papa became our hero. Tita and I adored him and to his delight put him on a pedestal. I came to emulate him, taking on his way of thinking and his opinion of people influenced how I viewed them.

Every morning our father drove us to school, and every afternoon the driver picked us up. At night, Papa checked our homework. On weekends we ate and watched television together. Our father intently listened to our stories about what had happened in school, the things we learned, the friends we made. Papa wanted his children to be independent and self-sufficient. He didn't want us to rely on anyone financially. As we were his daughters, it meant there was nothing we couldn't do. He said it over and over until I believed him.

"Your first husband is your degree," he often said. Education was crucial and nonnegotiable. We would get a diploma even if he had to beat it into our system. In this respect, he was ahead of his time. Although the Malian government promoted the enrollment of girls in school, getting married and having children was still a more important priority but not to Papa.

Tita and I had good grades and that pleased him. Feeding on our need for approval, Papa used our school performance to create a rivalry that would keep Tita and me competing and fighting for his love and praise. Our worthiness depended on our rank in school as well as the respect and obedience we showed him at home and praise or reprimand was doled out accordingly. He rewarded us with words of validation and rivalry, encouraging Tita and me to tell on each other to keep him informed.

I didn't forget Babette and Jean-Yves. We wrote back and forth often. One summer they came to visit us in New York. The following year, Tita and I spent Christmas with Jean-Yves's entire family in his parents' home in France. We walked to church for midnight Mass then came home and opened our many presents. It was an unforgettable vacation because it felt like my 'family' was together. I didn't know it then, but it would be thirty years until we would be together again.

In 1972, when I was ten years old, Papa was assigned to a new position in what was then the Federal Republic of Germany. We were leaving New York for a place called Bonn Bad Godesberg. I was again sad as I loved New York but in my short life had an appreciation for the constant state of change our life entailed. Mama Fire would take a break from her studies and leave France to come live with us in Germany. Germany felt like a real foreign country and I found the language difficult, not a romance language, to this day it surprises me how Tita grasped it so easily. My sister is bright, I don't know how Tita managed to do so well in school despite all the changes in our young lives. While Tita applied herself and learned to speak German, for me learning it became a strenuous and unrewarding process. That was the year I witnessed a shift in Papa's behavior and a downward spiral in my confidence. Tita had now become his favorite child and Papa began to whisper in her ear that I was unworthy. Our relationship became an open rivalry, fueled, and encouraged by Papa. It would take decades to mend our distrust of each other.

The end of our first year in the Bad Godesberg section of Bonn was awful. My report card showed what I couldn't hide: I had failed almost all my classes and would have to redo the year. Papa shook his head, signed the card, and without uttering a single word, handed it over to Mama Fire. She shook her head, "This is so disappointing."

I took my report card and walked away, ashamed yet relieved that I wasn't beaten. Later, when Tita came into our room, I knew by the beaming smile on her face that she had been showered with compliments and praise. At dinner, Papa was in a strangely good mood. He made jokes that weren't funny, which we still laughed at. Finally, at the end of our meal, Papa said it was time to be serious. There was something he wanted to say. I wasn't worried because he had tried to lighten up the evening until that very moment.

First, he turned to Tita, "I'm very proud of you. You did very well in school, and you are a good girl at home. You respect your parents...you make me proud." Then he looked at me. "Unfortunately, I cannot say the same about you."

Panic poured in. Papa didn't raise his voice. He was calm and cutting. The rancor in his voice was beyond what I could fathom.

"You are the big sister, but it's Tita who looks and acts like a big sister. You are a failure in school and a failure at home, just like your mother. Do you know why we split? Why I threw her out of my life and out of my house? Because I didn't want to take care of a worthless human being who brought nothing but problems to me. And you are turning out to be just like her. I'm warning you, Anna, you better be careful. You better get your act together and change. Because if you keep being the failure you are now, I will not put up with it. I will throw you out the way I kicked out your mother. I will not, you hear me, I will not continue to feed and shelter a disappointment in my house. Now maybe when you grow up and become nothing, maybe you can go beg Tita, and she'll have pity on you and take you in. But you will not stay in my house."

There was frightening silence during and after his tirade. Tears streamed down my face. No one stopped him. No one came to my rescue. Papa left the dining room. Mama Fire followed him. My sister and I cleared the table, washed the dishes, and went to bed without talking. The next morning, Mama Fire made some omelets for breakfast. Tita and I set the table. We all came together, sat, and ate as if nothing had happened. How could Papa not understand! I did well in school when I studied in French, shouldn't he be a little more understanding. Papa's words cut me to my core and the events of the previous night marked the beginning of my fall from grace, a time that would stretch from my teens to my young adult years.

Chapter Five

THE YEARS OF THE LONE PECULIAR STRAW

The one who walked alone—the lone peculiar straw.

Thorn firmly piercing my heart, the year was 1974. Tita was ten and I was twelve. Papa was at the end of his diplomatic assignment in Germany. We were going back to Mali. Mama Fire was going to France to finish her studies. I was overjoyed. We were going home and I was going to see Lalla.

But Papa had other plans. Our father was still determined to be our sole parent. We remained isolated from our maternal families. As we settled into our new home in Bamako, our paternal uncles, aunts, and cousins—who were teenagers about the same age or slightly older than Tita and me—all came back into our lives. Every Sunday, from morning to late afternoon, we spent the day cooking, chatting, and telling jokes while Papa, his cousins, and friends carried on their own conversations on the side of our yard. I did not go to live with Lalla as I had hoped, instead our family grew when Mama Fire returned home and gave birth to a baby girl, our sister, Mimi.

Papa never had to say it—Tita and I were too scared to ask if we could visit our maternal relatives. I missed my grandmother terribly. I don't know how Lalla found out we were back, but one beautiful afternoon after school, we walked into the house and found my Lalla with her sister, Fanta sitting on the veranda. Looking back, I know my grandmother was hurt. She didn't understand Papa's rules. But both Lalla and Uncle Layes—Maman's brother—were intent on two things: to give Papa his *due share of water*—meaning always remain respectful and mindful of his ways; his ways; and to be present in whatever manner they could in my life. Thus, they came to see me as much as they could.

"I knew your father when he was a villager from a place no one in our family knew," Lalla liked to say. "He was the one who needed me then. But he's your father; and as long as he has you, there are things I cannot say to him."

I wasn't born when Papa first met my Lalla and my grandpa who died a year after I came into the world. But according to the story I heard from Lalla and the family at Duba, my grandmother was a force to be reckoned with. I didn't comprehend the extent of the power my grandmother wielded in Bamako the capital of Mali, as a councilwoman who was very close to the Presidential couple at the time, Modibo Keita and Mrs. Keita.

Lalla had never been to school. She didn't know how to read or write. When my grandmother came into the world, Mali was already under French rule. The military penetration, or forced colonization, began around 1890. But after World War II, when many West African nations were still considered French colonies, the rise and popularity of national political parties who demanded independence worried and frustrated the occupying force.

"When the war ended, our leaders began to organize and rally for independence," my grandmother said. "But France was not having it. I used to attend our clandestine meetings. It is there that I entered politics. Our leaders were accused of being Communists. They were arrested, jailed, and tortured; others lost their jobs. I saw wives, mothers, and sisters become the sole bread winners of their entire families for a long time. In the end, our struggle prevailed, and in 1960 Mali gained its independence. Soon after, I joined your grandfather"—her second husband and the love of her life—"and campaigned for him. You see, he was educated, but he was not a good public speaker so I used to speak on his behalf. I helped him organize his meetings and conferences. We won. Your grandfather became a senator, and I was elected a council woman for our district."

Shortly after, Papa who was an undergraduate student in Paris, came back home for his vacation. A mutual acquaintance introduced him to the powerhouse couple, who then had two children one being my mother, and a son, my uncle Layes. The rest, as they say, is history. But my mother had long since left my father and was living in Senegal.

In the middle of that first year back in Mali, the one person I never expected to see came back. Maman, who now worked and lived in Senegal, took her vacation, and came to spend it with Lalla. She called Papa and asked his permission to see me. This was the second time. There's a picture of Maman and me when I was about four or five. But in my memory, this was a brief meeting. He agreed but didn't tell me. I was visiting my grandma Fanta when she asked, "Did you see your Maman?"

"What?"

"You know Rokia is here, did you see her?

"No. Where is she?"

"She's staying with Lalla."

My heart beat with excitement and fear. My Maman was here, but how in the world was I going to tell Papa?

Grandma Fanta was Lalla's little sister, and as an elder, was given the moniker grandma. "Please, please," I pleaded, "Tell Papa and ask him if I can go visit her."

Grandma Fanta agreed. Two days later, she stopped by our house.

"Mama Fanta, how are you?" Papa greeted her.

"I'm good. Listen, I don't know if you already know, but Rokia is here."

Papa interrupted her: "I know, she called me and asked if she could see Anna. I already said yes."

My grandmother politely thanked him and left.

That Saturday afternoon, Papa called me. He was standing in the middle of the living room. "You know your Maman is here. I don't know why you would want to see a woman who has never done anything for you. But it's your decision. If you decide to go see her, I'm not taking you, and I'm not giving you bus fare. It's your problem. So, what do you want to do?"

I said, apologetically, "I'm going."

Papa walked away. I didn't have any money so I went to see Grandma Fanta. She asked Grandpa Seybou, her husband, a taxi driver, to take me to Lalla's new home. My grandmother had moved from Duba when one of her brothers asked her to be the landlord of his new property. I was torn between fear and excitement. I had no clear memory of Maman. And I worried that if there were strangers in the house, I would not know who my Maman was.

As Grandpa's cab approached the house, I grew restless. The front door was open, and sitting alone at the end of the veranda was a woman.

"Oh, look, here's Rokia, maybe she was waiting for you."

I shook my head no. I was convinced she didn't know I was coming. The car stopped, I jumped out and ran to her. Maman opened her arms wide and held me tight. Grandpa Seybou followed, laughing: "I'm just the chauffeur today. Anna, you forgot your bag."

"Go get it. I'll wait for you," Maman said.

I dashed to the car, grabbed my bag, and ran back to Maman. We were both ecstatic. Maman was tall. She was beautiful, and without knowing her, I worshipped everything about her: her contagious laugh, and the way she talked. She gave me an image to hold on to. I really had a Maman.

Lalla teased me, "Anna, now that your Maman is here, you forgot about me."

"Never, never." I hugged Lalla.

She laughed. "Go talk to your Maman. I know you missed her."

It was the beginning of our loving, complex, and turbulent relationship. For the next two months, I spent every weekend with Maman and Lalla. Maman was kind. I held her hand, I sat by her side. And on many Saturday evenings, Lalla and I listened, as Maman recounted for me the tales and songs of her childhood.

"*N'zirin!*" Maman said, beginning her tale in the traditional way.

"*Namu*, we are listening," Lalla and I replied.

"This is the story of the fight between Long Tail and Long Tongue. Long, long ago people and animals used to live together in the villages. They understood each other because they spoke the same language. In these villages, people lived in huts with straw roofs. The homes were close to one another. Children and animals—rooster, hen, ox, horses—wandered free, except for the dog who was the guardian of the community and could usually be found resting at the entrance to the village.

"Every dawn, the men went to work in the fields. Women stayed to clean, fetch water, and cook. Later, around noon, they took the food to the men in the field, and while the husbands ate, the wives did the farming. The elders stayed behind and watched over the grandchildren.

"One early afternoon, when grandparents and grandchildren were napping, and the village was quiet, Long Tail and Long Tongue—two small lizards—came down from the roof where they were enjoying the sun to run around the cooking area looking for forgotten leftovers. It was their lucky day. They found a spilled bowl of rice near the kitchen that no one had cleaned up. And for a while, Long Tail and Long Tongue were busy running back and forth from the bowl of rice to the roof, taking as much grain as they could to feast on later. But when it came time to share the meal, the two lizards could not agree on the portion of rice each should get. And so, the fight began.

"Long Tail and Long Tongue kicked and tried to scratch and bite each other, their tails furiously pounding against the roof. The dog, the guardian of the entire compound, heard the noise and called on the rooster, 'There's a lot of noise coming from the roof and grandmother is sleeping. Do you know what's going on?'

"'Oh, it's nothing, just two lizards fighting over food.'

"Please, Rooster, go and ask them to stop. And if they don't, do something to end the fight."

"The rooster was outraged. 'You want me to get involved in a fight between lizards. Really? I am the king of the henhouse.'

"The rooster walked away full of pride. Soon after, the dog saw the ox and made the same request. He got a similar answer: The ox couldn't be bothered by such a thing as the fight between two insignificant lizards. He was an ox.

"Meanwhile, the battle between the two lizards had intensified. It was clear this spat over food was not going to end well. The dog tried one last time to avoid the worst. He didn't know what it would be. He just knew it wouldn't be good: 'Horse! Horse!'

"What's going on, Dog?"

"Can you please, please go and separate the two lizards fighting on top of the hut?"

"Really, Dog," neighed the horse. You want me to intervene?"

"Yes, I have a bad feeling about this fight."

"Well, if you do, why don't you stop them?"

"I can't. Master said to guard the entrance."

"Well, stay there and leave me alone!"

"The horse majestically ran off. By now Long Tail and Long Tongue were exhausted. One faux pas during an attack and they both fell through the small hole in the roof into the oil lamp, breaking it. The elder jumped, but it was too late. The flaming wick fell into the mosquito net and caught fire. The elder screamed and the children screamed, 'Fire.' The dog barked furiously to sound the alert. The young people, women, and men who weren't far ran back and used all they could—tree branches and buckets of water—to extinguish the fire. The home was destroyed, but they were able to save the elder.

"The village healer came and prepared the ointment the family would apply to her badly burned body. And because it would be some time before she could eat, he prescribed chicken broth soup as her daily meal. The rooster who refused to intervene in the fight between the two lizards became the main ingredient for the potage.

"As the elder continued to battle for her life, the clan decided to send someone to inform the rest of her family living in different parts of the community. A young man rode the horse as it had never been ridden before, making it wish it had done something to stop the unfortunate fight.

"The grandmother's entire family rushed to be by her side. The ointment healed her burned body, and the broth gave her back her strength. The village helped her children rebuild her hut. To celebrate her recovery, and thank all the villagers for their help, the family decided to have a feast. The entire community came and they sang songs, danced, and prepared a festive meal of rice, vegetables, and ox meat.

"The people were grateful to the dog for his loyalty. It was thanks to him—his barking gave the alert and told them something was wrong—that they came on time and saved the elder. To thank him, the villagers brought him a large plate of bones so good that he forgot the sadness he felt when the ox disappeared.

"In the end, the rooster, the ox, and the horse all paid a price for not wanting to be bothered. Only the dog, faithful to his duty, emerged unscathed from this turmoil and even found an unexpected reward."

Maman concluded, "When I was a little girl, your grandmother and the elders used this tale to show how destructive conflict can become if you let it escalate. In this world, there are two things that can give birth to things bigger than themselves: fire and war. A fire can devastate and decimate an entire community, and a war can bring the world to its end. That's why, when there are disagreements in the family or in the neighborhood, people get involved and try to resolve them. Fighting is never good."

"Well, sometimes...."

"No, Lalla, fighting is never good."

They exchanged a knowing look and laughed.

"Your Maman is right, Anna, fighting is never good."

I loved and envied their closeness. Lalla and Maman acted more like sisters than mother and daughter. For two months we spent every weekend together.. *hèrè*—joy and happiness— filled the house. I listened and laughed as Lalla and Maman gossiped about family, friends, and neighbors.

As the end of her vacation neared, Maman decided one Sunday afternoon to take me home. The taxi stopped in front of the house. We walked in together.

"Hello, anyone home?" Maman asked.

"Yes, we're here. So, you finally decided to come visit?" Papa teased.

They laughed and hugged. I was in shock. *Papa didn't hate her.* Maman declined to stay. She just wanted to bring me home and thank Papa for allowing me to visit her. Every week, Maman called Papa to ask permission for me to spend the weekend with her and Lalla. The three of us walked together outside, and the inquisitive neighbors came out one by one to say hello and find out who was the tall woman who was conversing with Papa.

A week later, I was waiting for Maman. We were going to spend her last afternoon together. The next day, she was going back to Dakar. How would I ever say goodbye to this woman I adored and needed in my life? I had put in an envelope all the pictures I wanted to give Maman so she would not forget me. I left the envelope on the dining room table to get something.

I heard footsteps and ran back. Too late. Papa had my photos in his hand.

"Who gave you the money to take these pictures?"

"Grandma Fanta."

"Where did you go to have them taken?"

"Uh, not far."

"Where? And when?"

"This week," I said, desperately praying the threat would go away.

"When this week? Did you cut school?"

"No."

"Since when do you think you can have this tone with me?" he demanded.

I didn't run fast enough. Papa grabbed my arm. As he pulled me closer to him, he twisted it while looking for the branch of a tree he could cut and use to whip me. I managed to free myself from his grip and ran to the door, yelling: "I've had it! I'm going to live with my Maman."

"Good riddance. When I come back, I don't want to find you here."

He left for work. By late afternoon, Maman hadn't shown up. Instead, she sent a friend with a note saying goodbye because she knew we would both cry. I wrote back that I needed her because Papa had just kicked me out of the house. I packed a few things and sat waiting. Tita watched me.

"Where are you going?"

"I'm going to live with my Maman."

I said it resolutely. I said it with confidence. But I wasn't sure. Soon the sun would set, and Papa would come home. I had to go. But where? Shortly before my father came home, I decided to go visit some friends for the evening. I stayed there late until they were ready to go to bed then took a taxi to Lalla's place. I knocked on the door and Maman opened it.

"What happened? What are you doing here?" she asked.

"Did you receive the note I wrote you?"

Maman didn't answer. Lalla appeared next to her. "Did your father throw you out of the house?"

"Yes."

"Go back to where you came from," Maman said.

What? Panic. Pain. I disintegrated inside.

"Wait," Lalla interjected. She went back inside and got dressed. "Come with me."

Lalla and I got back in the taxi and she had him take us to the home of her most trusted childhood friends. She asked the couple to keep me for the night. The next morning, Maman left for Senegal. That evening, Lalla and a group of the elders took me home. Papa had an audience: Lalla and the elders; Tita, my baby sister; my uncles and their wives. We were all sitting on the terrace. Papa recounted his grievances: I didn't do well in school. I was disobedient. I talked back. The adults unanimously condemned me. Only Lalla remained silent.

But more than being embarrassed publicly by my father, it was Maman's reaction that left me wounded. How could the woman I'd come to idolize reject me? How could that wonderful reunion result in this devastation? Papa had always portrayed Maman as the woman who abandoned me. Lalla, on the other hand, spoke adoringly about her wonderful daughter. And before she left me behind again on that fateful night, I loved Mother. Seeing her and being around her had filled a deep emotional void. For the longest time, in school or at friends' houses, my eyes always seemed to catch those moments when mothers hugged and kissed their children. I watched furtively, secretly wishing I were the child receiving all that love and affection. In the short time we were together, I was the recipient of the love I had missed for all those years. Later, Lalla tried to explain that Maman didn't take me with her because she was afraid of what people would have said—of her coming in and taking her daughter after all these years. But she knew Maman loved me. I wanted to believe her. But being left behind and facing Papa's victorious speech as he humiliated me publicly made it difficult to feel loved or wanted.

Life went on. But my heart was broken. I was in a state of numbness that Papa, my uncles, and aunts called indifference. I didn't have the drive to be good at anything. While Tita continued to shine with top-of-the-class grades and outstanding obedience at home, my new normal was report cards filled with very average grades in most courses and regularly failing scores in math. Papa was furious. How could a child of his not excel in schoolwork? Eventually, he gave up on me. He turned to my sister, who became the sole carrier of the burden of fulfilling all his expectations, and he publicly nurtured the divide between the good child against the bad one.

Papa wanted to punish me. He sent me to spend my vacation with Lalla. He believed my grandmother's modest means would feel like a downgrade from life under his roof in a villa. He forgot the verity of the old saying: *The road is only long if you don't love the person you are going to visit.*

My grandmother's home was smaller. A tall wall protected the two rooms and private terrace my Lalla occupied, as well as, the three large single rooms with a shared vast open veranda, common kitchen, and bathroom that were rented out. My grandmother collected the rent. The veranda was the common area where everyone gathered almost every night after dinner to talk and listen to the public radio station until very late when we all went to bed. There was no television station at the time. It felt like we were at Duba. The one big change was that there was electricity in the house. One night, while Lalla and I lay side by side on the mat, the radio station played a traditional song, and Lalla sang along, "*It is good to want to learn how to swim or how to ride a horse. Yes, it is good to want to learn new things. But the best knowledge of all knowledge is knowledge of self.*"

She stopped singing, and asked me, "Do you know what this means?"

"Yes, I replied. "It means knowing who you are?"

"And who are you?"

"I'm your granddaughter, and the granddaughter of all your brothers and sisters."

"That's true, but that's not all."

"Tell me."

Lalla lowered the volume. She didn't have to say it—I knew she was pleased I had asked. My grandmother was always delighted when I had questions about our ancient things. And I was happy because Lalla was the best storyteller. That night, Lalla used the adage to tell me about her father—whom she adored. He was the first in their entire lineage who was born Muslim. My great-grandfather was the namesake of the visitor who, early on, had prophesied his arrival to his anxious clan. Lalla's grandmother had suffered several miscarriages, and when she became pregnant again, the elders watching over her were afraid she would lose this unborn life too. One day, a Muslim scholar who was traveling across the country, stopped, and asked if he could rest before continuing his journey. The family welcomed the stranger and invited him to stay as long as he wished. He lived with the clan for a few weeks and, before leaving, predicted that the new life would be a healthy baby boy. The father replied that if that were the case, the newborn would be named after the stranger—the bearer of good news. Months later, the presage came true and my great-grandfather came into the world. Seven days after his birth, he was baptized Umar, and because his namesake was a well-known religious scholar, the family nicknamed him "Teacher."

Lalla's father was the first member of the entire lineage to learn the teachings of Islam, as well as be initiated to *the good path*—the belief system and way of life of his elders. Later, my great-grandfather would move out and go on to have his own family. By that time, Islam had become the main religion of the country. Hence, all his children were born Muslim, but some of Lalla's siblings were taught and became the guardians of our ancestral traditions.

"I can't tell you everything," Lalla said. "I went through so many hardships." She went on to talk about her childhood. My great-grandfather had passed away when she was seven. Without him to keep her safe, some of her adult siblings no longer cared to watch over or protect her. Like the orphans of her tales, Lalla had suffered at the hands of adults who were supposed to care for her. My grandmother recounted the abuse she endured both emotionally and physically—the sleepless nights she spent babysitting the newborn nephew or niece who didn't want to go to sleep. The hunger from having too little to eat. The beatings she received for the small and big things she had done wrong. Lalla, my beloved elder, said that too many abuses at the hands of those who were older than her had forced her to become fierce and defiant. And after the difficult childhood came the unhappy young adulthood.

Lalla was in her early teens when one of her older brothers forced her to marry a much older man she didn't love. Together they had two children—Maman and Uncle Layes. But months after the birth of her second child, Lalla took her two children and left her husband, demanding the marriage be dissolved. At the time, divorce was an ignominy only men could seek, to punish an unworthy wife. But Lalla was defiant and she paid a hefty price: She was shunned and stigmatized by her own family. Still, she refused to give in or change her mind. And so, my proud, rebellious grandmother became a single parent—a father and a mother to her two children, and the sole provider of her small family. As she finished telling me her story, I wiped away silent tears.

"Why are you crying?" she asked me. "I don't tell you what I have been through to make you sad. I tell you all this so you know that pain didn't begin with you. I know your father. I know the way he talks—but you don't belong to him alone, Anna. And if he doesn't want you, we want you. That's why I tell you all this, so that you know you belong to us. I tell you this to *give you heart*—the drive and ambition to do and be better in the future.

"Now you know those from whom you are—the people you come from. You have to do better. It is the hope of every parent that their offspring do better than them. Don't underestimate yourself. Don't be afraid of the work ahead of you. Fear gives small things a big shadow—making them seemingly more difficult than they truly are. When you go back into your father's house, think of what I said and work hard."

Lalla reminded me of a popular traditional song that said, "As children, we each have three possibilities: Surpass the successes of your elders, imitate those who came before you, or accomplish less than your parents." The exceptional fit into the first category. To do less than your parents was a disappointment. All children are warned to avoid this shame and disgrace, for the successful child belongs to the community, and sometimes to the country; but the failures belongs solely to their parents.

She wanted me to work hard and become a success story so that she could continue to improvise lullabies—songs of praise for me—and boast to the clan and her neighbors. My successes where not mine alone; they were also hers to celebrate. I wanted to be who she wanted me to be but thorns riddled my body that was festering in shame and anger. For Lalla, I would try.

Another school year was about to begin. I dreaded leaving, but Lalla reassured me with these parting words, "*Lagaré*, everyone falls. Falling is not a bad thing; it's refusing to get up that is a problem."

I promised my grandmother that I would try to be good, both at home and in school. I would be obedient. I would work hard. I saw Lalla smile, filled with hope that I would keep my promises. Unfortunately, I couldn't keep my word. I no longer had the will to make any effort. I could stay still and listen to Lalla and the elders talk all day long but being in the classroom was another story and school bored me. I was easily distracted and because I couldn't act out at home, I did in school. I was an extrovert who did whatever it took to be noticed. I made my classmates laugh as the class clown with hidden tears. I didn't hate all of school. I loved history, literature, philosophy, and English, my third language after Bambara, my first, and French, our official language. But math, science, and physics were beasts I couldn't understand or conquer. And so, I lost interest. And while Tita remained top of her class, my failing grades in these three courses turned the year into a disaster. Especially for a man who was a mathematician.

"You are a failure," Papa said.

"No, I am not."

"What's the matter with you?" my angry grandmother asked.

"Nothing."

"Why can't you be more like Tita," both Papa and Lalla often said, or they would compare me to some other dutiful and submissive well-liked teen that had good grades, like Tita. I would just shake my head and stare down at my feet. I didn't have an answer to that. Or, more honestly, I did; but the response would have gotten me in more trouble. How could I tell my elders without sounding disrespectful that I had no desire to try to be like Tita or the schoolmate they were comparing me to?

Like a foul-smelling jar, I was the stinky jar in my family that they could not hide. These were the years when I didn't seem to be able to do anything quite right. These were the years when Papa and the elders could not find one good thing to say about me. Indeed, these were the years when being Anna was not a good thing to be.

Papa, my uncles, my aunts, and our close relatives agreed that I was the disappointment of the clan. It was resoundingly stated, and accepted by all—myself included—that I would be different and somewhat *less* than the rest of the family. Our neighbors began using me as the prime example of who they didn't want their children to turn out to be. Even Lalla, my enduring defender, began to doubt me. She was angry that I was such a difficult child. But most of all, my grandmother was torn. Because even during these challenging years, Lalla refused to totally give up on me. She went from one extreme to the other—scolding me when she was angry at me for not being all the things she wanted me to be, then telling me that I belonged to her. She couldn't disown me, no matter what. I didn't grasp what she saw in me then, but something in my grandmother refused to stop believing in me. She kept telling me that she saw that I would do great things.

Papa, Lalla, and all the elders of the community were trying to make me into the embodiment of their expectations. They forgot the sage truth that states: *You can give birth to a child, but not a replica of yourself.* I wanted to be me, even if I didn't know what that looked like. In the end, despite their pleas, anger, and humiliation, the elders in my family could not pull me out of what they saw as my irreversible indolence. To protect myself, I retreated inward, spending a lot of time alone living in my head, a safe place filled with the same family. Only in my stories I was everything they wanted me to be. They loved me, and no one said or did things to hurt me.

My apparent insouciance and laziness served me well. They hid my pain and made people believe that I didn't care. In the outside world, I was labeled as rebellious and insolent. I was the one who walked alone—the lone peculiar straw that didn't fit in with others. Coming from a family of fighters and high achievers, they were bewildered to have in the clan an underachiever who didn't have enough pride to fight to better herself. My frustrated elders speculated out loud what kind of adult I would turn out to be—for I behaved as if I didn't have their blood running in my veins. Their bitter words told me that unless I changed, I would never do or be anything they could be proud of. I had become a disappointing teenager who no one understood, and no one knew what to do with. Surely I would become a disappointing adult. I couldn't allow that to happen.

I promised myself that I would reverse the course. I would show them. One day Papa would be proud of me again. One day I would be so successful that my overjoyed grandmother would sing my greatness to the family and our neighbors again. One day the elders of our community who had lost faith in me would see. I would be somebody and they would recognize that their judgment of me was wrong. I would be the Malian child with the whole universe inside of me. I was a Bambara.

A few years later in 1978, when I was a young adult, Papa divorced Mama Fire and married Mama Deep Water. At sixteen years old, we are once again uprooted when Papa is nominated Ambassador of Mali in Ottawa, Canada, and the family moves to Canada for five years before returning to Bamako when I was twenty-one.

Our family had grown, and Tita, Mimi, and I had two more brothers and two sisters who would follow. We were now seven siblings.

Chapter Six

LOVE THE WORLD

*You have an image of yourself and then you work hard
to become that vision.*

I was now twenty-five, the firstborn. I was shaping up to be the Anna I wanted the world to see—a strong, happy, carefree woman in control of her life who didn't care what others thought or said about her. I had managed to complete a vocational school that gave me an associate degree in administration. Tita was twenty-three and doing well in medical school. Mohammed was fourteen; Mimi, was thirteen; Iba, eight; Fifi, seven; and Yuma, the baby of the family, was four. I had just joined the workforce as an office assistant to the program manager of the United Nations.

At work, I performed my day-to-day tasks, but I wasn't the best employee. I was the fun, eccentric worker who made everyone laugh. When my head was there, I was hardworking and produced some good results. But I wasn't reliable—no one could depend on me to show up or complete my assignments on time. In my personal life, I developed habits that made me everything a woman was not supposed to be in the traditional society we lived in. Contrary to the faith I was born in, I was a heavy smoker, both at home and in public. I enjoyed drinking when I was out and loved to party. I had none of the qualities that the traditional men of our culture and their families looked for in a future wife, but I also had no interest in getting married.

I was born into a Muslim family but I didn't know much about Islam. The Creator was an abstract concept that I couldn't grasp. When I asked Lalla and the elders who or what was this Daba? Where did the Creator come from? Where did Daba live? They all had the same response:

"Daba was the Uncreated Creator. And when Daba created humankind, the unknowable Creator said: I am Daba the Creator. I Am One. I wasn't created. I didn't come from something. I am not in the sky. I am not on Earth. I cannot be measured in time. I am not liquid, and I am not solid. I am not night, and I am not day. You can't see me anywhere, yet I am everywhere. Nothing happens that I don't know. And nothing happens without me allowing it to happen."

Tell me, what do you do with that? How do you process this and make it into something you comprehend? When I pressed for more explanation, my elders described Daba as a rewarding and punishing Almighty. It was blasphemy to disagree with or criticize Daba's will because just like our parents, the Creator could and would make things worse. Hence, my image of Daba was of an authoritative figure much like Papa, Lalla, and the elders, but with powers that were far beyond what I could grasp. But if nothing happens without Daba allowing it to happen, how then did Daba explain me? And since he'd allowed me to be me, Daba was someone on whom I could depend.

Papa, Lalla, and the elders didn't pressure any of us to regularly pray the way they did. And so, I prayed when

I wanted something—to keep my job, to find a way out of an embarrassing situation usually revolving around money I owed. My pleas were usually answered quickly and favorably. I was grateful. I thanked the Creator effusively and moved on to other things. Daba was a distant protective parent and friend I could call on when I needed something, and that definition of the Creator suited me.

I was young, and I was adamant about living my life the way I wanted to—in complete freedom. I didn't want to answer to my elders. Lalla and her teachings were no longer relevant to the world I wanted to create and live in. I didn't have time for her or her stories. I had one purpose: to impress with generosity. Yet I realized it was impossible to sustain my financial generosity with Papa, my family, the elders, friends, and colleagues.

My relatives and friends kept telling me that they were worried about my future. You're not taking life seriously enough, they said. You are always making mistakes. You're always in some sort of financial trouble, they lamented. It was true—I didn't have a good relationship with money. I spent most of my earnings buying gifts and helping people I believed were in need.

If a friend needed money to help pay the rent I was there. If a recently separated or divorced relative needed money to buy food for the family, I was there. If uncles wanted money to put gas in their vehicles, I was there. I was there for everyone who asked. I was continually money-strapped because of my insatiable craving for love and acceptance. My generosity was a plea—even though I refused to admit it—the truth was deep within; I did care about what others thought of me. My offerings were appeals that said, "*See, I'm not that bad...there are things about me that you can love.*"

Lalla didn't complain. She let me enjoy my new job and the freedom it brought me. She didn't make me feel guilty for promising to visit her and then never showing up. She didn't question or criticize the way I lived my life. She let me be. I was living in my Father's house. She would forever be the unassuming, discreet presence who stepped in to defend or help me out of trouble when I needed her.

One night my friends and I were in the club drinking and dancing. My cousin Fatou, who was there, saw me with a cigarette, and thought it would be a good idea to tell Lalla. She went to see her, and on that day, my Uncle Layes, who told me the story, was also there.

"I was surprised to see Fatou because she rarely visits us. Your grandmother was in the kitchen. She said she needed to talk to her, that you were both in a nightclub, and she didn't like what she saw. I tried to dissuade her. But she was convinced she was doing the right thing. When your grandmother finally joined us, Fatou told her that she was shocked and outraged when she saw you smoking. She wanted Lalla to talk to you and make you stop this unbecoming and shameful behavior."

"What did Lalla say?"

"Hmm, Anna, the *lioness* came out." We laughed.

"Poor Fatou."

"No, no, don't say poor Fatou. She brought it on herself. I tried to warn her. She didn't listen. Your grandmother said: 'You came all the way from your home to tell me this?'"

"Your cousin looked my way. I looked down. I wasn't going to get involved. Lalla said: 'Anna smokes, right? Why shouldn't she if that's what she wants to do? She has a job. It's her money. Tell me did she ask you to buy the cigarette she was smoking?'

"Fatou answered, 'No.'"

"Lalla said, 'If you didn't buy her cigarettes, what is your problem? What she does with her money is none of your business. If you want to come visit me, you are welcome, and I'm happy to see you. If you come to talk badly about my Anna, I don't want to see you in my house.'"

"Fatou didn't know what to do. I kept my head down. She was in trouble—I had no intention of adding myself to it. Everybody knows that you cannot say one bad thing about you to your grandmother."

We laughed.

Still, the quest to be forever the kind and generous one to my friends and relatives came at a cost. I was in debt. But I couldn't stop giving away money I didn't really have. The amount I owed ballooned and my creditor – a childhood friend who loved me dearly, and wanted to believe against all odds, that I would eventually pay him back, finally became convinced that I couldn't pay. So, he went to see my grandmother and asked her to talk to me. Lalla called me. The conversation was simple:

"Your friend came to see me. He said you owe him money."

I was both fuming and ashamed. How dare he drag Lalla into this?

"How much do you owe?"

I told her the amount. It was substantial. She didn't get angry. She didn't ask what did you do with the money? Instead, in a reassuring voice my grandmother said, "We're going to pay him back. How much do you have?"

I had about a quarter of what I owed. Lalla went into her savings and paid the rest. I didn't know what to say. To ease my guilt my grandmother said, "You will pay me back later."

Lalla's quiet intervention shook me to the core. I was mortified by who I had become. My ill-fated attempts to be loved and accepted by showering people with gifts they didn't ask for had backfired. Yes, my grandmother had paid my debt, but I was acutely aware that I was not a trusted person. I was branded as unreliable both in my professional and family life. Yet I didn't agree with all the negative statements made about me. Yes, I was impulsive. But everything I said and did came from my heart. My spontaneity was the one thing I liked about myself. I was scolded many times for saying the wrong thing at the wrong time. But they weren't lies. And what if at times I was unpredictable? Who in this world was perfect? I wanted to fight the stigma that came with being Anna by proving that there was absolutely nothing wrong with me. I was fine the way I was. The people I loved just didn't understand me.

However, deep within, I was also afraid I would remain the oddity that no one wanted to be like. My self-inflicted visceral fear of remaining forever a failure gave birth to an absolute need to become what no one expected me to be. "One day," I used to promise myself repeatedly, "I will show them."

My head was filled with dreams of conquest. I wanted success—a happy, fulfilled life with wealth that would make me the Anna everyone would love and admire, when they would again tell me, this time with awe and pride, "Anna, you are unlike anyone in our family."

I would work hard. I would not give up on myself. And I was going to do all this far away from them—in New York City, the only city in all my travels I'd fallen in love with. The Big Apple always made me feel at home. It made me feel anonymous and gave me a sense of freedom. New York was a protective citadel where I could be free to be Anna. I'd always known that one day I would come back to stay for good in this city. It was the perfect place to be me.

At thirty-one, it was time to say goodbye. I knelt in front of Lalla and bowed my head. I felt my grandmother's strong hands on my head. Her voice quivered with emotions as she recited blessings asking Allah to keep me safe. She held my face in her hands.

"Anna, the world is too vast for you to have to stay in a place where you are not happy. I pray that where you are going, you will find all the happiness you want. Don't forget me. Don't forget where you came from."

It was time to say goodbye
With tears in her eyes,
My grandmother implored me to be wise,
And once in America,
To do as you Americans do.
She said to thank you for your hospitality.
Because your kindness would be a debt
She could never repay.
But you would always
Have her undying gratitude.
Choking back a sob
My grandmother said
She might not live long enough
To see me come back
With a piece of the American Dream.

I smiled bravely
And forbade her
To go anywhere before my return.
I would be back
With her part of the American Dream
And together we would share it,
Sitting down under the shade
Of the big mango tree.
She smiled with all her heart
And promised she would wait.
Only then did I fly to you.

My pursuit of happiness officially began on a very cold December 29, 1993. At the end of a seven-hour flight from Paris, I stepped out of the plane at JFK. I walked out, knowing that a new life awaited me.

I came to do all the things that seemed possible only here.

I came to reach all the goals that could only be attained here.

I came to live my vision of a life that was my American dream.

My American Dream. What was it?

A vision—my model of a perfect life.

Build a career that I alone believed was possible.

Be a success that I alone thought was attainable.

Conquer a wealth that I alone assumed was realizable.

Find a love that I alone felt was probable.

I was excited. With my head and heart overflowing with joy and anticipation, I felt an acute pressure to work hard and do whatever it took to exceed all of my self-imposed expectations.

I vowed that I would not let myself down or get discouraged. This was my final destination—the make-it-or-die-here city, because going back to Mali or starting over in another country were not options.

Life is a struggle…but will is a powerful support for the ones who use it. Indeed.

It was not the New York of chauffeurs and maids and a big house in Bronxville but it was everything else. Over the next nine years, I stayed the course. I worked hard, patiently chasing the vision of the life I believed that I should have. For nine years, I experienced the different meanings of these four simple words: *Life is a struggle.* I swung from temporary jobs (babysitting and housekeeping) that paid less than minimum wage to secure positions (entry-level receptionist) that paid only a little more to long and short periods of unemployment in between. There were days when all I could afford was a cup of coffee and a bagel a day. But I also met extraordinarily kind people who fed me and offered me shelter when I most needed it. The incredible generosity of people I couldn't repay made my heart overflow with gratitude. Their kindness made me believe in Daba and in my pursuit. Gradually, prayer became part of my daily routine.

Patience is a tree whose roots are bitter, but the fruits are sweet. For nine years I embraced and immersed myself into life in the Big Apple. I was intent on being a New Yorker. I was one of the millions of people from around the globe who all came to live in the big cosmopolitan city. And like my contemporaries, I learned to adapt, adopt, and live in the rhythm of the hustle and bustle of the restless city that never sleeps.

For nine years, I was undeterred, never doubting my decision to chase my dream in the big city. I made plans that I followed through to completion. For each dream, I remembered to be patient when things didn't go as planned. I learned to accept delays, changes, and failures without losing sight of the goals I had set for myself. I knew I could surmount any difficulty that came my way. I was a fighter, a fixer, and a problem solver. I had followed in Papa's and Lalla's footsteps in those regards and I never quit. And it was this patience and obstinate tenacity that had *crumbled and collapsed the wall of struggle.*

I was part of a group of volunteers assigned to stuff envelopes for the entire mailing list of a company. The first day I walked in the office I loved the energy. It was a non-profit organization working for the prevention of HIV/AIDS in faith-based communities in the U.S. and parts of Africa. One of the senior staff liked me and convinced the CEO to hire me as his assistant.

Finally, after too many trials and tribulations to count, I was working for an organization whose mission I believed in with a passion. I was in a good place. I had found what my heart and my pocketbook needed. I had job security and a steady income. *This is the beginning*, I thought. Hard times were over. Life would only get better. And in that moment, my pursuit of happiness—all the plans I had made in my head—seemed attainable.

It was a special time.

I loved the world, and the world loved me back.

Chapter Seven

A WOMAN OF MY TIME

*It is true that you cannot be patient and
wait all your life, but you still owe it to yourself
to wait until you reach your goals.*

The year was 2005. We all watched as the resilient and enduring city recovered from 9/11 in 2001 when George W. Bush was first elected president and now here in 2005, he was officially being sworn into office for his second term as president. Condoleezza Rice became the first African American U.S. Secretary of State. This was also the year Angela Merkel became Germany's first woman Chancellor and Ellen Johnson-Sirleaf was elected President of Liberia, becoming Africa's first elected female head of state. Encouraged by the prowess of women, I was running, pushing, and rushing, certain I was going somewhere.

You cannot add water to a jar that is already full.

I only had one ear—I could only hear myself. I was a woman of my time living in a world that seemed obsessed with managing and controlling time. Like the people of my era, I was fixated on spending my time efficiently and wisely, so I could have enough time to have some quality time.

I was a woman of my time moving in a world where everything was under perpetual scrutiny—from the most mundane to the life altering. Thoughts, theories, phenomena, people, discoveries, experiences, past, current, and future events: All were examined and judged, studied, analyzed, measured, and evaluated and reevaluated with the understanding that the conclusions would also need more follow-up, more studies, and more investigation.

And like the people of my generation, I lived my life under perpetual self-scrutiny—constantly analyzing, judging, and criticizing myself before anyone else had a chance to do so. I told myself that it was "constructive criticism" so I could find and change what I had done wrong and improve what I could have done better. I had an opinion about everything; and in conversations with friends, colleagues, and loved ones, we shared our overcritical views of each other, our neighbors, our coworkers, our families, and the world surrounding us. I was as resilient as the city I lived in, a world that was in a state of impermanence.

The world has become a boiling porridge.

And I can't find a spoon to cool the porridge down.

I was a woman of my time living in an unstable world plagued with two viruses: terrorism and war. Viruses that spread like wildfire throughout our global village. The wars and their atrocities had given birth to an unforeseen, appalling, and destructive consequence: the intensification and spread of terrorism—a transcontinental network of violence and hatred that couldn't be eradicated because it enrolled and rallied to its cause all the discontented, dissatisfied, and desperate citizens of the world. Citizens that sometimes turned out to be our very own next-door neighbors. *They only saw today—they didn't care about tomorrow.* Their fight presented an unmatched challenge for our time, for they were willing to commit suicide as long as their horrendous act also murdered the largest number of innocent people—men, women, and small children.

But the elders warned us that the use of brutal force to combat terrorism only temporarily buries the evil it wants to fight and destroy. The evil seed is tenacious. Once buried, it grows in secret, and appears stronger than before somewhere else.

What would be the consequences of this never-ending, senseless destruction? What world would we pass on to our children and grandchildren?

Yes, I was a woman of my time living in an uncertain and unstable war-wracked global village, a world connected by twenty-four-hour news cycles fiercely competing for our attention and our loyalty by presenting the worst images, the chaos, the horror of the world. The sensationalized headlines sending shock waves of dismay and disbelief were at times simply too difficult to watch. But I was a woman with a purpose.

2005 was the year when a new technology emerged, further blurring the already very thin line between our public and private lives—YouTube was launched. A time when in the midst of our daily routine we paused to watch, listen, and comment on the latest news of the hour. We smiled, grinned, or frowned at the announcement of the engagement of Charles, Prince of Wales, to Camilla Parker-Bowles. My friends and I held our breath, crossed our fingers, closed our eyes, and then screamed, laughed, and danced when Jamie Foxx name was announced as the winner of the Best Actor Award at the 77th Academy Awards for his portrayal of the late Ray Charles.

Things are happening here...
Disturbing things are taking place here.

The levee broke in New Orleans. News reports and images of Hurricane Katrina and its devastating effects in Louisiana sent shockwaves of dismay and disbelief around the world, followed by anger and outrage at the government's insufficient preparedness and inadequate response.

You wander without knowing where you're going.
Life has become a never-ending crisis that has left everyone
Rich and poor baffled[2]...

It took us a while to shake off the anger and powerlessness we felt deep inside, but, ultimately, again we had to go back to our personal lives, our daily routine.

It was my third year working for the HIV/AIDS organization. In that time, I had been promoted and was now the office manager and French translator of all the educational material for our partners in West Africa. I loved my job. Our team, in partnership with the faith leaders of the churches and mosques, developed culturally sensitive resources they felt comfortable using to start the conversation about the virus—how to fight it's spread, stigma, and shame—in their respective communities.

For the first time in a very long time, I felt secure in my life. Back home, I had redeemed myself. My accomplishments had helped me climb the ladder from being the disappointing kin to becoming a beloved member of the family. Papa, Lalla, our relatives, and the elders were in awe of how I had turned my

---

[2] Translated lyrics of the song "Koyan" by Salif Keita. Reprinted with permission from Professor Cherif Keita author of the book Outcast to Ambassador: The Musical Odyssey of Salif Keita.

life around. I was proud. At last, my family embraced me; and that, in turn, made me feel worthy.

And, as the icing on the cake, a colleague introduced me to his dear friend, thinking we would be a perfect match. We were two kind, intelligent, and ambitious people looking for our someone to settle down with. And when we actually hit it off during our first meeting, we were sure this was a love story in the making. Indeed, as Lalla and the elders often said, faith combined with hard work, patience, and perseverance, had pleased Daba, who was rewarding me by granting all my wishes. And I was a train on a track—gaining speed—advancing toward achieving my goals of success and happiness, certain I knew what my future held.

For thirty-six months, the bumps in my life—"the small stuff" were resolved without me worrying about them. I was no longer apprehensive about tomorrow, for tomorrow was as good as the day before. For thirty-six months I lived and breathed good days that unfolded the same way every day.

I was a woman of my time moving in a world that no longer deferred my dreams and my aspirations. My life knew no delays. My prayers were answered; my wishes materialized. And slowly, those simple, ordinary, happy days became my expected routine. I just knew I was going to be happy living the life I was supposed to live. And so, as I looked back and remembered all the hard work and the difficult times before the last three years of respite and relief, I couldn't help but smile and be happy with myself. *Yes, it hadn't been in vain!*

When December 31, 2005, arrived, my friends and I gathered to celebrate and welcome 2006. I had no doubt the new year would be an even better year—a year of more stability and joy where nothing would derail my peace of mind and the pursuit of my happiness. Gone were the days of sleepless nights wondering what jobs to apply for. Gone were the panic attacks in front of the ATM machine showing my very low balance. Gone were the self-encouragement moments when I had to convince myself to stay the course, because I had come too far to give up now.

The countdown began. The ball was coming down. Ten, Nine, Eight... My friends and I watched it on TV. Seven, Six, Five...We were counting with the hundreds of thousands of people from around world that were gathered at Times Square to witness the ball drop. Four, Three, Two, One.... The people on TV, my friends and I all jumped and screamed together, "HAPPY NEW YEAR!"

We hugged, laughed, and made a toast to the New Year. 2006 was here. *And everything old is new again.* It was a new year and we could have all the new beginnings we wanted. The New Year, like a new child, contained all our shared and secret hopes for love, joy, and success. We talked about the books we would read, the seminars we would attend to get better at our jobs and achieve new personal goals. We wanted to transform ourselves. No more excuses. We were determined. A few minutes in, we were committing to making 2006 the year of fresh starts, the year of change. *And everything old is new again.* We would not diet, because dieting didn't work for any of us. Instead, we promised to eat healthy. Some friends promised to go back to the gym; I promised to walk more often. We said it: 2006 would be the year where we would make things happen for ourselves and for our loved ones. I was becoming Lalla's Anna.

Nothing good lasts forever.

Our love story didn't last. Despite our best efforts to put-up with each other's sweat—our true characters and bad habits—we couldn't make each other become the lovers we longed to be with. I tried to be patient. I suppressed my frustration because I wanted to believe that, with time, we would work things out and get to live the perfect love story I had in my head. In the end, it didn't work. Still, when it ended, I wept.

It is while enjoying the bright, sunny days that you prepare for the rainy days.

I didn't see it coming. In the office, it began with a few words that came and went without anyone paying attention. True, the CEO said them—but it was something to think about. No one thought it would really happen. A few months later, the words came back. They were said again. This time we, the staff, took notice. We were in shock. Suddenly the rumbling groan of fear rose from within, but I quickly suppressed it with reassuring words: *This is just another idea; it would never materialize.* Something inside me whispered *but what if...?* I couldn't imagine the rest, so I shut down the warning voice and told myself I was worried for nothing.

But the words had caused commotion, and for weeks, we all whispered our unanswered questions and speculations passing in the hallways, or late at night in the elevator. After weeks of waiting, when nothing followed the announcement, the words were forgotten. Lalla and the elders of our community said, "*If you pay attention, you will notice that in every difficult situation, just before the denouement, fate usually provides some sort of ironic or comic relief to distract you and ease your anxiety. It is fate's gift—a breather just before you are hit with your worst imaginable or unimaginable fear suddenly becoming true.*"

We were called again for an unscheduled meeting, and there the words were said solemnly, "The organization was relocating to a less expensive state, Virginia, and we could go with the job or stay behind and find another employer." Silence. My colleagues and I looked at each other. We needed time to process. The words we had speculated over for months had materialized and become our new reality. We could move with the job. But how many of us wanted to do that? Who really wanted to start over in a place where you knew no one? And if I chose to stay behind, how soon would I find another position? Because *nothing good lasts forever*—2006 had also been the year that saw the U.S. housing bubble begin to burst, causing home prices to decline. The job market followed. Demand for work was much stronger than job openings. Recession hadn't hit yet, but anxiety was spreading. *How long until I found work?* The company moved to its location. I didn't follow. I was a New Yorker and I had no interest in starting over somewhere else.

Oh no, not again! my entire being cried out. This was not what was supposed to happen ever! I had been out of work before—many times, as a matter of fact. I couldn't picture myself going through the anguish and the despair of looking for another job or reliving the restlessness that came with looking at postings for hours, hoping to find a perfect match for my qualifications. The time spent applying for positions and trying to write appealing cover letters that would catch the eye of the people in charge of selecting the lucky candidates. The distress and dread that came with waiting for a call-back. The nerve-racking wait, torn between the hope of being hired and the disappointment that began to settle in once I realized too much time had passed—they must have chosen someone else. The panic of seeing the money slowly dwindle out of my bank account every time I took out some cash, knowing I hadn't made any deposits in a while. I had experienced this scenario too many times. I didn't want to go through this again. And what would my family think of me? Another lost opportunity. Another failure.

Over the years, I had experienced many setbacks. As the old saying goes, *one step forward, two steps back.* Only this time I was thrown ten steps back. Losing my job was not supposed to happen. As a matter of fact, being unemployed was not something I expected to experience ever again. But the reality was that I was out of work. Becoming jobless chopped and shredded my previous accomplishments into pieces. I didn't understand my life—how could this happen to me now? I was beaten, but I was not defeated—not yet.

The stressful search for a new job began. I was on edge—afraid I would not find work quickly enough to stop the hemorrhaging of funds from my bank account. My mornings started with words of encouragement to myself: *Just stay the course. You have come too far to give up now. It will get better—I know it. I promise. Just stay the course.* As days turned into weeks, it became increasingly difficult to find the will to look for a position. Still, every morning, I searched for postings and sent copies of my résumé to a world that didn't answer.

I was a fighter. I was no quitter—I knew that. *Hush,* something inside of me said. I knew all the words. But right now? No. I was too tired to hear them. They took too much energy—energy I didn't have at that very moment. Right now, I was in pain. Right now, I didn't understand. I was baffled by the turn of events. Let me just lie down and sob. I knew tomorrow or the day after, or maybe in a week I would…I didn't care what I would do—it didn't matter. Right now, I was heavy and I didn't want to think. I only wanted to lay my head on a pillow, close my eyes, breathe, and be alone. I needed time to nurse my ailing will back to health. I was a woman of my time watching in disbelief as my life unfolded in the opposite direction to where I believed it was headed.

Walking in the dark makes you see things more clearly—for hard times sharpen your understanding, making you wiser.

I could testify to that. Every challenge I met in my life had made me stronger and wiser. But within months, I had lost both my relationship and the job I loved. How could this be? What was the purpose of this new trial after I had already spent so much time proving myself again and again? What could it possibly teach me that I didn't already know about myself? I didn't have answers, and it didn't really matter because my daily survival was my most pressing need. I had to find work.

When the world turns, turn with it.

I was a woman of my time who knew how to quickly adapt to changing new circumstances. I was proud of that fact and had it written on my résumé. And this time was no different. I couldn't find a job equal to my last one, so I resigned myself and took a position as an entry-level salesperson, making half the salary. I wasn't happy, but I was relieved to be working again, and the job was stable and secure. Work quieted my fear and doubts and reasserted that indeed *no matter how big a pot is, you can always find a lid to cover it—for there are no problems without solutions.* Still, I felt sore and frustrated with my life.

When the time comes to ask questions, don't ask the world; ask yourself.

At first, I was too exhausted and couldn't muster the will to think. Letting go of my job and having to settle for work that paid close to what I made when I first began working in the U.S. wounded me deeply. *Nothing happens without a reason.* Why was I starting over? What was I doing wrong? What would my father, my elders think of me now? Shame and guilt overwhelmed me. I no longer had a vision of my future—all my dreams and projects were put on an "indefinite hold." I avoided thinking about the past because it was a bitter reminder of the letdown I had become in my own eyes.

I apologetically told my family I was laid off because of the recession. The clan was sympathetic and understanding. But their compassion hurt, for despite their kind concerns, I knew they saw me as a failure. My siblings all seemed to be excelling and thriving in their respective fields and paths. Their futures looked bright. Tita was a doctor working for an international organization. Mimi, our second sister, was in France, preparing her doctorate thesis in economics. Iba, our brother, was in London studying for a master's degree in finance; Fifi was studying to be a certified accountant; and Yuma, the baby of the family, had just finished high school and was getting ready to go to college to study law. I was happy and proud of each one of them. I didn't want their lives. I believed in my pursuit. I just wished I were in a better place. After those conversations, I called only occasionally to reassure everyone I was still alive, I was doing fine. *You don't tell the reason why you fell into the bottom of a well until you come out.*

I wasn't fine, but that was my problem.

I wasn't fine, but I didn't want help from anyone.

I was a fighter. I was not a quitter. And even though I didn't have the energy to be those things yet, I knew my resilience and zest for life would eventually come back.

"*Pray!*" something deep inside of me said. With this simple directive, all the knots within disappeared. I exhaled. "*Pray,*" the voice insisted. Prayers had worked before. But I had been negligent. Guilt washed over me. And all of a sudden, I understood. This was Daba reminding me to come back to the Creator. The years when life was a struggle, I began to pray faithfully and sincerely. But when happiness appeared, the Creator became less of a priority. I didn't stop worshipping altogether, but the need and the will to pray lessened. *Depending on how you tend to it, your faith will turn into warm or cold charcoal.* My faith hadn't turned cold, but it definitely needed my renewed dedication.

I needed help. Who else could change my luck, turn things around so my life would be everything I imagined and wanted it to be? Only the Creator.

Pray! The voice repeated with confidence. *You know that Daba never refuses to answer a prayer.*

Chapter Eight

DABA OF FEAR, DABA OF GUILT

Daba being indefinable and imperceptible,
the Creator can only be imagined—thus every person
creates their own image of Daba.
Lost in the clamor of my mind.
Cold tears and unsoothing relief.

"A large hot apple cider, please."

"Careful ma'am. It's really hot."

I smiled vaguely. It didn't matter. The hot cup warmed my cold hands. Before carefully taking my first sip, I inhaled scents of apple, cinnamon, and all the spices that made hot apple cider my favorite drink.

Hot apple cider. For me it was one of the best traditions of the season. Already two years had gone by and 2009 was about to dawn.

'Twas again the season with its wintry temperatures, and all its customs and rituals.

'Twas the season with all its good cheer.

New York was beaming with lights, decorations, carols and jingles, and Santa Clauses of all shapes and sizes. Family and friends reunited to wrap presents and celebrate this special time of the year. Coworkers gathered for office parties and gift exchanges. In building lobbies and homes, you could find the traditional tree adorned with colorful bright lights and under each, a few wrapped gifts.

'Twas the season for elaborately designed department windows depicting Santa riding with reindeer in a carriage filled with presents. Standing at the door, inviting passersby to come in was Santa himself with his trademark bell ringing and a "Ho, Ho, Ho, Merry Christmas!" Inside, long lines of parents and grandparents waited their turn to see their little ones sitting on Santa's lap as they took pictures of the moment for posterity. Outside, there were artisans, food, and flea markets all adorned with bright lights and festive ornaments. My email account was overrun with online promotions and last-days sales to acquire trendy gifts for the very special people in my life.

'Twas the season of joy to the world!

But the world wasn't happy.

There had been a man-made calamity: The housing bubble burst. The media, global economy experts, and political leaders around the world proclaimed the looming financial disaster. The blame game began. Whose fault was it? Culpability fell immediately on the financial companies who knowingly lent large amounts of cash to people who not only didn't have the means to pay back the money, but also didn't understand the terms of their loans. No one—neither the lenders, the economic experts, the political leaders, nor the media knew or wanted to acknowledge the extent of devastation this collapse—called the mortgage crisis—would have on so many companies, jobs, and lives around the world.

'Twas the season of joy to the world!

But the world wasn't happy.

And neither was I.

Don't be ungrateful! It's better to wear rags than walk naked, I kept reminding myself. *Almost two years now—early 2007 to end of 2008—I was working. One must know how to be content with what she has,* I would lecture myself every time I felt glum. In these times of disaster and tragedy, where every day on TV I saw images of people who had just lost their jobs, their entire savings, and their retirement funds, I knew I should be grateful for having a position that provided me with an income. It was not the position I wanted, but it was what I had and it shielded me from the fear of unemployment. But accepting this new chapter of my life was more difficult than I had imagined. I found it hard to live on a salary that was half of what I used to take home. In addition, there was no room for growth— no possibility for me to move up or be transferred to another position. This was it.

Do not put a year's worries on a single day. You are not sure of what can happen during an entire day, and you want to worry about the whole year? This was what I told myself. *Take a breather, enjoy the holidays. In a couple of months, you'll see. Maybe things will get better by then.* I didn't want to feel sorry for myself. I didn't want to feel beaten, but it was not easy to find reasons to be happy for the end-of-year celebrations. I didn't know what to do with a holiday I wasn't looking forward to.

Pray! The voice inside of me had said, *for Daba never refuses to answer a prayer.* But like my powerless and hopeless state of being, my supplications were dull. I prayed out of obligation. I prayed in doubt. I prayed because maybe it was true that the Creator never refused to answer a prayer. But my dispirited attempts to implore Allah didn't bring peace or solace. They didn't take away the wall of uncertainties I faced.

The dreaded holidays arrived. I attended parties, smiled, and made jokes as if I were having the best of times. And a day after 2009 arrived, I resumed my monotonous routine. Most evenings I stayed home and watched TV, flipping through the channels until I fell asleep. Amid this purposeless, emotionless life, I turned to the one thing that didn't change—the one thing I did still control. The one thing that made me happy, that helped me cope: food.

Food was my blanket. Food was my refuge. Food gave me comfort. My meals were a brief escape from the present. Three or four evenings a week, I would overeat. And it usually happened the same way: I ordered dinner from a local restaurant that delivered to my apartment. The portion they gave was too much for one person. I knew that—I knew I had too much food on my plate, but it didn't matter. I had in my medicine cabinet a box of antacids that would help relieve any heartburn, any indigestion. I took my plate and ate while watching TV.

I ate because I loved food and enjoyed a good meal. I ate to feed and nourish my body. I ate even when I wasn't hungry. I ate to empty my plate. I ate because food temporarily covered and buried my sadness, my fears, and my worries.

I didn't realize it then, but I subconsciously associated the act of eating with happier times. Eating took me back to my past, when special occasions—marriages, baptisms, and religious holidays—brought family, friends, neighbors, and the entire community together. Happy times spent talking and laughing while feasting together. Even today, my adult siblings and their respective families, and my dearest friends still love to get together and share good food as we catch up with each other's lives or fervently discuss the events of the world.

Yes, food was the perfect companion to make me forget all that was not working well in my life. And so, what if a few nights every week I ate more than I should? One day I would stop. More than twenty years had passed since I quit smoking. I'd been a heavy smoker and I noticed I'd begun to cough more frequently—a cough that hurt my chest. I developed a shortness of breath and could no longer walk long distances, and I loved to walk. I got scared and made the decision to quit before anything bad happened. One night, right before midnight, I lit what I promised myself would be my last cigarette. Now, two decades later, I still didn't smoke. I could do anything I set my heart to do. One day, I told myself, I will stop eating so much at night, but right now, it was one of the very few things I still enjoyed. I had gained weight and felt heavy, but I wasn't ready to give up overeating.

Very often, it is when you are at the height of despair that Daba breathes into your spirit the light that will enable you to find a resolution.

One night, I overate again. And to make matters worse, I ate late in the evening, shortly before going to bed. To hush the guilt and the scolding I felt rising within, I told myself I would eat less the next day, and maybe also walk a few blocks to slow down my rapid weight gain. But tomorrow was still to come and, in the meantime, I had to deal with the discomfort my excessive consumption of food had created. I tossed and turned, hoping to find a position that would ease my stomachache and allow my bloated belly to feel relief, but nothing worked.

The heartburn persisted and kept me awake. Finally, I got up and took an antacid and while waiting for the medication to bring some relief, I turned on the TV, absentmindedly flipping through the channels. I wasn't looking for a particular program. Suddenly, something made me pause. First, it was his appearance—the way he carried himself. An impeccably tailored suit and measured steps that showcased his confidence. Then I noticed his voice: poised, dignified, and calm. I watched the TV screen as the religious teacher looked directly at me and spoke in an assuring and soothing tone about my life, and my problems. His words resonated with me:

"Maybe you are out of work...?" Yes, I had been out of work.

"Maybe you don't like your job...?" No, I didn't care much about my new position—the only reason I was there was because I couldn't find anything better, and the salary did pay my bills.

"Maybe you are going through financial hardship?" Yes, I nodded, frustrated. After my monthly expenses, I had no money left for anything extra.

"Maybe you loved your life—you were doing fine, and everything was going well for you; and all of a sudden, events turned your life upside down and you lost everything you had, and now you have a hard time coping and understanding what took place, and why did it happened to you at this time, when you were doing so well...?"

I couldn't believe that someone who didn't even know me could describe my life so accurately. I listened, eager to hear what words of comfort or solutions he would offer.

"This is not the time to give up." The religious teacher then went on to solemnly tell the very old story of the good family man who God had allowed to be challenged beyond what many of us living in this present day could bear. He had lost everything. And while describing in detail the many losses this God-fearing man had endured—health, wealth, and children—the religious speaker would from time to time slow down and look straight into the camera as if to make sure we were following and understanding the message—*for the eye is the light that clears the way for the tongue.* In the end, the religious leader concluded the Creator had rewarded the righteous man—giving him back much more than what he had originally lost.

Many in the audience nodded as they were in total agreement with the words of the teacher. Some had tears in their eyes. The moral of the story was that no one should ever despair because of struggle. As Lalla and the elders often said, *"Life is made of many tomorrows and no one knows if today's struggle will lead to tomorrow's richness."*

"You see, you are not alone," the teacher said. "This is your opportunity to hold on and show your unwavering faith in the Creator."

Whether it was coincidence or fate, that night the charismatic religious teacher on TV confirmed what Lalla and the elders often said: Daba always tested one's faith, and the Almighty would only reward those who, in the face of hardship, showed total trust and submission to the All-Powerful will. They all assured me that the bigger the hardship, the greater the reward would be. I should not be afraid, worried, or discouraged, for God never challenged anyone beyond what they could endure.

"Pray!" the elders said. "For Daba never refuses to answer a prayer."

"Won't you please join us now and pray," the religious leader concluded in a calm and compassionate voice, still looking directly at me through the screen of my TV.

"You should really pray more sincerely," something inside of me scolded.

It was late in the evening. The preacher's sermon had just ended with soothing music that seemed to invite one to reflect on the message received. My stomach ache was gone, and I went to bed convinced that God had just given me the answer to my problem.

In life, there are no coincidences. I was certain everything that had happened that night: eating too much, then suffering from an indigestion that would not go away, turning on the TV, and changing the channels until I stumbled on the program—all these were signs that the Creator really wanted me to pray. Daba heard my pleas and was showing me the path to take. Tomorrow was a workday. But something was bubbling inside of me and I knew tomorrow would not be another uninteresting day.

Yesterday was gone. I was standing on today, acknowledging that tomorrow would belong to Daba.

Yes, I must pray! Something deep inside of me echoed. I opened my mind to the possibility that God had made me lose everything I valued to make me pay attention. *When blessings are extended over a period of time, we tend to take them for granted until we lose them.* I needed to change my straying ways and seek the forgiveness and the favor of the Creator. My faith had been a dimly lit ember for quite some time. How could I have been this unwise and imprudent in my judgment? My faith was being tested. I believed the words of the religious teacher who assured me I would experience what it was like to have

Daba's favor in abundance, but only after I came back and put the Creator at the center of my life. This was my opportunity to hold on and show my unwavering allegiance to the merciful God who always forgave and helped the remorseful sinner.

Tomorrow—the word filled my entire being with hope and joy. Tomorrow—the word contained all my urgent dreams and desires. Soon I would see the end of the tunnel. I could see my imminent bright future. I stopped myself. Not yet. First, I needed to make amends. I was going to relentlessly pursue the Creator until Daba forgave me.

Life is made of many tomorrows; and each day begins with its own sun.

I woke up the next morning, happy to see the sun was shining. I felt light and cheerful. I had a simple and good plan. Thus, began my mission to please the Creator, be blessed and regain the approval and the favors of the Almighty.

I prayed every day in the morning, in the middle of the day, in the afternoon, in the evening. I prayed feverishly, I prayed zealously. I prayed adoringly, I prayed devotedly. I prayed faithfully and dutifully. Prayers of repentance, prayers of praise and hope to the Creator. My piety quieted and made my fears and doubts disappear. Prayers gave me a sense of being virtuous. I was doing the right thing, my being asserted. I was pleased with myself—I was the remorseful sinner; and I was convinced my supplications satisfied the Almighty. And because I was on the righteous path praising and adoring the All-Powerful the way Lalla and the elders had taught me, I knew I would be rewarded. I had no idea how or when it would happen; but that wasn't important because when Daba wanted to bless you—as *sudden as a fine rain*—the Creator poured favors on you without warning and without waiting.

With my daily devotions, Daba became the center of my life. My faith became a demanding fire that consumed my entire being. I prayed nervously, I prayed restlessly—my head and my stomach buzzing with impatient expectations and wants. I prayed apprehensively, I prayed fearfully. I prayed timidly and tensely, and in my quest to become a better person, the subway station peddlers, the young people selling chocolate, the good and bad singers, and the young break-dancers all became the beneficiaries of my generosity. I parted with my few extra dollars because, in my eyes, they were the less fortunate.

Months passed. I was consistent, disciplined, and methodical in my pursuit to please the Creator. But nothing happened. Inexplicable, Impenetrable, and Baffling Daba. I was mystified. I didn't understand why things were at a standstill. My life was no better and no worse. Something inside of me began to crack—anger flared. I suppressed it. I wanted to hold on to hope. I wanted to believe in the possibilities of a new tomorrow.

Life is made of many tomorrows;
Every dawn begins with its new sun;
And every sunset is followed by a different moon.
Days follow one another, but no days are really alike.
Happy sunny days are preceded or followed by sad sunny days.
Standing on today, who can be certain of what their tomorrow will be?[3]

I stubbornly and desperately wanted to remain on what I believed was the good path. I wasn't going to stray. For months, I had worked hard to become a good, obedient servant. Now

---

[3] Words found in many teachings and traditional songs—they help explain that everything in life is a cycle.

was not the time to lose my temper and risk unleashing God's wrath. I would stay the course. *To the ant, the morning dew is a flood.* Daba didn't need a reason to take away—and even though the Creator didn't give more than one could bear, I knew my will couldn't handle the slightest setback. My life hadn't changed yet, but nothing bad had occurred either.

I continued my pursuit of Daba, and for months afterwards, I prayed dutifully. In my prayers, I cried, I pleaded, I got annoyed, and I got mad. Afterwards, I would immediately repent, afraid the Creator would get angry and punish me for having so little faith.

What frightened me most was to have to accept that I didn't know what to make of my life. I was in a long tunnel of unknowns and I could not get out. I could no longer make plans because the things I relied on to plan my life—those things I believed made me the person that I was—my job, the money I made, and the love I had—no longer existed. Even my unwavering drive had abandoned me. Every day started and ended the same way. Each day brought nothing memorable, nothing to be excited about, except for the fact that I was alive, in good health, and on Earth for another day. I had never experienced anything like this: I was a breathing, functioning human being who clung on to a routine that didn't demand a lot of thinking. I wasn't working toward a goal, I wasn't waiting for something to happen, and I wasn't trying to accomplish anything. My head was still on my shoulders, but it was numb, a muddled container that no longer seemed capable of producing clear ideas. At times, I wanted to summon the courage to think or try something new. *For what reason,* the voice of fear would ask? *So, you can fail again? What can you think of that you haven't tried already?*

Why was Daba not answering my prayers? Was I not praying ardently enough? Surely the Maker of uncountable and sometimes unimaginable wonders knew how much I needed to see a sign. But how can you tell if the All-Powerful has heard your prayers? How do you feel the presence of the unfathomable, inconceivable, unexplainable Almighty? Where do you find within, no matter how tired you might feel, more faith and devotion to show God? *Daba was inexplicable; and Daba was impenetrable* and everyone—Papa, Lalla, the elders, and even the religious leader—were afraid of the Creator's wrath. But which Daba? Maybe I was praying to the wrong Daba!

Missionaries brought Christianity to Mali when they first began to arrive in 1870s and built their congregations in remote parts of the country. The adults were already following *the good path*, the Bambara beliefs of elders, and showed no interest in learning about a new religion. The missionaries turned to the youth. They hired children and offered them small jobs—running errands and washing dishes. They paid the children very little and gave them treats—candies, chocolate, and small toys—to motivate them to keep coming to church despite the condemnation and punishments of their families and communities. Still, the income the children took home was welcome for a number of struggling families. And while the children were working, they were also taught to read and write. Then they were catechized, baptized, and encouraged to evangelize and gradually bring their whole families to the church.

By the time the first Christian missionaries arrived in Mali, Islam was well established in the country. From around 801–900, Muslim North African traders coming from Morocco,

Algeria, Libya, and other countries played an important role in introducing Islam into the region. The merchants brought salt, horses, dates, and camels and traded them for gold, timber, and foodstuff from Mali. Gradually, the Muslim merchant-scholars became influential advisors and scribes to the kings. Over time, people began to select, adopt, and make certain aspects of the faith their own.

Both Muslim scholars and Missionaries came with the purpose of replacing *the good path*—the ancestral teachings they labelled as regressive and unholy. In their arrogance, they were so convinced of their superiority that it didn't occur to them that it was impossible that a world that had existed for thousands of years wouldn't have some knowledge and some truths to offer. The Dogon people were well aware of the Sirius star system and followed it long before the French claimed to have discovered this star system in the 1930s. The French anthropologists who claimed discovery were, in fact, awed by the Dogon people's advanced astronomical knowledge of the solar system despite their "primitive" lifestyle.

They discovered that the so-called primitive people they came to civilize and enlighten, had centuries of customs, traditions, and philosophy of life that taught them how to be truly human. These people considered all beings and things sacred and lived in harmony with their environment. In lieu of books, their teaching tools were what they observed in human behavior and Mother Nature. *For all things in you and around you have been created to teach you about yourself, the universe, and ultimately bring you closer to Daba.*

Daba was my Daba.

The one Lalla and the elders spoke of. They often said there is only one Summit—one Daba—but the paths to reach the Creator are as many and as varied as humanity. Hence, there was no right or wrong way to approach the Almighty. After years of hostility between the three faiths to keep or convert believers, the people of the *good path*, the Christians, and the Muslims had to learn to live together, for no one was going away. They found similarities in their beliefs that allowed them to see and respect each other. For regardless of how they practiced their faith, their respective truths taught their followers the same lessons:

There was only One Creator you called Daba, Allah, or God.

One path to reach the Master of the Universe: faith, submission, and the practice of a religious tradition.

And the *griot*, the storyteller, sang:

Tuned instruments make beautiful music,

But no harmony equals in beauty that of the agreement amongst human beings.

Hence, let us cultivate tolerance, compassion, peace, love, forgiveness, acceptance of others, and solidarity within our community.

This acceptance to live in good accord with your neighbors, whatever their faith, was passed on from generation to generation. It made religious freedom and tolerance a way of life that explained why Papa, Lalla, Maman, and Uncle Layes never imposed their spiritual views on me. I was encouraged to believe and eventually practice a faith. I naturally embraced Islam as my religion.

The majority of the people in Mali became Muslims but some without abandoning the good path of their elders. As Christians and Muslims, we celebrated our different religious holidays by sharing meals and sometimes praying together. When hardship or disaster occurred in our communities, the voices of wisdom of the three faiths came together to comfort and counsel everyone to accept the situation because what the Creator allowed to happen was always good. It was unimaginable to question Daba, just as it was unthinkable to doubt the elders' actions and decisions.

This was not my first crisis of faith. Five years before I left Mali, the unimaginable happened. Suddenly the image of the distant yet protective Creator shattered in my mind and the Daba of fear appeared, bringing me pain, anxiety, fright, and panic attacks all at once.

The green fruit can fall before the ripe fruit, but it is not the proper order of things.

My brother was supposed to come see me that afternoon. When he didn't show up, I found it odd. He had never missed our get-together before. But I didn't think more of it. Later, friends close to the family came to see me. They sat me down. They were grave, carefully searching, struggling to find words. I became frantic.

"What? What's going on?"

"Calm down, Anna."

I stood up.

"Sit down."

"No, tell me what you want to tell me now."

Another silence. Then: "When was the last time you saw Mohammed?"

"Eh, I don't know, Tuesday. We were supposed to meet yesterday, but he didn't show up."

"Anna, Mohammed had an accident...and he died this morning."

Who? What Mohammed are they talking about?

"Who? Who died?"

"Mohammed."

I screamed.

"No, not my...*my* brother cannot...my brother cannot die!"

Arms wrapped around me and held me as I wept. How could something like this happen? Death happened to others—old folks or people I didn't know or didn't care about. Death didn't touch young people. Less than a month after he had turned sixteen, my brother was gone—killed in a motorcycle accident. Death took my brother. Daba allowed it to happen. All at once, I understood all too well why the Creator was to be feared. My brother's sudden death crushed my beliefs—being young, healthy, and vivacious weren't enough—they didn't guarantee the long life I thought my siblings and I were entitled to.

Man walks owing to the contradiction of his feet—for when one foot is up, the other is down. This symbolizes the great law of dualism—that all opposites are complementary. Thus, when life appeared, death followed. "But death is forever something new," the elders sighed, "for it always shocks and upsets."

Mohammed was my brother, not by blood but by marriage as he was the son of Mama Deep Water before she married my father. But he was every bit of a brother to me.

Gone was his laughter. Gone were our long conversations where we made fun of the rest of the family, and where I listened as he confided in me and shared everything going on in his life.

Gone were his protective hands that were so quick to hide my cigarettes from the prying eyes of family and neighbors. I adored him. And he adored me back.

You offering sympathy will not bring back the dead; but it will preserve love and fondness among those who remain.

People came and grieved with our family. Mama Deep Water grieved her first born. People came and offered support. They came and offered sympathy. My eyes remained dry; I couldn't cry.

The sun didn't forget to shine, and so life went on.

And we carried on vain conversations so people would not think we were sick. Or going crazy. We ate to prevent neighbors from worrying. We prayed to show that, in spite of our pain, we kept our faith in Daba.

The sun didn't forget to shine, and so life went on.

We: his mother, his father, his sisters, his brother were not fine; and for a long time, we would not be fine. Still, the sun did not forget to shine and life went on. And with each day, we slowly and painfully learned to go on without him.

We laboriously got used to not seeing him. We missed his laughter but couldn't bring ourselves to talk about him. We learned to get used to not hearing his voice. We shared silences filled with thoughts of him—awkward, excruciating silences, because someone almost said his name.

But because *the sun didn't forget to shine, life went on.*

We each found our own way to cope, accept, and grieve the loss of our Mohammed. His sudden and brutal passing had created the fear of death in me. And soon after his funeral, I began to be afraid to die. I spent months sleeping with the lights on.

Over time, my fear of death transformed and turned into panic attacks. The elders said that prayers would help. I needed to commit to my religion so Daba could help me through this difficult time. I began to pray fervently and dutifully every day. Prayers did bring me some solace, and so I continued my devout practice all through the years when life was a struggle until happiness rained on me. During all those years, I prayed every day, in part because of my rekindled faith, but also because the Creator had become the Daba of guilt when I felt shame and remorse for missing prayer time. Indeed, I chastised myself, what was the purpose of reaffirming my allegiance to Daba and promising to be pious and follow the teachings of the sacred book if I didn't scrupulously practice devotion, no matter how inconvenient?

More than two decades had passed since my brother's death, and once again my relationship with the Creator was at a crossroads.

"Put your faith in Daba instead of people," the elders often declared, "for people will disappoint you, but the Creator is always there and never disappoints the true believer."

I had done that. I had been persistent in my devotion. Still:

Daba didn't answer my prayers for a new job.

Daba didn't answer my pleas for financial blessing.

Daba was silent to my tears.

Daba could move mountains, but Daba didn't want to move me.

Daba could shake the Earth, but Daba chose not to touch me.

Daba seemed unfazed and undeterred by my pain and my worries.

What do you do when the power you were taught to put all your hopes on remains hidden and silent? I could pray and wish for all the things I wanted, but I could not make them happen—no matter how often and hard I prayed and no matter how much I wanted these things. *You are powerless—there's nothing you can do, Anna. Only Allah!* I repeated those words until they pressed and drowned all signs of impatience.

I kept praying despite myself. I was afraid the Creator would punish me for not being pious enough. I didn't want to give up. I prayed until I couldn't pray without feeling angry or resentful. I prayed until I couldn't find words to pray.

I was tired. I didn't want to upset the Almighty, but Daba's silence made me ask: why was I praying? What was the purpose of being such a devout person if Daba wasn't hearing me? But, if I were a true believer would I have these questions, these doubts?

Pushing stops at the wall—for you cannot go beyond your own limits. Moons of unanswered supplications took me to the limit of my endurance. I ran out of will and out of patience. I needed a break. I stopped praying, not only because I was angry—even though at the time I denied and quashed those feelings out of fear of reprisal—but most of all, I stopped praying because I didn't know what else to tell Daba. In spite of all my efforts to please and gain the favor of God, my prayers and good deeds didn't bring the life transformation I longed for.

Strangely enough, I had the obscure belief that I would be fine. Deep inside I had this "knowing" that Daba was there, even if I didn't figure out how to reach the Creator. Still, in the back of my mind, I kept looking for signs of punishment to come. But nothing happened—nothing good and nothing bad. Life went on. I was still stuck in a job I didn't like but was afraid to leave because it gave me the security of a fixed income. In my own eyes, I was a failure and kept my distance from my relatives to avoid hearing the disappointing confirmation that I was the forever letdown—the one who would remain less than the others.

I stopped watching the programs of the charismatic preacher. I didn't want to see or hear anything that had to do with trying to be a good devout person, a dutiful and obedient servant. I had tried that, and it hadn't work for me. In the end, I lost my appetite, because even food failed to provide the comfort and solace it usually brought me. Aside from my routine—going to work and coming home—I didn't want to do anything. I didn't want to think—fill my head with the plans and dreams of an unattainable future. I didn't want to read. I didn't want to watch TV. I wasn't used to silence in my head. I wasn't used to having nothing to do, nothing to plan, and nothing to worry about. This was not normal.

I wasn't aware that I was crashing. Slowly. The events that were about to unfold would take me to the limits of the Anna I knew how to be.

Bamako, Mali circa 1960

From left to right: Maman, Papa and their friend holding baby Anna.
Paris, France 1962

This is one of my favorite pictures of
Maman. She looks happy.
I don't know when or where this
photo was taken.

Maman and me at 4-years-old.
Bamako, Mali 1966

Me at 7-years-old.
Bamako, Mali 1969

118

Me and Lalla in Lalla's home.
Bamako, Mali 1988

Maman at 34-years-old,
working as a nurse.
Pictured at home.
Dakar, Senegal
1978

Family photo. From left to right, standing: me, Uncle Layes, my brother Soul.
Seated: Uncle Layes's wife with her niece, Lalla, Maman.
Bamako, Mali 1988

Lalla and me. I went to Dakar, Senegal to see Lalla to say goodbye before
leaving for the U.S. 1993

Maman posing for
the camera as a
beautiful DIVA.
Dakar, Senegal
1993

Me and Lalla in Dakar,
Senegal during my
vacation there.
2012

Me and Maman in Dakar. She was so vulnerable a few years
after having a stroke. 2012

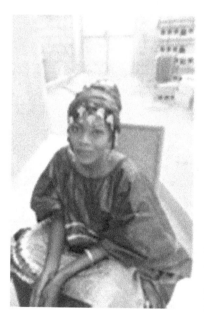

Mariam, Lalla's caretaker.
This photo was taken a month
before Mariam's untimely passing
at age 25. I considered her to be
like "My First Daughter."

Lalla, our Matriarch.
Early 2000's

Chapter Nine

TRYING TO FIT IN SOMEONE ELSE'S SKIN

You think you are about to rise when fate abruptly stops you in your tracks—holding you back because you do not have all that you will need to thrive.

Once upon a time, after years of hard work, patience, and endurance, I had been in a good place. I loved my work and I loved my life. The era of struggles I had known for so long were over. I was like a train on a course that nothing would derail, running toward the pursuit of all my goals of success and happiness. Then and there, I was thunderstruck. I lost all that truly mattered to me. I found myself starting over almost at the same level with the young people I was supervising and who, for the most part, had recently joined the workforce. This was where I was with all my years of experience and perseverance. There was no sugar-coating it. There was no way around it. This was my reality. And there was no foreseeable drastic change— no vision, no plans—to change my future. Yet, there was this "knowing" within, a stubborn belief that I would be all right. But when?

No matter the events and circumstances of my life, I always refused to see myself as a victim. And this time was no different.

To shake off my gloomy mood, I decided to join some of my colleagues when they got together for drinks after work more often. I was a forty-six-year-old woman going out with twenty- and thirty-somethings, young people who thought of me as their aunt or big sister—someone they could come to for advice, someone they were not in competition with. I was the sensible, levelheaded supervisor they trusted with their personal problems—their daily challenges and struggles, their dreams of who they were going to be after they left their current position for one that would be much more rewarding financially and more in tune with their ambitions and aspirations. I wasn't trying to be trendy, fashionable, or current; I just wanted to do something that would make me forget time. I quickly found myself bored.

In spite of my colleagues' kindness and willingness to include me in their outings and conversations, I really didn't fit in. I didn't enjoy the scene—the loud music, voices shouting to be heard, and the constant exchange of bad, silly, and tasteless jokes. I no longer enjoyed drinking. All those things were my déjà-vu—my "been there, done that," not interested in doing it again. I was surrounded by young people in an environment that cheered for me to relax, have fun, but I remained jaded. I thought I might as well be home. If I were going to be this uninterested, let it be in the silence of my apartment. And so, after a few polite "no's" in the face of their insistence, my colleagues stopped asking me to go out with them, and I was happy to return to my uneventful existence.

Spring was here. I could put away my coat. The sun shone longer, which meant it was still light outside when I left work.

Spring—the season that symbolizes the rebirth of nature and the return of the warm temperatures—influenced my mood and made me feel somewhat lighter, as if I too might experience something new and good. I no longer had an excuse to not exercise. I needed to try to lose some of the weight I'd gained—the unflattering pounds that made me refuse to wear form-fitting outfits.

Your habits are your refuge, for they give you a sense of security. I had my routine, which gave my life some order and some certainties. I rose early in the morning to go to work. I spent my day concentrating on the things I needed to achieve to do my job efficiently, and at the end of the day, I came home, had dinner, and watched TV until I fell asleep. I didn't want to go out. I didn't want to see people or talk to anyone. I just wanted to be alone. To be alone was calming. To be alone, surrounded by the familiar walls and simple décor of the place I called home was easy. I didn't want any other presence in my space and I didn't feel lonely. From time to time, my craving for food would sneak back, and I just couldn't resist.

I was a person of habits and that evening was no different. It was late, I didn't want to sleep, and so I began to change the channel looking for a comedy show or a program with no drama. I didn't want to see violence, trauma, or the charismatic religious teacher's program. I was about to give up and go to bed when I heard: "I know what it's like…I know how you feel. Remember, before all of this, I was you. I was where you are now. I've walked in those shoes."

I felt the compassion in the reassuring voice—and watching the live audience acquiesce as they reverently hung on to every word confirmed what I felt: These were not just words of comfort, but the speaker meant what he had just uttered. The close-up view of the simple yet cozy set, the speaker's serene presence—what was this oasis of tranquility? The pleasant speaker, who exuded confidence, ignored the camera, and spoke directly to the live audience.

"I've been there. I know what it is like. I know what it feels like to not be in alignment with your purpose—the things you were put on this Earth to do. I know what it is like to work at a job you do not like, to not make enough money…I've been there. But tonight, we're going to change that—I am going to help you change that. I am going to tell you how you too can become the master of your destiny. I'm going to help you have the life you've always wanted but didn't believe you could have. Trust me, I've been there, and just like me, you too have the power to create the life you really want, you deserve, but you just don't know how yet… That's why I wrote this book—to help you achieve and be all that you are meant to be—by giving you the tools that will help you unlock, unleash, and use the potential some of you don't even know that you have.

"If you follow these rules and guiding principles, I promise that you will start to see change, and soon you will begin to live the life you've always wanted for yourself but didn't believe you could have. It happened to me. It can happen to you."

"Really?" I couldn't help but smirk a little. I didn't want to believe, to be that gullible and simply accept everything the speaker said as truth, but at the same time, I was a little curious, and a little envious. The speaker was poised, confident, and looked like someone who indeed had everything. I couldn't help but wonder, how did he do it? How did he get so lucky and so blessed? It was as if the educator-on-life knew my skepticism, and my doubts:

"You know, what I found is that sometimes we are our own worst enemy with our negative thoughts and our deeply rooted belief that nothing good could possibly happen to us. Stop thinking and believing that you don't have what it takes or that you cannot achieve your goals, or that good things only happen to other people. I'm here to tell you that you deserve to be happy. You deserve to have your dreams fulfilled. Each of you, you are so much more powerful than you give yourself credit for. You are so much more. But first you have to stop the negative thinking. Look at me, I'm the living proof that good things can happen to anybody, because it happened to me."

The teacher-on-life looked into the audience, then right into the camera, and forcefully said: "Starting this moment, I want you, the folks here, and you watching at home to trust that good things can and will happen to you to. Would you do that?"

The live audience enthusiastically said "Yes" to the invitation.

Regardless of where and how we live, we often face the same problems.

We were the people of our time running and rushing, chasing the things we believed would give purpose and meaning to our lives.

We were the people of our time, looking to find ways to realize our unfulfilled dreams and aspirations.

My contemporaries and I were the people of our time looking for answers; and that night we watched and listened to an educator-on-life assure us that he had found the solutions that could help us transform our daily existence to happy, fulfilled, and successful lives.

Every day your ear goes to school, I told myself philosophically. Lalla and the elders often said that, provided we pay attention, we can learn something new about ourselves and the world every day. And here a total stranger was telling me he could teach me how to discover new things about myself. What could this man—so sure of himself and of his words—possibly tell me about myself that I didn't already know? *I've got to hear this.* I waited, ready to deride and dismiss his message as "feel-good words" intended for those who liked to believe those sorts of things.

He surprised me by talking about his personal trials and tribulations—a career that was going nowhere, the missed opportunities, the setbacks, and the disappointments that led him to a full-fledged crisis. The hardship forced him to take some time off to do some soul searching, which led him to the discoveries that would change his life. Then, drawing from this experience and the lessons learned, he authored a book detailing his journey and the set of rules and guiding principles that helped him transform his life. The purpose of the book was to help others who were facing similar struggles achieve their own success stories. *Expertise needs to be based on experience to be reliable.* My skepticism and my doubts were gone. The educator-on-life's journey was proof that a happy, successful, and fulfilled life was attainable.

He promised—and I wanted to trust him—that his book would be the solution to my problems. He vowed—and I wanted to accept his words as reality—that if I read and scrupulously followed the rules and guiding principles detailed in his book amazing things would start showing up in my life. I wanted to believe I had found the solution—the book of the educator-on-life was the missing piece that would let me rise and thrive as I created my new life.

When the program ended, I turned off the TV and went to bed, my heart light and full of hope. I felt the fresh air fill my lungs and I exhaled. Something inside of me had lifted and the heavy wall within had disappeared. Tomorrow I would buy the book and read it. Then I would follow its rules and guiding principles; and once I start seeing the promised results, then I would let myself go and be elated. But tonight, I needed to be cautious, even as I hoped I would find the tools and advice that would help me transform my life in the book.

The next day marked the beginning of my new journey. The first step that would open the door to this new quest was to buy the book, which I did. I also acquired books from several other authors about how to have a happy, successful, and purposeful life. I read all of them.

The different authors' words resonated with me because they described and addressed issues very similar to those I was dealing with, such as the relentless pursuit of elusive dreams and ambitions that refused to materialize and the pain and frustration of trying to settle for a disappointing life, which I knew all too well. The authors admitted that, like me, in the beginning of their respective journeys, they had been tenacious, but their hard work and dedication didn't bear much fruit. They fell short and wanted to know why. What were they doing wrong? And it was this quest for answers that had led each one on a path of soul-searching where they encountered wise spiritual leaders whose knowledge guided them through their transformational journeys. The lessons learned had, in turn, become teachings tools they offered to help all those who were going through similar situations.

The various books offered some common rules that readers were meant to follow. I had a notebook. Inside, I wrote the guiding principles that most spoke to me. I called them IT. They were that I:

1. Change my attitude—the way I thought about, saw, and did things. They stated that once I started to recognize the glass was always half full, I would appreciate what I

already had and this new attitude could help me become a better problem solver.

2. Make an inventory of my ambitions and aspirations. What did I want? Then create a detailed plan of action— breaking each down into smaller steps—the things I needed to do to make my goals attainable.

3. Be disciplined and stick to the plan. Yes, there could be delays or distractions, but never lose sight of what I wanted to accomplish. They insisted that I never give up on my dreams. They wanted me to believe in myself, have a positive attitude, and remind myself I could do anything I set my heart on. And I should surround myself with people who could understand and support me to help me stay optimistic.

4. Measure my progress monthly by regularly reviewing what I had done.

5. Be proactive—always think of what else I could do to bring me closer to my goals.

And with IT, I was ready to begin the journey to my life makeover.

The following weeks and months, I worked relentlessly following IT. The new set of instructions that ruled my life revived and brought back in full force the fighter, the fixer, and the problem solver that were dormant in me. My young colleagues were impressed with my enthusiasm and the fact that a mature woman (translation: old) was not afraid to question herself and try to change the things that didn't work for her. I recommended the books that I loved. I talked about the results of this new adventure as if I were already living my dream life. IT reaffirmed what deep within I already knew—that I was in charge and in control of my destiny. IT made me worthy in my own eyes once more. I was doing the right thing. I was being assertive and I was taking charge. I learned to refuse the train of negative thoughts—I didn't want to be my worst enemy by thinking that I couldn't achieve something. I told myself over and over I could do anything I really wanted to do. Yes, I could quit my job anytime I wanted. But I was also a responsible adult with bills to pay, and a responsible adult made compromises; and that's why I needed to find another position before I could leave the one I had.

The practice of IT helped me put the circumstances of my life in perspective. Things were not as bad as I sometimes wanted to believe. I had no doubt that, with patience, the practice of IT would ultimately transform my existence. I was excited. I was enthralled with IT. How had I managed so long without IT? What took me so long to find IT? My life would have been so much easier if I had found IT earlier. IT was the wonder that was going to allow me to rewrite my life. I was confident that as I followed the rules and stayed the course of this new way of approaching and dealing with the events of life, I would reap the benefits similar to the love, success, and happiness these authors were experiencing in their own respective lives—no doubt I would become the decider, ruler, and controller of my own destiny.

In the beginning, my daily routine became more exciting as I studied and applied IT. The new rules were meant to mold and reshape me into a better, more positive version of my old self. And when I first put the advice into practice and experienced the predicted results, I was ecstatic. The new rules calmed my anxiety and gave me back a sense of control over my life. As a result, I was relaxed, almost serene. I managed to work up the courage to ask and obtain a raise at my job, which although less than I wanted, I learned to appreciate. Those wins reinforced my conviction that I was on my way to creating a bright new future for myself, that the steps and guidelines were working. I felt good about myself and about the direction my life seemed to be taking.

However, the world was still in crisis. Barack Obama—the candidate who embodied hope and change—had made history by becoming the first African American ever to be elected president of the United States. But the presidential election took place while the country and the world were in the midst of the worst recession since the great depression of the 1930s. The collective restlessness of our global village made all my fear and worries reappear.

There were no rules or guiding principles that told me what to do in an era of recession where my age—forty-six—and my years of experience didn't make me the most competitive choice in a job market where offers were scarce. I was vying with young college graduates that were more eager, had more drive than me, and therefore were far more appealing to hiring managers. What was I supposed to do? I couldn't picture a brighter future that would make it easier to accept my reality. This was another impasse. I knew what I wanted: peace, happiness, and money. But it was difficult to see how these wants would materialize when everyday thousands of people were losing their jobs and willing to accept positions with significantly lower wages than they were used to.

I was grateful to have job security. And so, as I embraced the saying *it was better to wear rags than to walk naked*, I realized that in choosing to stay where I was until the world got out of recession, I no longer had a reason or a desire to practice IT.

In trying to fit in someone else's skin, you will find that if the skin is not too large, it is too tight.

So much effort and so few results to show for it! I had applied myself to adapt and conform to these instructions, hoping that becoming more like the educator would help me achieve the goal of attaining a life similar to his—filled with accomplishments and happiness. I did all this because I so much wanted to be a success story.

My commitment knew no end. I was obsessed with creating my success story. I was fervent, zealous in my dedication to scrupulously follow this detailed roadmap toward a life of bliss and triumph. I molded and reshaped my entire being—the way I approached, thought, processed, and reacted to life's events and circumstances—to imitate and be in line with what the educator said he had done when he was confronted with similar situations. All that work for the promise of a better existence that, in the end, didn't materialize. The transformation that the educator-on-life and his contemporaries had promised in every single book I had read didn't become a reality. It was a harsh reminder that *no one truly gets to live the same life as their fellow man; and no one gets to experience the same fate and destiny as their neighbor.* I could try as much as I wanted to mimic the things they had done that had changed their lives, but the outcome would never be the same.

When I was a young adult, Lalla used to make fun of me whenever she saw me emulate the way someone I admired spoke or did things. She would say: "Anna, why do you like to create so much trouble for yourself? Haven't you learned yet?"

Then she hummed as she mocked me: "Imitator! Imitator! Don't exhaust yourself trying to be someone else, Anna. Just be you."

The experience of others was only supposed to help me better understand what was going on in my own life. The knowledge of others was meant to confirm that something could be accomplished. That was why Lalla and the elders were always reluctant to tell the young adults what to do. Instead, they drew parallels with the events of their past, so that we realized others before us had faced comparable situations. They said we should not do what they had done for what is knowledge if not a succession of errors?

No one really gets to live the same life as their fellow man.

And no one gets to experience the same fate and destiny as their neighbor.

I turned against myself. How could I have been so naïve, so gullible? How could I have spent—no, *wasted*—so many months doing things…I couldn't finish the sentence. I couldn't describe what I had spent so much time doing. All I could think about was the time and the effort. So much work…so much expectation. I had a lump in my throat. I didn't want to say it, yet I couldn't avoid it. *This was, yes, Anna, say it, another FAILURE.* What a disappointment! It didn't matter that no one knew. I knew. This was one more idea, one more plan, one more execution that didn't work.

I was bitter. So much hope and dedication, and so little result to show for it. So, what if most days I knew how to chase away negative thoughts and avoid office gossip? So, what if I had managed to get a raise? These small victories were petty compared to the life-changing experiences I had dreamed of. I was filled with frustration. I was lost in the chaos of my mind, at the mercy of thoughts that were berating me and telling me what a letdown I was.

Patience cannot win over what drags on forever.

The persistent, unanswered question surfaced once more—what was I doing wrong? I didn't know, and I no longer cared. I gave the books away and threw out the notebook. I didn't want to hope and I didn't want to dream. I told myself that the entire experience was a failure—my failure. I was hurt to have tried and put so many expectations on something new that, in the end, didn't deliver all its promises. I was also angry to have been so naïve, to actually believe that someone else's solutions to their personal problems would be a perfect fit for me, that they could somehow solve my own issues.

The teachings were not "THE ANSWER" I had hoped for. And so, now what? Where was I supposed to go to find the will to overcome this crushing setback? What new ideas could possibly emerge that I hadn't already thought of or tried? The only thing I knew was that I didn't know anything anymore. Fate had stopped me on my path so many times that I had no choice but to stay still because, this time I was not only beaten, but I was also knocked out.

The Anna I knew how to be had reached her limits. My operating system, the dos and don'ts—the road signs that had guided my life—were useless. They no longer suited my life. The fighter, the fixer, and the problem solver vanished, for there was nothing to do, fix, or make better. The devout and righteous being, the spiritual seeker had all been shattered. I was scattered into pieces that no longer fit together. I didn't know who I was, and what I was supposed to want or be.

What you have learned and taken from others, is it worth what you don't know of yourself?

I had learned and practiced all that I could absorb, all I had been given to imitate. For the longest time, I had lived by these rules and principles and they had taken me to the frontiers of a life that existed solely for the outside world.

Lalla and the elders cautioned that the seeker of self and the seeker of the world are two different things. The first wants peace, the second confusion. Indeed, I was in a state of total commotion. I had sought the approval of my family and the world. I had taken from others and planted in me their knowledge and beliefs. But they didn't help me find my seat. I wasn't happy. I had learned a lot and knew how to talk with confidence about knowing yourself, being comfortable in your own skin, knowing and going after what you really want in life. Yet, I had not acquired the abilities on which I so expertly gave my opinion.

One must know when to look back and lean on the ancestors' truths. For everything you are, others were before you.

Soon after, on a gloomy Sunday afternoon, desperate to flee from my despair, I finally had my long phone call with Lalla and she imparted the wisdom of the elders, telling me I could only figure out where I was going if I knew where I came from.

I had to let the solutions come from my gut. I was shocked to find that the only reason I wanted wealth and professional success was to prove myself to the people I loved. And now what? What did I truly aspire to be, and why?

Lalla and the elders taught that the world of the eyes, the nose, the mouth, and the hands is the world of appearances. It is a world that everyone knows and understands. But you are more than that. *You are one and many—for there are many you in you.* Inside each of us lie hidden powers that you must learn to know if you ever want to find your seat—be grounded and settled within and live comfortably in your own skin while navigating life's twists and turns."

I was entering a new phase. The events of my present daily life would be the catalyst that would make me dig within to unearth the powers at work that triggered how I received, thought, and reacted to life's events. The process would bring forth the unhealed wounds of my past. Slowly, I would discover the true Me I was clueless about. It all started with an incident that was really nothing.

Chapter Ten

WHAT BOILS WILL EVENTUALLY OVERFLOW

If you say it's nothing…
Know that in life it is the nothing that always starts
something.
Therefore, be aware because from your nothing
So many things can arise.

*I*n the beginning, it was nothing. A difference of opinion between two coworkers that could have been easily settled. Instead, it grew into full-fledged war because we didn't like each other. The argument became the weapon we used against one another to finally settle once and for all who had the most power, who had the backing of the heads of the company, and who would, in the end, be able to tell the other what to do.

The afternoon of our final disagreement, we were going back and forth, exchanging escalating angry emails until he crossed the line. His words made my blood boil. *Who did he think he was with his condescending tone? Did he think he was in charge?* I didn't respond right away. I didn't want to be unprofessional. I needed time to gather myself and my thoughts. When I regained my composure, I replied that I would not continue the conversation until there was a meeting with the head of our department. It was her elusive and ambiguous attitude that had contributed to putting my colleague and me at odds, creating a rivalry for the only supervisory vacancy. I demanded that the manager decide who was in charge.

Fear gives small things big shadows, for it creates images of things that do not exist.

That night I went home and became increasingly anxious about what would happen the next day. What had I done? Did I really need to send that email? Did I really need the head of our department to intervene? My angst grew. A tight ball hardened inside my gut. Fear had my heart racing, and my mind feverishly replayed the words I had written in various emails, as well as everything I had said or done on previous days. I hadn't done or said anything wrong. Still, I wanted to be prepared. I began to focus on the worst-case scenario: Would someone find something I did or said to use against me? It was an emotional mayhem: My head spun anxiously, zealously raging to think and rethink all the decisions I had made. After several hours, I was exhausted from interrogating myself, trying to anticipate what more could happen that I didn't see.

Very late that evening, as I got ready for bed, I told myself I should still be prepared for the most dreaded outcome. The head of our department could take my colleague's side—promote this man I really didn't like and make me report to him. That would be a nightmare. He seemed to be the kind of person who would hold a grudge and I was sure, if promoted, he would find ways to humiliate me. What would I do then? I couldn't quit, not with the state of the economy. I promised myself I would make the best of it like I had always done. I needed to work, and no matter what took place, I would find a way to keep my job.

I didn't sleep well. I had nothing to blame myself for, yet I prepared to face the day as if I were guilty of something. Indeed, one can feel guilty without being guilty of anything. I went to work full of anxiety and fear, ready to defend myself, but also ready to compromise if things didn't go in my favor. An hour after I arrived at work, I received a phone call from the principals of the company who had been copied on our email exchange. They thought I had handled the situation professionally and told me I had their total support. Later in the afternoon there would be a meeting with the head of the department to address and settle our dispute. After I hung up, I heard myself sigh and relax. I was so relieved. I paused. I needed a moment to fully absorb that I had won the battle, I had won the war, and I was in charge.

Hours later, there was a face-to-face meeting with our direct supervisor. She repeated what the leaders told me during our phone conversation. My colleague seemed to be in a state of total shock and dismay—as if he had been told a different story. He remained silent. When the short meeting ended, I officially became the supervisor. I spent the rest of the day amazed by this happy turn of events.

I couldn't believe I had won the fight. I had stood up for myself, and this time it didn't backfire; I was not shushed or embarrassed. I spoke up, and this time I had the last word.

It never occurred to me I could really win—that someone would in fact take my side. *But why wouldn't you have*, something deep within whispered? Throughout the several weeks of bickering and discords, I had remained professional. That was why the voices in my head couldn't find anything to reproach me. That evening, I was still savoring what I considered to be my big victory. I was happy, grateful, and proud.

See, you were worried for nothing. Again! I was a little annoyed with myself to have let the situation upset and disturb me to the point that I had lost sleep. It wasn't the first time. But it was the first time that I didn't brush it off, that I paused and wondered why was I so worried? Why did I make such a big deal of this situation? Why did I always zero in on the worst that could take place? I didn't like where this line of questioning was taking me. What was the matter with me? I had always been this way—I always wanted to be prepared for the worst that could happen. *When you fall, always get up ready to explain and justify yourself.* That was exactly what I did. I faced the situations head-on, ready to defend my words and my actions. It seemed, however in hindsight, that both my practice and this situation were ordered steps to get me to look inward.

Back then I was reluctant to question the ways I had always done things. I was a no-nonsense woman—everyone knew that. I loved my reputation of a "tough, no-nonsense person." I loved that people—myself included—thought nothing could break me. I had perfected the art of hushing and suppressing certain emotions: pain, anger, fear, despair, tears—feelings I considered to be signs of weakness. These sentiments allowed people to either mock you or think less of you. I wasn't weak. I didn't break down in public. No one was allowed to see me sweat.

Being critical of myself came naturally to me. I was stubborn, opinionated, sometimes loud and exuberant, but I wasn't weak. No doubt about that. My harshness toward myself was my understanding of what it meant to be tough and real. But this last incident had drained and exhausted me more than any previous experience. And I wondered why it didn't cross my mind to think about being on the other side—the side where good things happened? The side of best-case scenario. I had never questioned my defense mechanism before. But the questions came: *Why are you always accusing yourself of wrongdoing even when what is going wrong has nothing to do with you? Why do you always believe you are at fault—that it must be something you have said or done?* Why, in my mind, was I always the bad person? I didn't like the truth this inquiry exposed, showing me how little I thought of myself.

I am a fighter, a fixer, and a problem solver, I forcefully reminded myself. Still, in spite of my best efforts to quiet it, something kept bringing the questions back into my mind. I didn't know how to erase them. What was going on with me? Why all of a sudden was I questioning a behavior that had protected me against pain for so long? True, the last incident with my colleague had been difficult and very draining emotionally, but it was over, and I had won. What was the big deal?

The big deal was that my body, my entire being, was tired. *You push and push until you are up against the wall.* With this last incident, my body seemed to have reached its endurance limit. Years of preparing for the worst had taken its toll and I'd had enough. I just couldn't do this to myself anymore. And so, now what? I was tired, but I didn't know how to relax. It was then that I remembered Lalla, and our last conversation.

"Don't rush, don't force, and don't rationalize. Let the answers come from your gut," she had said. It was time for me to stay still and let something, anything come from my inside. It was time to go back to my breathing exercise and *seat my mind.*

The thorns can only be pulled from where they penetrated...

The head of the department called me late one evening to tell me my colleague had just resigned. I wasn't surprised, and I wasn't sad to see him go, but I felt compassion because this was not a good time to be looking for a new position. I was also informed that starting the next day I would have to work extra hours until a replacement was found. I was home, resting on the couch, absentmindedly watching the images on my TV. I had turned off the sound to answer the phone and didn't turn it back on. My thoughts drifted to my ex-colleague. I felt sympathy for him because I knew how upset and powerless one can feel when things go wrong. I had been there, many times. My mind drifted to an unknown place—to blankness. I shook my head to bring myself back to reality, and that's when out of nowhere scenes from my past came tearing out of my gut.

"Soon," he said, "as soon as I see a taxi."

"Anna, come here... explain to me how you broke this glass," Papa said while removing the beating belt from his pants. "Stop crying. You are nothing. You are the big sister, but it's Tita who looks and acts like a big sister. You are a failure in school... and a failure at home...just like your mother."

"Go back to where you came from," Maman had said. "Anna, do you know that once your name is said, no good words follow. Anna, why can't you, for once, do what is expected of you! Are you really set on killing us with embarrassment?"

I had to sit down and hold my head in my hands. I didn't know how to stop the memories from invading my mind. *Small events can carry big scars.* They were the fragments from the sad episodes of my youth that helped create a character built on expectations, pressure, and fear. To avoid being hurt, I began to laugh at all my flaws before anyone else could. And because Papa seemed to call me only when I had done something wrong, it was easy to assume that every time someone called my name, it was because I had done or said something wrong. As a result, I was continually apologetic, even when there was nothing to apologize for. I didn't need to be at fault. I just didn't want anyone pointing their fingers at me and blaming me for any mistakes.

I was addicted to my fear and doubts. Happiness, serenity, peace, and quiet unnerved me. They were not my normal state. They never lasted. The people I adored were taken away from me—first a Maman I never knew, then Lalla, Mama Sweetness, and Babette and Jean-Yves—with every goodbye, my ache and anxiety of being abandoned and left behind grew, making me dread the unknowns of the world. I couldn't trust anything or anyone, but I could rely on the bombastic voice of worry in my head that warned and prepared me for all the possible messy situations. So much energy devoted just to avoid grief.

Then, there were the side effects. The fear of being abandoned tainted many of my relationships. Some people in my life were toxic, yet I couldn't let go because of my need to be needed, to not be deserted. I was overaccommodating in order to be accepted by others. Still, my need to be in total control of my life was not only caused by fear—it was also created by the desire to resemble the person I adored, Lalla. I emulated, and made mine, her traits, the things I liked most about her.

"Too many mistreatments forced me to be fierce," she'd said. *My* fear made me seem fierce.

Lalla was an uncompromising force of nature. Family and friends knew they could depend on her because she wasn't afraid to fight for the people she loved and the causes she believed in. For as long as I can remember, my grandmother had been this fearless woman who everyone, whether they loved, admired, or despised her, feared because of her unbending bluntness. Listening to her, adoringly watching her, I learned from her that strong, bold women did not break.

I stayed on the couch, too dazed to move. I massaged my stiff, aching neck and shoulders. Tense and rigid were my normal ways of being. I didn't know what it meant to relax. Remaining anxious and stiff inside-out was the price I paid for decades of living and breathing to the ticking of expectations, pressure, and fear within.

I was in shock! No, I didn't want to beat myself up for having always been so hard on myself. Instead, a kind-heartedness appeared and made me see the good in my intentions and my heart. I felt compassion for me. And I whispered a few times, as if to convince myself: "Anna, you're not that bad."

This simple statement startled me for two reasons: I had never actually expressed positive words about myself; and until that very moment, I never really liked Anna.

I didn't like the way I looked—I saw myself as unattractive. That was why I avoided my reflection in the mirror and I didn't like being in pictures.

I didn't like the way I laughed—I was too loud (Papa said I laughed like my Maman; and no woman should laugh like that).

I didn't like the way I walked—I was too brusque, not feminine enough.

The only things I liked about myself were what others had said were good about me: I was intelligent and kind.

This was my defining moment. I promised myself I would stop the never-ending disparaging judgment of myself. I began to see the Anna I had been as more damaged and vulnerable than I thought, and more caring than I wanted to show. I didn't value who I was, yet I no longer saw myself as an unlovable human being.

The ball of harshness and fear I had carried inside of me for years melted. I experienced calmness, which was unnerving at first. I wasn't used to going so long without worrying about worst-case scenarios. For a moment, I wanted to be restless—*this was not normal, better be careful!* But something in me didn't want to go back to my old normal. I didn't want to be afraid anymore. I didn't want to let my mind and the voice in my head drive my entire being into emotional mayhem. The constant suspicion of myself, the questioning and the doubts were exhausting.

The relentless scrutiny had to end. I was better than that, otherwise Daba would never have allowed me to come this far. I stopped. I hadn't acknowledged Daba in a positive way in a long time. A rush of love and gratitude washed over me, as I finally conceded that, during all this time, even when I didn't want to recognize it, the Creator had always been present. I had this "knowing" that all along the Almighty had been watching over me and would always be there. I promised to make a concerted effort to check myself—and stop myself whenever fear appeared in me. If a problem occurred, I would deal with it honestly, but I would no longer think about all the bad things that could happen, and I would no longer prepare for the worst-case scenario.

If you show patience and endure the smoke, in the end you will enjoy the fire.

I was no longer who I had been, yet I wasn't who I was going to become. For a while, I only had good days. Did things go wrong at work and at home? Of course, they did. Did I panic? Every time. But I was now aware of my nervous system—that quick heartbeat that first got my attention before fear appeared to take hold of my thinking and my entire being. I knew how to stop myself before the voice in my head had a chance to really spin the events into negative thoughts. First, I stopped everything I was doing. Then I found a place to be alone for five or ten minutes so I could think, breathe, and talk the situation through. I began by acknowledging that my fear was back—I was afraid. Then I intentionally breathed slowly in and out to calm my mind. Finally, I faced the situation and asked myself what had really happened and stuck with the facts. I refused to contemplate assumptions and speculations, for they were the treacherous thoughts that led to worst-case scenarios. That, in turn, helped me determine under whose watch the problem had occurred, and whether I bore any responsibility. If I had contributed to the issue in some way, the next step would be to figure out how I wanted to resolve it. If it turned out it was my responsibility to fix the problem, I would do it promptly so the matter would be closed. The process was intimidating, but I stayed committed and, in the end, I was relieved and a little surprised to find there weren't that many problems, and almost all of them were not of my making.

As time went by, my newfound kindness to myself spread into the different areas of my life. In my daily interactions, I attentively listened because I was no longer in a hurry to provide answers for the sole purpose of explaining and justifying myself. As a result, I seemed to now sense the small hidden things behind the words and actions of other people. Angry words lost their sting when it was clear they were hiding feelings of insecurity. Actions that didn't seem to make a lot of sense became clear when I understood that fear or the need for approval had triggered them. People's voices at times gave me clues to their emotional state. From time to time, I surprised myself when I was able to read someone well. I was in awe at how easy it was to diffuse disputes and challenging situations. How strange and natural it was to realize I worried less and less.

Compassion made me forgive. I forgave family and friends, but most of all I forgave myself and accepted that to have empathy didn't mean I was weak. I even started to find good things to say about myself—I was a hard worker, and I deserved the raise I had asked for and received.

As weeks turned into months, a transformation I wasn't always aware of was taking place. The change within manifested itself when I spoke with more assurance and sympathy than I ever had, and when I heard myself laugh wholeheartedly without fear of being too loud. I realized I had changed when my serene attitude left some relatives perplexed. Had I suddenly become wealthy? No. Then what was the matter with me?

I began to love the world and felt the world loved me back again. Things were good at work and I no longer hated my job. It wasn't my dream job, but I was grateful to be working and decided I would be the best employee I could be. I even started to be grateful and thank Daba for the things I used to take for granted: my good health; a few good and loyal friends. And then a job posting for an office assistant for the New York City government caught my attention. I applied for the position, and when I received a call asking me to come in for a meeting, I decided this time would be different. I wasn't going to overthink and overprepare for the interview. Did I want the job? Of course, I did, but I wasn't going to this interview with the sole goal to impress. I was going as Anna. I would be honest and let them decide if what I had to offer were the qualifications they were looking for. The interview went very well and the conversation went over the hour it had been scheduled for. I was calm and confident, and when I left, I was sure I would get the job. A few days later, I received a phone call confirming my prediction. Within weeks, I started to work in my new position. It was a new beginning with a transformed me.

I was in a good place. My need for control had subsided a lot. Yes, my past was painful. I wasn't unbreakable, but emotions and the unknown were not my enemy. I didn't know what tomorrow would bring and that was okay. I started to think about what I really wanted in life. What was I passionate about? I wanted to read more. I wanted to better understand my faith. Who or what the Creator was. I wanted to travel. My longing had nothing to do with career choices or where I wanted to be in the next five or ten years. They were all about quality of life—learning to better understand and love living.

It was at this stage of my journey that Lalla said: "Now you understand why we say the seeker of self and the seeker of the world are two different people. The first wants peace, and the second confusion. You were pursuing the world. You wanted people to approve of you. You have seen the limits of where that chase can take you, and how frustrated it left you. The outside world can't fulfill you."

"Why didn't you tell me this before?"

"Because you wouldn't have heard me or believed me. You needed to have the experience to accept this truth. I see you are ready to listen to your gut and let it guide you to the true you, that was dormant within. Anna, no one is ever complete. Yet, from my experience I can tell you that what you'll find inside of you are the things that will make you the most content. And if you keep digging, your gut will guide you to the source of all fulfillments, Daba. That's why our elders say that as adults we come face-to-face with two unavoidable beings we have to learn to know if we are to become our true selves. In the beginning we face and get to know who we are so in the end we gain our own understanding of the Creator."

"What do I do now?"

"Nothing. You are already on *the good path*. Stay on it. You are going to be just fine, *lagaré*. You know I tell you things as I see them."

That same Sunday, after our conversation, I met my friends for brunch in a café. We were talking about the books that had a lasting impact on us. I was very happy to boast I had read *Les Misérables* in its French original version.

"Enough, Anna," a friend teased. "Yes, *we know* you speak French…You are so full…."

"Yes, I am. And what's your point?"

We laughed.

"Why do you like *Les Misérables* so much?"

"I'm not sure. So many things. It's beautifully written…the description of the places and the events are so vivid and detailed you can actually picture them. And you are never bored."

My response was a partial truth that left out the most important reason why I loved the book. It was because of Cosette—the little girl who was ill-treated and exploited by the Thénardiers, who'd promised her mother they would take care of her while she went away to look for work. Cosette's pathos resonated with me.

"All joking aside, what made you love books so much?"

Babette and Jean-Yves. Instead, I lied, "In all the schools I went to there were libraries, and we were encouraged to read at least one or more books a month. I guess, it started there."

Later, thoughts of Babette and Jean-Yves kept coming back. One Christmas thirty-five years ago had been the last time we'd seen each other. Where were they? Did the family still gather together for the holidays? Did they think about me once a while? I wanted to find them. And I knew exactly where to start looking.

Chapter Eleven

AN UNFINISHED STORY

*L*ike the missing beads of a broken necklace, our storyline was filled with many lost bits. Tita and I had joined Babette, Jean-Yves, and their family for a Christmas while we were living in Germany. That vacation was the last time we'd seen each other. I was eleven and Tita was nine. For a year, maybe less, my sister and I kept in touch with them by writing letters that Papa mailed. And then the letters stopped. When did we stop writing? When did they stop answering? I was not sure. When I asked Papa, he said he had lost their address. He didn't know where they were.

Babette and Jean-Yves. For two years, they had taken the role of my primary caregivers and had become loving parents. *Good deeds should be housed by gratitude and recognition.* I wanted to make sure they knew I was grateful.

I had never said thank you for the love they poured into me.

I had never said thank you for making me part of their family.

I had never said thank you for showing me what good, decent, loving, and honest people were like.

I never forgot them.

The quest to find Babette and Jean-Yves began with a Google search. I didn't know where they were. I didn't know if they were still alive. The following three to four months, every weekend, I took time to look for them. My Google searches were unsuccessful. Few people shared the same last name as Jean-Yves, but each phone number I found and called failed to reach them. Then one day, I recalled the name of the village where their house was located. I Googled Jean-Yves's last name and the village and two phone numbers appeared. All at once the world stopped. I had found him. I was nervous. Butterflies in my stomach. I wanted to wait until the next day but couldn't. I surprised him by calling in the middle of the night.

"Are you Jean-Yves?"

"Yes.

"Did you live in Mali?"

"Yes."

"Jean-Yves, it's Anna. Do you remember me?"

"Oh, my God! Oh, my God! Oh, my God," was all he could say.

"You know, Babette and I often wondered about you. We never understood why we lost touch. We thought maybe we did something wrong."

I was stunned. "You didn't do anything wrong. I had to find you. I don't know if anyone in the family did ever thank you for all you did."

"That's not important. I just didn't know what we did wrong. So where are you?"

"I live in New York."

"Wow! I'm impressed. Are you happy?"

"Yes, I am Jean-Yves. I truly am."

"You don't know how relieved and happy I am to hear you say that. Tell me, and how is your dad?"

"Papa is fine. He retired a few years ago."

"Well, I'm retired too…but tell me, how is your little sister Tita?"

"She's fine, she works for an international organization in Dakar. But Jean-Yves, tell me, where have you been? The last time we saw each other was for Christmas in your parents' house."

"Well, you know they both passed away."

"I'm so sorry."

"Yes, but they were old. I'm so happy to hear your voice, after all these years! You have to come visit when you can."

"I will, Jean-Yves," I suddenly realized, "it must be late…."

"Don't worry. I'm so happy. I can't believe it. Will you call me tomorrow?"

"Yes, I promise."

He laughed. "Good."

We hung up. I was restless. I was too excited to do anything else. After thirty-five years, I had just reconnected with Jean-Yves. I didn't ask about Babette.

The next day I called. Jean-Yves filled in certain gaps. He and Babette divorced long ago and he was remarried, but they never stopped being family. He had been a school principal at international schools in the U.K. and then in Morocco. He came back to France and was a high school principal for years in Paris before retiring.

I didn't talk about my turbulent adolescence years. Instead, I told him how I came to the U.S. and my love for New York. We reminisced about the two weeks he and Babette spent visiting us in the Big Apple one summer—the first year after we all left Mali. He still remembered walking in Central Park, and the countless fearless squirrels he encountered. Jean-Yves, always thoughtful, asked if he could share with Babette that we had found each other and give her my contact information. She would be so happy to hear from me. Two days later Babette called. She cried. My heart ached. Her voice hadn't changed. She was still the buoyant spirit I loved.

"You know I have in my living room pictures of you and Tita when you were little girls. I tell my visitors you are my daughters. They smile...I know they must think I have lost it, but I don't care...you are and you will always be my little girls. I miss the life we used to have."

"Me too," I echoed. "It was simple...it was happy."

"When will you come visit me?"

"Soon," I said.

I kept my promise. I called Tita. My sister and I had grown closer with the years, and we trusted each other now that we weren't under our father's roof. She traveled often for work. No matter what part of the world Tita was sent to, she always let me know where she would be and for how long. I told her I had found Babette and Jean-Yves. She couldn't believe it. When I asked if we could go visit them together, my sister enthusiastically agreed. And then she did more. She used her many mileage points to purchase both our tickets to France.

A year after my call to Jean-Yves, Tita and I took the TGV, France's intercity high-speed rail service, from Paris to Lyons. A trip that would have taken four hours by car took two by train. Jean-Yves was waiting. I recognized him because he was wearing the same beret he had on in a picture he sent me.

Tita and I hugged Jean-Yves. He was frail. A flood of emotions overtook me, elated to have found my second father figure and sad to see that so many years had passed. Jean-Yves took a moment to look at us both. He was still water—managing to remain calm despite the flurry of sentiments that must have overcome him. We sensed the turmoil in him when he asked to stop a moment so he could catch his breath.

He drove us to the summer home he shared with his wife. I knew the house well, and one of the bedrooms was still called Anna's room. A few hours later, as we were about to get ready to have dinner, the phone rang—it was Babette. She wanted to make sure Tita and I were there and that we would visit her.

Tita and I had agreed we would spend a week with Jean-Yves and his wife, and the second week with Babette. We would then go back to Paris and spend some time with our friends before heading back, me to New York and Tita to Dakar.

That first night, Jean-Yves wanted to know everything that had happened in the last thirty-five years. We told him Papa had divorced and married his fourth wife, and we were now six siblings, five girls and one boy.

"While you all were in Canada, your father used to stay with us every time he was going or coming back from Bamako. That's how we learned he had a son. We used to live near the airport."

I was shocked. "Oh, I didn't know you and Papa had kept in touch?"

"For a while we did."

"Yes," his wife added, "your father used to stop by and spend the night at least twice a year."

Tita and I quickly exchanged a surprised glance. *What, Papa knew where Jean-Yves was? No, that could not be possible. Papa doesn't lie. I must have missed something.*

Tita and I spent an enchanting week with Jean-Yves and his wife. Every morning after breakfast we went for a walk in a different part of the village. Jean-Yves and his wife knew the history of each château, and every abandoned monastery we visited. Tita and I called them the walking encyclopedia. Early Saturday morning, we went to the farmer's market. It was 8 a.m. and the open space was buzzing with people pressing to come in. My senses were delighted by all the scents—warm French baguette, varieties of goat cheese, camembert, brie, and all sorts of locally made cheese that were not sold in big stores. Jean-Yves and his wife laughed in delight as they watched Tita and I go mad for the cheese.

And then there are the things you fathom without a single word being ever uttered. On our last night together, after dinner, Jean-Yves called me to join him in his office. It was the two of us. As if he was holding something precious, he slowly and carefully opened a box filled with the pictures of our life together. There were photos of Babette, Jean-Yves, and I sitting on the terrace at home in Bamako or walking in a street while vacationing in France. Picnics with the family. There were also pictures of them with Papa, Mama Fire, Tita, and I when we went to visit the Statue of Liberty.

I didn't have to wonder anymore. Jean-Yves never forgot me. I understood the immensity of his love, and the place I had in his life, watching how tenderly he touched each photo, asking me if I remembered when and where it was taken. Then, in a low voice, he shared:

"You know, a couple of years ago, your father wrote me. He asked if your brother Iba could come live with us. I believe he was in high school at the time, and your father was worried about his education because of the never-ending demands and strikes of the students and professors in Mali. The schools were often closed for long periods of time. My wife and I talked it over, and then I wrote him saying no…I'm sure Iba is very nice, but I didn't want to, especially after what happened with you."

My disappearance from Jean-Yves's life had been painful. He carefully put the pictures back in the box. I wrapped my arms around his neck. He smiled. He didn't complain, and he didn't say one unkind word about Papa. His silence spoke volumes about how hurt he had been, and how incomprehensible it had been to not know why we lost touch.

Papa had lied. I feared him, but I had also always revered him. He could do no wrong. In my eyes, Papa was a man of principle who didn't compromise and didn't tell fibs. In both his professional and personal life, my father worked hard to be seen as a straightforward, trustworthy, moral, and uncompromising man. Except now, there was a tarnish to that polished image— Papa didn't tell the truth when he said he didn't know where Babette and Jean-Yves were. I was hurt and angry, but not enough to dethrone him from the pedestal the little girl I once was had placed him on decades ago. I was flabbergasted but not enough to start questioning who Papa really was and why he had lied.

The next morning, Jean-Yves drove Tita and me to Babette's, a five-hour drive. Babette could hardly contain herself and began to cry before I got out of the car to hug her. We held on to each other.

"I can't believe you are here. Thank you, God…thank you. I can't believe you are here. Jean-Yves, thank you so much for bringing me my girls. By the way, I see you have a nice car, tell me, you must be rich now?"

"Yes, I am."

They laughed.

We walked in the house and Tita and I were taken aback. On a wall, Babette had enlarged photos from our forgotten childhood—the era when she and Jean-Yves were our neighbors. In the pictures, I was five and Tita was three and we were standing in front of their house.

"I tell everyone you are my two daughters."

Soon after, Jean-Yves left to go back home. When I walked him to his car, I sensed his sadness.

"Don't forget to email me as soon as you're back in the States."

"I will."

I watched the car disappear with a heavy heart. When I walked into the living room, Babette said, "I'm glad you walked Jean-Yves to his car. You know he was sad to go. He was happy to see you, but he's afraid he won't live long enough to see you come back."

I didn't know what to say to so much love and remained quiet. Babette reiterated what Jean-Yves said. "You can't imagine how happy Jean-Yves and I are that you found us. You know, you were...you are important to us. We never forgot you. We never stopped loving you. It was hard to let you go... we thought perhaps we had done something wrong."

The following five days with Babette were a flurry of storytelling and activities. She wanted to know everything we had done. Did I love my job? Did I love living in New York City? Was Tita happy in Dakar? She asked about Papa—how was he doing? She organized a party so her friends could see she had said the truth about her two daughters. She pampered Tita and me. What did we want to eat? She wanted to buy us clothes. Tita and I had to be firm in saying no, then letting us spoil her a little. Babette was grateful for every kind word we uttered, and every hug. At the end of our stay, my sister and I were emotionally drained, yet I felt I had come full circle.

Tita agreed. "Anna, this trip was a great idea. There are no words to describe what took place. I am so glad you took me with you."

"Me too. I don't know what to say or how to feel right now. Papa…?"

"Let it go. He did what he did, and that's on him. This moment is too important to dwell on him."

Tita was right. Our storyline was complete. Our reunion with Babette and Jean-Yves was all that mattered. Too soon it was time to say goodbye. Babette drove us to the train station. She made us promise to come back, if not the following year, then when we could. We promised. I fought back the tears as I embraced her tightly and murmured, "Maman Babette."

It was the end of a journey. The trip had been a rollercoaster of emotions for all of us. I looked forward to returning home so I could have some time alone to process it all. I thanked Tita for making the voyage happen. Yes, it was my idea, but she had bought the tickets that made the reunion possible.

I had set out on this journey to find Babette and Jean-Yves to say thank you only to find they didn't want gratitude. They just wanted to know I loved them, and I was happy. After I returned, I emailed Jean-Yves. It was the beginning of our online conversations. One day while on the phone with Jean-Yves he asked, "When will you be back to visit? It's been a year and I really would like to see you."

"I'm not going to make any promises, but I'll try to come next summer."

"That would be wonderful…."

It was the end of October. My life was like a peaceful streaming river—the calm before the storm.

Chapter Twelve

THE RUSHED, UNPLANNED TRIP

*The unexpected always annuls and ends
all that was planned.
The universe gives warning signs.*

*L*alla and the elders often said all major events in our lives are preceded by warning signs, provided we pay attention. I must not have paid attention because the first major event seemed to have come without warning.

It was Veterans Day, and I had the day off. After a late breakfast, I decided to call Maman. She wasn't home. I was surprised; it was midafternoon in Dakar, a time when she, now retired from nursing, was usually home. By late that night, I still hadn't heard back from her. Another troubling first because she always returned my calls. Puzzled, I tried to reach her the next day, thinking maybe someone forgot to tell her I had called. The maid answered the phone again and told me Maman was not home. It was odd, but I didn't want to worry. Maybe she was out shopping. She loved to shop for fabric that her tailor would make into beautiful, intricately embroidered traditional clothes.

The next day, I woke up apprehensive. I knew something had to be wrong. I dialed Maman's number. The phone rang.

I held my breath hoping to hear her voice, laughing, and reassuring me. Instead, my stepfather answered and calmly told me Maman was in the hospital. *My Maman in the hospital? But the woman was never sick.* Before I could ask what was wrong with her, my stepfather answered my questions. Maman had suffered a stroke and had been in a coma for eleven days. I wanted to scream, *you didn't think to call me and let me know? Me, her daughter?*

But before you slap someone, wait, and hear what they have to say.

I remained silent and listened to my stepfather explain the reasoning behind his decision not to let anyone know. He didn't call the family when she had the stroke because he wanted to wait until she regained consciousness. He was really trying to protect us. He quickly added that he had some good news: Maman had woken up the day before, and the doctors were cautiously optimistic she would be all right.

I sighed, relieved. I can't recall much more of our conversation. But we agreed on the time I would call him every day for an update. When we hung up, I didn't move. I didn't know what I was supposed to do next. I had already used all my vacation days, so I could not travel.

I felt guilty. My Maman was in the hospital fighting for her life and I couldn't be there. What kind of daughter did that make me?

When there's nothing you can do, swallow.

I swallowed my fear—fear of losing my Maman. I swallowed my shame and my guilt for not being able to travel and show that I was a good daughter who loved her Maman.

I swallowed my anger—anger at my stepfather—for not telling me sooner. Didn't he get, after all these years of being married to her, how close the members of Lalla's family were to one another—*like the threads of one cover?*

But when there's nothing you can do, swallow. I swallowed my fear, my anger, and my resentment, and I called Lalla. At the time, my grandmother lived with Uncle Layes and his family in Bamako. I discovered they were anxiously awaiting my call. Like me, my grandmother and my uncle had tried for days to reach Maman to no avail. A little before my conversation with him, my stepfather had called Uncle Layes to tell him the same story he would soon recount to me. We were livid, but most of all we were afraid. *How could this be? What really happened? She was never sick.*

Lalla didn't swallow. Both my stepfather and my uncle experienced her wrath—my stepfather for his decision to withhold information, and my uncle for not getting the plane ticket fast enough. Lalla was adamant about going to Dakar right away. They didn't talk back. Instead, my stepfather and my uncle asked me to intervene and calm her down. I was the only person who could convince her to wait until Maman was released from the hospital.

I called my grandmother—the woman who didn't hide herself from me. Lalla wanted to take the next plane to Dakar to see "her child." She was worried and scared. I listened to her voice, filled with anguish, tell me she didn't sleep at night and wouldn't until she saw for herself what had happened to Maman. She wanted to go see Maman because she knew "her child" needed her. A slight silence followed, during which I heard my grandmother breathe and sigh. I knew she was fighting to keep it together so she wouldn't make me cry. In that instant, I wanted to be with her—to hold her and tell her everything would be all right. Instead, I cleared my throat and

asked her softly to let the doctors take care of "her child," and I
promised that as soon as Maman was well enough to leave the
hospital, she would be on the next flight to Dakar. Lalla was
calm and said she would wait because I had asked her to.

Days carry troubles you cannot fast forward through.

Our worries and fears made each day seem very long. Every
dawn, I woke up hoping and praying for some good news. I
called every morning and spoke with my stepfather, who
gave me a detailed report on Maman's health. Then I would
talk to my grandmother, my uncle, and my brother, and we
would share the conversations we had had with my stepfather,
comparing them to see if he had told each of us the same thing:
"Maman was conscious, but couldn't talk" and "Maman slept a
lot." It was my new morning routine.

I can't recall when Maman's health started to improve—
maybe two weeks, maybe more—but it did. The first time
she was strong enough to talk on the phone, we spoke for less
than a minute. She seemed exhausted and her voice was so
frail it was hard to believe I was talking to Maman. Her voice
made real how gravely ill she was. But it felt good to hear her
low, soft voice. Later, in my conversation with Lalla and my
uncle, I found out they too had spoken to her briefly. We were
overjoyed. The dread had come and gone. We were grateful to
Daba—Maman had pulled through. She was going to live. We
were relieved and full of hope.

A small intoxicating flame called Hope.

According to the elders, one of the most *important gifts
Daba gave humankind was Hope*—a small intoxicating flame
that reawakened our faith in ourselves and in life. My dawns
were filled with hope and answered prayers. Maman's health
was improving. A week after our first talk, Maman was released

from the hospital, and Lalla traveled to Dakar to be with her and take care of her. I listened to Maman's voice become stronger and stronger. Every conversation brought good news. Both she and Lalla told me repeatedly she was doing better. Maman hushed my concerns with words of reassurance. "I'm better…I'm good…I'm well," she often insisted, laughing.

Then Lalla would lovingly scold me, "Anna don't worry so much. Everything is fine here."

It was comforting and reassuring. I had no doubt Maman would make a full recovery. Lalla was there by her side, helping and supporting her. I had no worries for, as always, Lalla would know what to do to make things better. As time passed, and fear and guilt melted away, I began to call every other day. Maman laughed and joked on the phone and Lalla would then tell me to stop worrying—Maman was doing well. Then I called once a week. Things were good as I listened to Lalla and Maman tell me she was healthy again. In my mind that meant that Maman was her old self.

I called often, and I sent money to help pay her medical bills. Six months after the stroke, Lalla, Maman, and I rarely spoke about it except to acknowledge "the unthinkable could have happened—we could have lost her." And then we thanked the Creator for her recovery. My life returned to what it was before the stroke.

A month later, the *universe gave other warning signs*. This time I noticed.

Thursday, June 4th, 2009. I woke up and for no apparent reason felt dull. The morning shower didn't help me snap out of it. The beautiful weather—sunny with a small breeze—didn't make a difference. I didn't know what I wanted to do. I didn't feel like going to work, yet I didn't want to stay home.

I got dressed. My head was clouded with an unexplainable uneasiness as I traveled to work. Once in the office, I did what I knew how to do well: I ignored my state of mind, worked, laughed, had lunch and coffee as if nothing was wrong. I was convinced that at some point in the day the uneasiness would go away. It didn't. I carried my heaviness with me back home and, together, we went to sleep. I didn't ask myself what was wrong with me because I knew everything was fine. I enjoyed my work, and I was in good health. Maman was her old self again; I could hear it in her voice every time we spoke. I was certain a good night's sleep would make the gloomy feeling disappear.

The next morning, Friday, June 5th, my eyes opened and almost immediately, I felt it. The uneasiness was back. I went to work, but unlike the first day, I didn't try to curb it. I let it wrap itself around my entire being. I kept to myself and remained quiet, almost reflective all morning. But then, in the early afternoon, the heaviness and gloominess became darker. I felt helpless and profoundly sad, and for no reason, wanted to cry. *What was the matter with me?* I decided to fight back. I took a walk, hoping the exercise and fresh air would help get rid of my mood, but it didn't. I came back to the office, determined to ignore the troublesome dread in me. I looked at the clock on the wall. *What, only four in the afternoon! This day will never end.* It would be another two endless hours before I could go home. Suddenly a rush of anguish overwhelmed me. That's when my phone rang. Caller ID read "Maman." My heaviness vanished, and I exhaled, relieved. I picked up.

Daba had allowed the unexpected to happen.

"Hello, Maman?"

"Yes…."

Her voice was strange.

"Is this good?"

"No," she said.

"What happened?"

"It's your uncle…."

"What about him?"

"He was sick."

"How is he?"

"He didn't make it."

And what Daba allows to take place is always good.

The strange voice—Maman was crying.

"Lalla?" I cried out.

"She's here; talk to her."

"Lalla."

My grandmother was weeping and between sobs managed to say, "Pray for your Uncle Layes, Anna. You hear me? Pray for your uncle."

That's all she could say. *And when all is said, to talk is useless unless you just want to move your tongue.* The sound of sobs, then nothing. I believe we all hung up. Shock and pain settled in. Finally, the first tears came.

The green fruit can fall before the ripe fruit, but it is not the proper order of things. Indeed, a child can go before his parents, but it is not how we want things to be. My grandmother had just lost her only son.

Mother, oh mother, did you know that habits make parting difficult?

The world is not a place where we come to stay.

Indeed, mother, being used to someone makes going away so hard.

The world is not a place where we come to stay.

And just like all mornings turn into evenings.
The world is not a place where we come to stay.
All arrivals lead to departures.
The world is not a place where we come to stay.
But being used to someone makes parting so hard.
The world is not a place where we come to stay.

Uncle Layes was a schoolteacher. A few years ago, he had retired as the principal of a public school in Bamako. My uncle had eaten his share of salt and drunk his share of water; and without us knowing this was all the time he had, he had walked away into the long corridor to the world beyond, leaving us stunned and in sorrow. I went home and called Maman. Lalla couldn't talk, she was weeping and getting ready to fly back to Bamako the next day to see her only son one last time before he was laid to rest—given back to Earth.

The Earth eats many good things.

I worried about Lalla more than I did about Maman. This was too much. First, Maman's stroke, which had scared and shaken all of us, and now *this*. I didn't know how Lalla would cope. I wanted to be with my grandmother and make things better. I didn't know what that meant, I just wanted to be with her.

My first conversation with Maman after my uncle's funeral was the defining moment. I hadn't planned to travel for another year, but Lalla and Maman had gone through too much. I had to see them. Maman's sigh of relief when I announced my upcoming visit validated what I felt deep inside—*I needed to be there.* We decided we wouldn't tell Lalla until I could confirm my trip to Senegal where Maman was, then to Mali, where Lalla now lived in my late uncle's house with his son and widow.

On July 29, 2009, almost two months after my uncle's walk into the afterlife, my flight landed in the afternoon in Dakar. The day before my arrival, I was a little surprised to hear Maman say she couldn't make it, but my stepfather would be at the airport to greet me. I didn't think much of it; maybe she was tired. He was at the airport waiting and, despite the sad circumstances that had caused the rushed unplanned trip, we were happy to see each other. I was also impatient to see Maman.

My stepfather and I were in a cab on our way to the house. The drive was pleasantly filled with the words, "Happy to see you." "Happy to be here." "Your Maman can't wait to see you." We didn't talk about my uncle. The car stopped. A young maid came to open the door. I ran up the stairs looking for Maman.

"I'm here," she said.

I turned and saw her sitting on the balcony with the beautiful view to the sea. Maman wore a simple long traditional yellow dress with the matching scarf tied around her head. I ran and hugged her. She laughed and hugged me back, then pulled a chair closer to her, inviting me to sit down. As I sat, I was struck with the reality of her disability. I sadly realized what "I'm better, I'm good, I'm well" concealed. Maman had trouble walking.

I was with Maman. I was close to her, watching her, and because it was just the two of us, she opened up and told me about her life-changing nightmare. She recounted the day of the stroke—her falling down in the middle of the street, the ride to the hospital in a cab. She remembered being admitted into the hospital, the call to my stepfather to let him know, and then nothing afterwards. When she woke up eleven days later, she faced a new, harsh reality unknown to us: She couldn't walk.

What I didn't want to know...and what you didn't want to tell me.

For more than a month, Maman was bedridden. She was a nurse, so she knew exactly what had happened to her. My heart sank as I slowly understood the reality of the stroke and its damaging consequences. My mind replayed my phone calls and it dawned on me that in all our conversations, I never once stopped to question my Maman's statements, never insisted on knowing what "I'm better. I'm good. I'm well" really meant. It pained and embarrassed me to realize I didn't ask because I was afraid to know as the knowledge would have impacted my newfound calm and serene life.

No words of comfort came to mind as I listened to Maman tell me how painfully difficult it had been in the beginning to wake up each day and not be able to get out of bed, walk properly, or take care of her basic needs. My grandmother had made things easier. Still, she had been sorely trying to resign herself to this new normal. She couldn't tell me sooner because these were not things one talks about over the phone. They were too close, too personal. *I didn't ask, but Maman also didn't want me to know*, I pointed out as if to excuse myself. Regardless, I finally understood.

"I'm better. I'm good. I'm well." The words were shields used to evade questions that would have revealed how the stroke had hurt her. They were protection that avoided or stopped pity. Lalla and Maman didn't want pity from anyone. Why? Because *sitting pitifully will not lessen your pain or misery.* Thus, they put forth the brave, almost defiant front Lalla had instilled in all her family. Maman, with Lalla acquiescing by her side, invariably replied to all the well-wishers' and sympathizers' "How are you doing?" with "I'm better. I'm good. I'm well." I wanted to believe Lalla would fix it—Lalla was supposed to make things better—the way she had always done when one of her family members had a problem. But Maman's health and my uncle's death were both things Lalla could not fix—could not make better.

And so, our long-distance talks seemed to have been moments of respite—times when both Lalla and Maman chose to close their eyes to the illness, its pain, and all their buried emotions, and instead pretend everything was fine. It wasn't difficult to do because I was happy to imagine everything was back to normal.

Relief drenched in salty tears.

I must have remained silent too long. As if to reassure me, Maman said she didn't want me to be sad, sorry, or angry— she was really doing better. She had made a lot of progress with the physical therapy and reeducation and she no longer needed help to get up and get herself ready in the morning. She could also walk small distances. Maman seemed to have come to terms with her condition; but more than her words, the stiffness of her tone spoke of suppressed pain, anger, and resentment. It was with harsh pride that she talked about her unwavering faith.

"Through it all I never stopped calling Allah." She was holding on tighter to the Creator. She had pulled through. She was alive and fighting to reclaim who she had been. She was relieved she had made so much progress—but her relief seemed drenched in salty tears. She held on to the words like a leitmotif: *Allah had allowed this to happen; and what the Creator allows is always good.* I wanted to believe that, but I also had questions

I didn't dare ask: What happened when she was alone? Did she cry a lot? Was she angry, afraid, and resentful? Did she question Daba when she was alone when no one could see or hear her?

I was only preoccupied with being a good daughter to erase my own culpability. I felt sorry for Maman and guilty for not being present when she was released from the hospital. What would I have done? I didn't know, but the voice in my head kept telling me that not being present was wrong. And so, for the week I stayed with her, I did everything I could to be a loving, respectful, and submissive daughter, as if I could turn back the clock to become an eager, pleasing child for her. I didn't leave her side until she asked to be alone. I listened and agreed with everything she said. I was beating myself up for not being there, as if somehow I was at fault—as if my presence could have somehow prevented Maman from suffering a stroke. I couldn't forgive myself for not making the trip earlier.

Our relatives and close friends who visited didn't make me feel better. They came to welcome me with long faces expressing pity and sympathy and shared their account of Maman's stroke. They shook their heads in disbelief, still trying to comprehend how something like this could ever happen to someone who was never sick. They described it all in detail, weaving words with long sighs that overstated their grief and their pity, the eleven excruciating days when no one knew if Maman would make it.

And always in the end—no matter how sorry and sad they were, they would turn on me. With tones filled with silent reproach or disappointment, they stated—as if I had let them down personally—that they expected me to come sooner. Why had it taken me so long to be by my Maman's side? I tried to find words to justify my behavior—that my boss refused to give me permission to travel. Together, we denounced and criticized the heartlessness of certain bosses that could only be found in the United States, where making money was all that mattered. They appeared to understand, and even if some were not totally convinced, they all agreed it was a good thing I finally came. It was good for Maman's morale. More than words of comfort, my presence showed Maman that I cared.

Early one evening, Maman and I finally called Lalla, putting the phone on speaker.

"Hello?"

"Lalla, I have a visitor who wants to talk to you."

"Who?"

"Hold on."

"Lalla?"

"Yes?"

"Do you know who this is?"

Lalla was uncertain, hesitant, so she asked.

"Who is it?"

"It's me, Anna."

My grandmother broke down and cried. Maman wiped away her own tears.

"I'm in Dakar. I'm coming to see you soon."

"Daba, thank you. You don't know how much I prayed to see you before I die."

"Don't say that."

"When are you coming?"

"Saturday."

Soon, I will see my Lalla, and I will find words to comfort her.

Soon, I will be with my grandmother; and I will make things better.

Tired of living, but not knowing how to die—that's how I found my Lalla when I arrived in Bamako. For the first time in my life, I saw my grandmother broken, defeated, and there was nothing I could say or do to make things better. Life went on, but her child's death had stricken Lalla at an unimaginable place beyond her very core. The light in her beautiful eyes was extinguished. The green fruit was not supposed to fall before the ripe fruit. He was supposed to outlive her—not the other way around. She told me that on her flight from Dakar to Bamako to bury her child, all she wanted to do was to see him. She spoke of wanting to see her child as if her presence could have somehow protected him, maybe changed something; perhaps she wanted to see him to make his passing real. After her plane landed in Bamako, relatives took her straight to the morgue to see her child one last time.

"I held his hand. I massaged his arms and his feet. I called his name. Your uncle looked so at peace, Anna. He was smiling; and that was the only thing that made my pain bearable: to see him lying so at peace."

"Anna, everyone came. Your aunts, your uncles, and many of his former students. I didn't know most of them. But they all remembered him."

Uncle Layes was a secondary-school teacher for fifty years. Teaching was his calling. At the beginning of every school year, parents tracked him in school and at home to beg him to either take their children in his class or teach them after school. It seemed that everywhere my uncle taught, from the most remote villages, at the beginning of his career, to school principal in Bamako by the time he retired, he had left students and parents who remembered the devoted teacher he was. The former students had become fathers and mothers with offspring of their own, still they called him "Sir."

I listened grief-stricken, my mind a total blank. And there was nothing I could say or do to make things better. For the ten days I stayed with her, every day in the wee hours before dawn, I heard my grandmother's grieving, shushed sobs in the room next to mine, weeping while praying to Daba. I didn't move. I stayed in bed because there was nothing I could say or do to make things better. I worried about Lalla and I told her so. She admitted she was tired of living. Nothing appealed to her. She didn't know what to do with herself. My grandmother was inconsolable. And there was nothing I could say or do to make things better.

"Anna, this was my fate. This was my unfortunate fate."

To accept this unfortunate fate, my grandmother often said the rote words the faithful say when facing a sudden, awful event with crushing helplessness: "Allah had allowed it to happen; and what Allah allows is always good." I believe that Lalla repeated these words over and over to shush the whys—for it was inconceivable to question the Almighty's will. She said the words again and again to bend her loss and pain, turn them into total surrender—total submission to Daba, so the Creator would show mercy and make it easier to accept her unfortunate fate. It was heart wrenching. My Lalla was broken, and there was nothing I could say or do to make things better. She had always been an indestructible force of nature—a baobab tree whose shade had provided solace to all those who had confided in her. Now these many friends and family members took turns and came to visit and comfort her every day.

I returned to Dakar and spent a few more days with Maman then flew back home to New York City. I was drained physically and emotionally. I had mixed feelings about my rushed, unplanned trip. Going to Senegal, then Mali, gave me an eye-opening understanding of what Maman had suffered and what she was still enduring. And knowing the truth about Maman's health was useful. I also sensed how fragile Lalla had become and learning that was helpful too. But beyond that, what did my being there really do? I didn't make things better, as I had imagined I would. Things just didn't work that way. Lalla—my Lalla—was in pain, and there was nothing I had been able to say or do to make her feel better. Maman was struggling to regain her mobility and there was nothing I had been able to say or do to make her feel better. I was overwhelmed with feelings of guilt, and uselessness. What good did I do?

Later, I was on the phone with Lalla, and as if to answer my unspoken question and free me from my tormenting doubts, just as we were about to end our conversation, my grandmother simply said, "Anna, it was so good that you came."

That was all I needed to hear. Indeed, *offering sympathy will not bring back the dead; but it will preserve love and fondness among those who remain.* Relief washed over me. So that's why I needed to go: to be there. It was not to make things better or easier. Lalla and Maman didn't need words. Still, my rushed, unplanned visit said I care.

I was present when Maman and Lalla needed to see me.

I was present when my elders wanted me close by.

I was present, and that showed Maman, Lalla, relatives, and the entire community that I was a good daughter, a good granddaughter.

I was present, and in the end, that was all that mattered.

When you fall asleep, your soul leaves your body to visit the parallel invisible world. Dreams are the remembrance of what it saw, and sometimes this vision can be a forewarning of what is to come. The soul has the power to meet the ancestors and to mingle with the beings in the afterlife.

Two or three nights after I returned from my trip, my soul traveled to an unknown place while I slept. I was part of a crowd. We walked in line, one behind the other. I believe it was flea market day because there were stands with all sorts of merchandise, and in the middle, there was a ladder placed at the opening of a large round tunnel that went up to the heavens. Light was coming down from the heavens.

The people I was in line with were pushing to access the ladder, but not everyone could reach it. I was a little far and apprehensive. I wondered how I was going to get through this crowd and have a chance to get up on the ladder while carrying a bundle of dead wood on my head. To make matters worse, the strap of my right sandals broke. Then I saw him. He called my name and we walked toward each other; neither one of us was surprised to see the other. I realized most of us were dressed in all white.

Without saying hello, I told Uncle Layes my concern: my broken sandal. He calmly told me to take the sandals off—that he would find another pair for me. He helped me get closer to the entrance of the big round tunnel. Finally, we were close enough that I could see the inside. It was an open passageway to the heavens with rays of soft white light coming from the sky; and in the middle of this tunnel was a ladder that went up to the light—to the heavens. It was very inviting. But I was nervous, for I didn't know how I would manage to climb with the dead wood on my head. As if he read my mind, Uncle Layes removed my burden—he took the dead wood away. With no broken sandal and no dead wood to carry, I started to climb the ladder. I recall reaching the top that opened into infinite light. There was no space, no beginning or end; just infinite soft light. I don't know how long I stayed up in the light, but when I came down, my uncle had disappeared. I didn't go looking for him either.

I walked through this limitless space feeling light and free. I remember that I was surrounded and enveloped by a quiet and serene atmosphere. I felt good. And it was from this peaceful place that my soul came back and settled in my body, allowing me to wake up in the world of beings and things. I was surprised at how light I felt—calm, and relieved.

I stayed in bed, trying to understand what had happened. I thought about my uncle and the strong bond we shared. Through our ups and downs of fights and misunderstandings, he had always remained constant. Uncle Layes was a solid presence in my life. I could depend on him. Our last phone call had been a happy one.

"How's everything?"

"Everything is good."

"I received my gifts, thank you."

"Oh, that's nothing."

"It is something. I thank you and you have my blessings—may Daba grant you success in everything you do. You have my number?"

"Yes."

"Well, you can call me anytime. I always have my cell on me."

"Good. I will. Goodbye, Tonton."

"Goodbye, Anna."

It was a mundane conversation, which made us happy because, in their delivery, the words carried all the love we had for each other. My dear beloved uncle—Maman's only brother and Lalla's only son. I remembered that during my trip to Mali, after he walked away to the afterlife, I went to the cemetery and a breath had quietly whispered: "You know I'm not here." And I silently replied: "I know." I smiled inside and still prayed. This dream was my first encounter with Uncle Layes's spirit; it wouldn't be our last. But that's another story, which I will tell later.

That morning after the dream, I realized the bundle of dead wood my uncle took away from me really made me feel lighter inside. A load had been taken away. I had been released. *I'm free,* I said to myself. The thought made me happy. I smiled. *Free of/from what,* my mind asked? How would this new freedom manifest itself and what would I do with it?

Chapter Thirteen

WHEN THOSE WHO KNEW YOU NO LONGER RECOGNIZE YOU

*Much of our existence is lived in planned
repetitive cycles. Thought and action patterns are
repeated each day and, thus, become habits or routine.*

*D*ays after the dream, I woke up every morning with the same feeling of being lighter. I would glance out my window and feel soothed by the park across the street with its well-kept green grass and the leaves gently blowing from a small breeze. But that was not what made me feel relieved.

I was content. And as the days unfolded and turned into weeks, my attention shifted back to my daily routine.

My days always began with a cup of Starbucks coffee. On weekdays, I sipped the coffee while reading and replying to emails before moving on to my many work tasks. On weekends, I savored my coffee while writing my list of things to do: chores, events to attend, dinner or get-togethers with my friends.

You're identified and appreciated for being a set of things.

I was known for being dependable. I was always available for my friends and my family, and because I was accessible, naturally, I became the one they relied on to wipe away their sweat.

I was known for being a good listener and a problem solver. No matter how big a pot was, I always found a lid to cover it.

I was known for being supportive for I managed to always say the right words at the right time that made the people around me feel better.

I was known for being "the strong one"—the tough woman who could handle and get through the most difficult situations. I was loyal. These were the set of things—the qualities that friends, coworkers, and family knew, recognized, and appreciated about me.

It was an ordinary weeknight, so ordinary that I couldn't remember the day. Long after dinner, the phone rang. I saw the name and sighed, exasperated before I even picked up. I wanted to scold myself for feeling the way I did because it was her. We were friends. *The one who was there with you and helped you drink your water when it was sweet should also be there to help you drink when your water turns bitter.* Through the years, we had shared enough sweet and bitter water together—we had been through enough good and bad times, shared secrets, falling in and out of love. We gossiped, laughed, and had a few differences of opinion in between that turned into arguments. Then we were mad at each other but never for too long. We remained friends even when we were envious of each other's accomplishments. We stayed friends even when we didn't like each other very much. We remained friends even when we betrayed each other by briefly replacing one another with new, seemingly more exciting, friendships that didn't last.

There weren't many people in my life I called friends—only a handful I had known since our days in school when we were teens. A small group of individuals scattered around the world.

We could spend months without talking, followed by hours of conversation as if we had just recently seen each other. She was part of this small group of chums who shared an unbreakable bond—a love and fondness that made us sister-friends.

Yet, on that very ordinary night, so ordinary I couldn't remember the exact day, when the phone rang and her name appeared on the caller ID, my entire being groaned, *not again!* I knew why she was calling.

She was calling so she would not have to think alone.

She was calling so she would not have to doubt herself and despair alone.

She was calling so she could have me echo, approve and reinforce her truth.

She was calling to have me agree, legitimize, and empower her and her wants.

I knew all of this—and picking up the phone, and saying hello, we would begin again at the same place we left off the night before: the same old story. But *a friend is someone who wipes away your sweat*. I was annoyed with myself for feeling frustrated, but the need to answer the phone—the need to be there for my sister-friend was stronger than my annoyance. This was what I was known and appreciated for—being there for the people I cared about. It was what made me dependable, the tree for them to lean on. Yet it had never felt like a burden before now. I forced a smile—*c'mon, Anna, you cannot do that to her*—and finally mustered the will to answer the phone.

"Hello."

"Hi. I was about to hang up. Where were you?"

"In the kitchen washing the dishes. It took a minute to dry my hands and find the phone."

"Oh, sorry, want me to call you later?"

"No, no. So, tell me, how are you?"

Long sigh, then, "The same. How about you?"

"I'm good."

"I envy you. You're always so optimistic. It's me and my issues that never seem to go away. I can't sleep, all I do is think about it. I don't know what to do. You must be tired of hearing the same thing all the time, right?"

"It's okay," I lied. "What's the problem?"

"Nothing has changed. It's just that I don't understand...."

For a while now, every other day, sometimes twice a day, we spoke of the lover she had done so much to please, but who was slowly abandoning her. Her lover had made her embrace his ideas of what a relationship should be. He had rearranged her, making her agreeable, more submissive to him. And then, after transforming her into who he wanted her to be, he started to pull away. He took his time to answer her calls, and at times went an entire day without calling.

Her lover made her doubt herself, feel insecure, feel afraid of losing him. She wanted to know what she was doing wrong—why was her lover aloof all of a sudden? Why was he moody? Why was he evasive? Why was he losing interest in her?

I was the voice of reason, the one who always knew the words to calm and soothe her fears and give her hope until tomorrow. Words that assured her nothing was totally lost yet—things could turn around and be good again. I knew what to say to make her laugh and feel better, and I enjoyed being the sister-friend who knew how to lift her spirit. But that evening I was tired. For some reason it was mortifying to acknowledge this, as if I were betraying her in her time of need. I was needed, three words that made me feel good. Only this time, the voice within muttered, *No, you're not.*

"Anna? Anna, are you listening?"

"Yes, yes, I'm here."

Sister-friend kept talking: She wanted to have a serious relationship; he was not ready. He had made some vague comment about being pressured into something he was not ready for. And from that moment on, they had been playing phone tag. This was maybe our third or fourth conversation in the week, dissecting word for word everything she had said, trying to figure out what she said wrong or could have said differently or not said at all. Every phone call I had hushed and suppressed my growing impatience to snap at her. Instead, I had told her over and over she had done nothing wrong.

I was dumbfounded—my sister-friend, a beautiful, successful, highly respected career woman was lost trying to manage her personal life. I had run out of suggestions; trying to reason with her was useless. She couldn't take in anything that was contrary to her thoughts. I told her the one thing I knew she wouldn't do. I said: "Return the favor—do what he does to you. Next time he calls, don't answer. Two can play that game, you know. If he tries but can't reach you for a day or two, I guarantee you, the next time you call, he will pick up. You'll be surprised at how fast he will pick up. The phone won't have time to ring."

We laughed, and then she said, "But what if he doesn't pick up? What will I do then?"

I wanted to yell, "Then you move on!" But I didn't. No matter how strong I wanted her to be, no matter how much I wanted her to have confidence in herself and leave this one-sided relationship, I also knew that *you cannot borrow someone else's guts to cross your river—no, you cannot transfer your will into someone else's heart.*

What good is the sun to the one who keeps their eyes closed? I was exasperated, and I didn't want to shush my irritation. As usual, sister-friend didn't want to hear what I truly thought; she just wanted me to comfort her, tell her this wasn't the end. Something would happen that would make everything all right. I felt depleted; nothing more could be squeezed out of me. I was done. I had no more words that would soothe and quiet her worries. And so, to end the conversation, I firmly said, "I don't know what else to tell you."

"What do you mean? I don't understand."

"What is it you don't understand?" I asked, barely containing my frustration.

She was shocked. I sensed anger in her silence.

"Listen, listen to me. I can't do this anymore. I'm tired. This situation has been dragging on for too long. And it's time for you to make a decision. If you want to stay with him and put up with his arrogance, fine. If you want to leave because you deserve to be with someone who will treat you better, that's also fine. Either way, I have nothing more to add to what I have already said over and over to you. It's time to change the subject."

"Fine. I won't bother you again with my problems. Goodnight."

"Yeah, goodnight."

She was upset and I didn't care. I was exhausted, and I was upset with her, with myself, and with my circle of family and friends who somehow expected me to always stop what I was doing to tend to their needs. I had given all I could give. There was nothing left in me to give.

Something inside me cracked. Something inside me was rebelling and I no longer wanted to be what I had always been—an enduring, understanding, and supportive ear. "Your freedom stops at the doorstep where mine begins." Oh my god! I burst out laughing. *I can't believe this just came out of me! Oh, my God,* I repeated to myself in disbelief. *No, no, no...Anna, you cannot turn into Papa.*

How many times had I heard Papa say these words? Too many to count—all through my teenage years. It was the verdict that ended all discussions, all negotiations. This sentence was usually followed by a variation of: "The day you leave my house, you can do anything you want. But as long as you're under my roof, your freedom stops at the doorstep where mine begins."

I never imagined I would one day let these words out, yet they perfectly reflected my sentiments. I felt as though for too long I had been taken for granted. I had been too accommodating— too eager to be present, too willing to provide support, and too ready to please. That was how I became good Anna—the one they could always call, the one they could unload their problems on because she had nothing better to do.

This was new—I was rebelling against the role I had played for the people I cared about. I no longer wanted to be good or nice, and I didn't care what anyone thought of me.

Enough, Anna. You have done enough...

I had done enough to prove I was a good daughter.

I had done enough to prove I was a good sister.

I had done enough to prove I was a loyal friend.

I had done enough and now it was time to think about me.

I had done for others; it was now time to do for me.

It is time for you, Anna, to be a priority in your own life.

I stopped. Stunned. The voice inside my gut was clear: My wants and needs were as important as those of the people I cared about. My head and my gut—two normally opposing powers—came together, colluded, and kept me up most of the night, taking turns affirming and insisting that I be important in my own eyes. Lalla would say: *You can love someone, but you shouldn't love anyone more than you love yourself.* My earlier conversation with my sister-friend had thrown me over the edge of my patience. I was still irritated at me, at her, and at the people who made up my world. When sister-friend and some of my loved ones called, it was mainly to talk about what was happening in their lives. It was assumed things were always good with me or I was someone who didn't like to talk about herself. Still, I faced challenges. I didn't know how yet, but the time had come to reshape and redesign the boundaries of these relationships. Going forward, I would decide how much of my time and energy I would dedicate to every person soliciting my attention or my help.

I had created this situation. I had spent most of my adult life chasing the love and approval of family and friends. I had turned my attention solely to them. I had gone in debt for them. My main priority was making sure those closest to me were alright, even if it meant pushing aside, neglecting, or ignoring my own needs. I acted as if the only reason for my existence was to make other people's lives easier. My loved ones knew they could count on me, and I was happy and proud to have been there for them. But after years of giving all I had to everyone and everything, I was drained. I too needed some of the love and attention I gave to others.

In some ways I was emulating Lalla and Papa, who were both very reliable. They were the tree that others leaned on. My revered elders, the most influential people in my life, were often sought out for assistance, wisdom, and support. I wanted to be the parts of them I loved. But Lalla and Papa were never afraid to speak their minds about what they expected from themselves and from others. In imitating them without taking on their imposing presence, I had unintentionally made myself smaller and smaller until I became invisible to all, and most importantly to myself. My needs and wants didn't matter. Lalla and the elders would say I was trying to *be like water*. I shaped myself into what I believed others wanted or expected me to be for them.

Perhaps I had been too nice, too accommodating. But I refused to beat myself up for it. My last conversation with sister-friend had fueled the voice inside my gut that demanded I think more of me. It kept reminding me I was important. *You have earned this. This is your time.* I vowed that going forward, whatever time I had remaining on Earth belonged to me. I would no longer force myself to do things just to please others. I was accountable to no one, only Daba.

I made a proclamation: People were free to call, and I was free to not pick up the phone. People were free to want to talk, and I was free to not be available. Freedom—a powerful word I never knew could apply to me. I now had choices I never thought about, never considered.

My excitement and determination were dampened by a lingering fear that didn't want to let go. One moment I was savoring my new sense of freedom that I had paid my dues and had nothing to prove to anyone; the next moment, the little pernicious voice of fear rose to question how I was going to do this. How was this new Anna going to be received? Who would be left to love her if her new attitude angered, disappointed, and frustrated everyone? Still, the desire and the resolve to be this new Anna was stronger. And it was at that moment I finally understood the dream. In it, Uncle Layes had taken away the bundle of dead wood I carried on my head. The dead wood symbolized my duties to my family, my friends, and all the people I cared about. Its removal signified the release of all my self-imposed obligations. My uncle had removed my burden and I was finally free.

Free to put myself first.

Free to become significant in my life.

Free to reach the light.

I was taking my first deep, long breaths of the new free me, resolutely vowing to never again pressure myself to do what was expected of me unless it was something I really wanted to do. The voice in my head raised its objections. I struggled with my affirmation.

Wouldn't putting myself first be selfish?

Wouldn't becoming a priority in my life be too self-centered?

And if I declared I was important, wouldn't that sound a little too narcissistic?

Each question was answered with a resounding *"No"* from the voice inside my gut, along with a few more no's for the things I used to be and do.

No, I didn't have to drop everything I was doing just because someone wanted something from me. I didn't have to always run to the rescue so I could be called dependable, reliable Anna. Some people would have to start relying on themselves.

No, I didn't have to put up with folks inviting themselves to come visit and staying interminably in my home.

No, it was not my job to be the one who always remained calm and made others feel good. And, No, I would not deprive myself of funds I needed and send money just because someone asked or expected me to provide for them.

And once I gave my opinion on an issue, I would not engage in endless and fruitless discussions.

The voice within my gut wasn't concerned about the struggle going on in my head—the fear of what people would think or say when facing my new attitude. The mysterious voice was taking the lead and slowly becoming the ruler of a new burgeoning operating system—the way I was beginning to see and react to life's events. The voice overruled and pushed back against every warning and every fear my head imagined. It was driving me out of my comfort zone, out of the way I knew how to be. Ready or not, my life was going to be about me. I wasn't entirely sure of what this meant, but I knew at that moment, it meant I was ready to be honest, and say no to the things I didn't want to say or do—even reluctantly, and even when I feared others' reactions.

You're identified and appreciated for being a set of things. The day you stop being those things, you become unrecognizable to those who know you.

At first, my new attitude shocked and sometimes mortified my inner circle of relatives and friends. They didn't recognize me and didn't understand why I had unilaterally decided to change the boundaries of our relationship when they had done nothing wrong. Some questioned my sanity. Others challenged and denied my choices, as if changing the tone of their voice and becoming abrupt, demanding, angry, insistent, or—when all failed, pleading with me—would compel or coerce me to change my mind.

"Oh please, please, please, why can't you do this for me?"

"When was the last time I asked you for a favor?"

"What? What do you mean no?"

"No? I didn't expect to hear that from you."

"Really, you think I'm wrong? Did you really listen to what I just said? Well, you just don't understand...."

"You're my last hope."

"You know I wouldn't ask if I didn't have to...."

"But I have no other choice. Please?"

"How can you say no after all I have done for you?"

"Very well, I will never ask a favor from you again."

I was calm, clear, and sympathetic when I maintained, "I'm so sorry, but I can't do what you want me to."

When I occasionally felt inclined to give in, I did so under my terms.

Surprisingly, I didn't feel uncomfortable or bad. The anger, outrage, disappointment, resentment, and frustration in their voices didn't make me yield. Somewhere from deep within, the words of my favorite American idiom rose and spilled over: *It's not about you.* I loved that saying because it was the perfect disclaimer for my new way of being. *It's not about you* reminded me my views, my words, my actions, and emotions were mine alone and they mattered

It's not about you meant, people's understanding, opinions, or interpretations were theirs and theirs alone. I was not going to let their words affect me because it was no longer my duty or responsibility to make myself fit their views or perceptions.

And so, as I applied myself to acknowledging and taking my wants and needs into account before making my choices, the phrase *it's not about you* became the refrain that helped me find the words to respond to the demands of those who knew me but no longer recognized who I had become. It also helped put their reactions into perspective. I pretended I didn't hear the whispers.

"What's the matter with her?"

"How could she talk to me that way?"

"Better be careful…you cannot ask her anything these days."

"Never say you know a person because you can never really know someone."

You can never really know someone. I smiled as I recall that these were the exact words Lalla and the elders said when confronted with someone who was saying or doing things that were out of character. I had changed, but I couldn't measure how much. The forever accommodating and agreeable Anna I used to be was no more. Still, I didn't know how to define this being who was blooming within.

Lalla and the elders taught that you can never totally know yourself. Why? Because when Daba created humankind, the Creator deposited in each of us a tiny part of all living things. Consequently, our bodies became the temples that contained all the different elements of the universe, making us the conduit of all cosmic forces and influences. Both our greatness and our madness come from this condition. We are the meeting place of contradictory forces in perpetual motion, much like the universe itself. Thus, from the day you are born to the day you leave the Earth, every experience will shape and change you in ways you won't always see, expect, or understand.

A single event can awaken something totally foreign in you.

In my case, two sequential events had profound consequences. My conversation with sister-friend took an unusual turn and became a defining moment when the voice inside my gut rose to demand I be attentive to my own needs and become a priority in my life. And before that, the dream that had awoken me to the fact that there was life after life. This realization—of an invisible parallel living world—had made Daba a more complex reality than how I had previously viewed the Creator— simply as a punishing or rewarding All-Powerful. Who was Daba?

I was born a Muslim because Islam was the religion Lalla, Papa, Maman, and Uncle Layes practiced. I knew when and how to pray. Every year I fasted during Ramadan. I had stopped drinking. These were the things that allowed me to identify myself as a practicing Muslim. And then the challenges of my life, the unfulfilled dreams and ambitions had reinforced the image I had of the Almighty—the indescribable and incomprehensible Creator who inspired fear or guilt. I prayed to either obtain protection and favor or to avoid the wrath of the inscrutable Daba.

Still, there was a longing that my rigorous allegiance to the religion didn't fulfill. I wanted more. And this feeling of something lacking made me question my faith. What did I truly know about Islam? About Allah? Did I want to remain Muslim or explore other faiths?

The questions brought to my awareness my lack of knowledge about my religion. Aside from the basic dogmatic precepts I had been taught long ago and some prayer verses, I didn't know much about Islam. Many relatives, friends, and colleagues were from different faiths. And observing how they practiced and talked with profound love and conviction of their beliefs made Buddhism and Christianity appealing choices. Even my elders said: "There is only one Summit—One Creator—but the paths to reach Daba are as many and diverse as the human race."

However, before I could make the life-changing choice of remaining Muslim or converting to another faith, I owed it to myself to try to learn and gain a better understanding of the religion I was born into and taught to worship. I didn't want to make a rushed decision that I would later regret. I was going to educate myself. It was around this period that Jean-Yves and I began to discuss this important topic. After Tita and I rekindled our connection with them in France, I'd kept in touch with both Babette and Jean-Yves.

With Babette, there were phone calls because she refused to use email. We reminisced often about our lives in Bamako when she was a schoolteacher loved by her students, and things were good and simple. Adjusting to retirement had not been easy for Maman Babette. I could feel it even though she refused to "bother" me with the details of her daily life. Our conversations were bittersweet.

Jean-Yves and I communicated mainly by email. He was a very active retiree in his community. He volunteered with other seniors as mediators who were called upon to de-escalate public housing residents' small-scale disputes. And he took Arabic lessons twice a week to help him read online newspapers from Morocco. I felt safe with Jean-Yves. He had an encyclopedic knowledge of world history and geography that was hidden behind a genuine humility. I wanted to have his opinion, and maybe some guidance for my faith in transition. Hence one Sunday afternoon the conversation began.

"Jean-Yves, do you mind if I ask you to give me your personal opinion on something?"

"It sounds serious. Are you alright?"

"Yes, don't worry. I'm fine. It's just…it's kind of a sensitive and very personal subject."

"I'm listening."

"It's about religion. I'm at a crossroads. You know I've always been a Muslim. But now I'm questioning, what does it mean? I must admit, I don't know much about Islam. I don't want to worship just because that's what I have been taught and told to do. I want more. I want to understand what Islam is. I also want to know more about other religions and maybe then decide if I want to stay Muslim or convert to another faith. What do you think? Am I making any sense?"

"Yes, I understand. And I agree with you. I think it is critical to understand your faith, so you can choose how best to practice or not practice it. Especially in today's environment when extremists of all beliefs have altered and distorted the messages of the Prophets. It's a challenge for all of us, not Islam alone. I live in an environment where religion has somehow become an old, outdated thing. Sometimes, even I don't dare say that I believe in God."

"Are you serious?"

"Yes, very."

"What do you do? I remember when we were in Bamako you used to go to church every Sunday."

"Unfortunately, I don't go that often anymore. Still, I believe in God. But I am surrounded by people who think that religion is archaic. And it feels like it's easier for them to disparage and vilify faith than to try to understand it. I'm not saying that's what they want to do. It just feels that way. To keep the peace, I keep my faith to myself."

"So, Jean-Yves, what is faith? I mean we say we are people of faith, but what does that mean? What's your definition of faith and religion?"

Jean-Yves laughed. "*Oh là là*, I don't think we have enough time to talk about it today ...."

I realized that it would be late at night in Lyon. "What if I email you my questions?"

"Great idea. I'll take my time to answer them as accurately as I can."

I could sense his delight in being asked to share his thoughts. I think we were both in awe to find that beyond our deep love for each other, the man I considered my second Papa and I had one more thing in common—the belief in the Divine Presence—even if our acts of devotion were different. The next day, I sent Jean-Yves my questions. I eventually received his reply.

> *Dear Anna,*
>
> *I was slow to answer you, I had no idea that the questions we had been talking about on the phone would lead me to think more carefully than what is usually given to a simple conversation.*
>
> *Giving my "personal interpretation" as you ask, I will try to clarify, in a first step, what I mean by faith, by belief or religion, the three words being used, often, as synonyms.*
>
> *The word faith, in French, means fidelity, and it seems to me that the English word "faith" has the same meaning.*
>
> *Loyalty to what? To whom?*
>
> *The three monotheistic religions describe, with variations, faith as fidelity to the covenant between God and Abraham:*
>
> *In the Tora, Abraham undertakes to worship only one God and to submit to his prescriptions, which will be specified to Moses, in exchange for eternal life. The*

double sign of the "signing of this contract" is the circumcision and the rest of the Sabbath.

In the Gospel, the same idea of covenant (called the new covenant, is confirmed by Christ.)

In the Quran, Abraham, Moses, and Christ are prophets in the same way as Muhammad, the Prophet of Islam. This idea of a perpetual pact or alliance also exists. The word "faith" in Arabic (Iman) refers to the idea of "agreeing," close to the idea of alliance or pact.

Someone who has faith, that is, a faithful, is one who trusts in the word God has given to humanity. For me faith can be compared to electricity: a continuous current that reminds us of the Alliance and its obligations to humanity. Who can say that they are in continuous relationship with God?

The word religion had bad press throughout the 20th century. For Marxists, it was (and still is) "the opium of the people." For Freudians, it is an "illusion" (Freud's book is titled "The Future of an Illusion"). As for the word belief, you can stuff anything into it, it doesn't necessarily imply faith, you can believe in a lot of things!

Hugs, see you soon, do you have your plane ticket to come see us?

Lyon, Oct 26,2009
Jean-Yves

I was in awe of the information Jean-Yves gave me. I thanked him from the bottom of my heart. I wanted to make sure he knew that I valued his knowledge.

While my communication with Jean-Yves was going on, friends who knew of my quest for answers offered me what I consider to this day to be an excellent interpretation of the Quran. For months I read every night until I finished the sacred book. Later, the Quran would become one of my bedside books—one I don't read every day but repeatedly go back to when I find writings that help explain the symbols and messages behind the literal meaning of the words.

Three books turned out to be life changing. The authors were Persians, great thinkers of their respective times. The most influential was the 13th century poet Rumi's work, the *Discourses of Rumi (Fihi Ma Fihi)*. Then, 5th century philosopher and theologian Al-Ghazali's, *The Alchemy of Happiness*. And finally, 14th century poet Mahmoud Cabestro's, *The Secret Rose Garden*.

Their work introduced me to the sacred and inner aspect of Islam. Their wisdom filled my yearning for whatever was missing in me. It was the beginning of my spiritual education, one that made me cognizant of concepts that were foreign to me—the existence, purpose, and functioning of my own inner being and its connection to the Creator.

One of the most important lessons was that each one of us is invited to seek the Creator through a direct personal experience of Allah. Why? Because according to Islamic theology, the Creator said, *"Know me before you worship me, for if you do not know me, how could you worship me?*[4]*"* I remembered Lalla

---

[4] According to Sacred tradition of the Hadith Qudsi.

saying: "You'll become your own compass when you understand why you believe in Allah."

I was excited and relieved all at once. Faith and worship were quests and private conversations with the Almighty. Nowhere in the teachings was I asked to be perfect or righteous. The scholars' writings all portrayed the Creator as loving and forgiving and human beings as seekers who wanted to experience that divine love, to know what sensing the presence of Daba would be and feel like. The elders who didn't have words to explain the Creator said that we each had to find our own way to experience the presence of the Divine in our lives. Hence, faith was this inner light that the believer needed to nurture through prayers so its flame would not dim or be snuffed out under the demands of our daily lives.

I loved the Islam that Rumi, Al-Ghazali, and Shabestarī conveyed in their writings. Their teachings encouraged me to know myself so I could gain a deeper understanding of the divine, while also stressing I should remain true to who I was. I was a work in progress. I would continue to pray imperfectly— praying too late at times, too zealously, or too distractedly due to other demands or hectic moments.

Lastly, the writings asked that I look beyond what I already knew about myself—all the things I believed made and defined me. They asked me to turn my attention inward so I could come to know the powers at work within me. These concepts were comparable to the teachings of Lalla and the elders who said, *"You are one and many—for there are many beings and things within you that you must learn to know and understand."*

I had always been divided into two distinct selves, a body, and a mind: a body I was taught to dislike and came to disregard and neglect; a mind I had trained to be restless, always anticipating how to protect and defend myself against pain. But while *shaking the bush* to find the roots of my unhappy life, I had awakened to a third element of my being: the voice inside my gut. It wasn't the familiar bullying and threatening voice of fear, pain, or anger. No, the voice inside my gut didn't try to manipulate or control me. It simply stated the way things were with compassion and unshakable assurance. And when I listened to it, I found it was never wrong. Slowly, the voice changed my operating system—the way I perceived events and reacted to them—by making me turn my attention to it for guidance. I learned to stop conforming to the eyes of the outside world, the thoughts in my head, and the constraints of fear I had relied on for so long. I was more than that. Acknowledging and listening to the voice in my gut was the beginning of recognizing and accepting that there were unknown powers at work in me. For *everything visible has a connection to an invisible force that is its source. In each of us, there is another being we must learn to know.*

Indeed, the voice in my gut surfaced and made me aware of my buried being. It brought back to my consciousness hushed and suppressed events, and all of the angst from those times. My conversation with Jean-Yves, his email, and the readings from the Persian scholars had deepened my need to have a more profound connection with this hidden part of my being who was also supposed to be my direct connection to the Creator. Lalla and the elders taught: *Know yourself and ultimately you will have your understanding of unknowable and indescribable Daba.*

But to whom or to what did this voice in my gut belong that made me rethink the way I saw myself and lived my life? It sounded like me, but the unwavering calm and certainty was nothing like me. It was unflappable and knew me in ways I didn't know myself. Where was it taking me? The voice simply replied: "Just let the answers come from your gut." *I can't wait!*

Chapter Fourteen

WAKING UP AND MORNING,
THE NEW BEGINNINGS

In each of us lies another being we must learn to know.
It speaks to us and tells us it sees us very differently
from what we believe we are.

I wanted to understand the mystery of the voice within, so I did what came most naturally to me: I let my head go to work. Its mission: Find a clear and simple definition and/ or explanation for what I sensed and experienced but had yet to find words to express. To help me think, I began a new routine: Every evening after work, instead of taking the train, I walked home and tried to listen for the voice. On my one hour long trek I would ask:

How long had it been there? *All my life*, something in me said.

How come I hadn't heard it this clearly before? Silence. *Because you didn't want to.* My body stiffened, unable to find words to deny this truth. I changed the subject.

Focus, Anna, focus. Who or what was the voice inside of me?

"Don't rush, don't force, and don't rationalize. Let the answer come from your gut."

Hope reappeared. I had this knowing deep within that if I stayed the course, I would find answers. After all, *the river pierces through the rock using perseverance.* Emboldened by optimism, I had an idea: What if instead of trying to find words to describe the voice, perhaps I would just go with what I knew and watched what happened? I tried to gather thoughts and ideas. What did I know about this familiar yet indefinable living thing inside of me? Total blank.

"You are so…," I stopped. I wasn't going to utter anything derogatory or unkind to myself. Still, the word came out, "Ignorant."

Strangely, I wasn't perturbed. I had heard the term before, many times as a matter of fact, and it wasn't said to attack or castigate anyone. In fact, it was part of a teaching. It was so unexpected that I blurted: "Are we really going there tonight?" This was not what I thought would happen. Okay, I'm going with this. In life there are no coincidences.

I had in front of me the word 'ignorant' and it was a perfect description of how clueless I was about the voice inside my gut. And so, I began to repeat, "Ignorant or was it ignorance?" I was onto something. What was this expression tied to? Words were trapped. Words were on the tip of my tongue, caught in my mind, unready to release them. Ah! How could I be this excited and frustrated at the same time?

"Ignorance and life or life and ignorance."

"Life is a struggle against ignorance."

Yes! That was it! At last, words of our tradition were now rushing and pushing to come out: "Life is a struggle against ignorance—it's the lack of knowledge of our true nature that obstructs and distorts how we see ourselves, the world, and Daba. As your elders, our responsibility is to help you wake up—*kunun*—open your eyes and senses to the worlds outside and inside of you."

I learned this the year when Papa thought that sending me away to spend the entire three-month vacation with Lalla in her humble home would be punishment for my mediocre school performance. It turned out to be an essential and needed education on what Lalla and the elders called *Learning to be Human*. During my stay with her, my grandmother and her elder neighbors made it their mission to teach the youth of my generation about the *good path* that had been passed on from their forefathers. I loved the stories of my elders but didn't understand how their ancestral philosophy of life could possibly relate to me.

Seriously, how could seniors who had never set foot in school, and many of whom had never traveled outside of Mali, possibly know, or tell me anything useful about the issues I faced as a modern teenager? Going to school in different countries; finding a way to fit in wherever you were in the world; being likable and making friends easily; not caring about being the best in class; being fine with being the lone straw that nobody believed could possibly come from a high-achieving and well-respected family...how could they tell me about this, and so many other things?

Even so, I fondly recalled how Lalla and the elders, in their unassuming way, feigned not to see our pompousness as my peers and I listened in delight to the stories of their lives while maintaining that we were almost adults who had it all figured out. It didn't occur to us that *everything you are, others were before you.*

Lalla used to prepare too much food on purpose. And after every meal my grandmother neatly placed all the leftovers in a clean bowl which I took to the neighbors. It was a large family with many small children. At night, I walked in: "Good evening, Lalla said to bring some food."

"Thank you," the wife replied as she stood to take the bowl. Her husband asked: "How is your grandmother?"

"She's fine."

"How are you?"

"I'm fine thank you."

By that time, his wife had transferred the food into another container, washed the one I had come with and returned it to me. I said, "See you later" as I glimpsed the children eating the food I had brought.

This was my daily routine. There was an implicit understanding and expectation that you took care of your neighbors. Sharing what you had didn't make you superior, and those benefiting from your generosity were not less. And so, every morning, on her way to the market to buy food, the mother of the children stopped by to talk with Lalla about what was going on in her life or in the community. And every evening, an hour or so after dinner, our neighbors and their teenage children would come together on our terrace under the moon and the stars for an evening of storytelling.

Lalla and the elders always began by talking among themselves about their day, the news, or what was going on in the community. Our elders were people of the same age group who strongly believed *because they are the closest to you, your neighbor's home should be the first place you run to for help in your time of need. For your relationship with your neighbor is like the connection between your mouth and your hand. When your hand hurts, your mouth blows on it to soothe it. And when your mouth hurts, your hand pats it.* And the traditional song went:

It is true the Creator made all human beings the same way.

But, just like the ten fingers of your hands, the Almighty didn't make them equal.

Be kind and good to the less fortunate.

Your act of kindness today is an investment in the other world tomorrow.

Lalla and the elders explained: "Yes, it is true the Creator made all human beings the same way—meaning Daba created all souls the same way. Therefore, no soul is better than another soul. But, *just like the ten fingers of your hands, the Creator didn't make them equal* implies the fate and the future of people are not identical. Still, we are bound and connected to one another. We need and complete each other.

"Your act of kindness today is an investment in the other world tomorrow—it means be kind. Don't be indifferent to other people's suffering; help when you can. Because you don't know if tomorrow you will be in need of kindness yourself."

And right after the refresher course on what it means to be a good human and a good neighbor, Lalla and the elders decided to go over another essential teaching: the meaning of the word *kunun:* wake up. Wake up—open your eyes and your senses so you can see what is in front of you, what is surrounding you, and what is inside of you.

The elders went on to say that the day we came into the world, we awoke in a family and a community we knew absolutely nothing about. We didn't know who we were, where we were, or why we were put on Earth. And it was this unawareness that Lalla and the elders of the community helped us wake up to. It was their duty and responsibility as parents and grandparents to *shape the fresh clay*, to train us to open our eyes to see ourselves, the people around us, and the countless ties that bind everyone to the world surrounding them. It was during these times I heard my elders remind me repeatedly to "Wake up—open your eyes to see, pay attention to where you are going, what you are doing and saying. Wake up—open your eyes and see the consequences of your words and actions. Wake up—open your eyes and observe the faces of your elders—and know when it is a good time to approach them to talk or ask questions, and when it is better to just leave them alone."

Wake up—*kunun*—was a crucial state that applied not only to us human beings. Like mankind, all elements of the universe were first created by Daba then awakened by the Creator. Lalla and the elders said *kunun* was the first inner pulsation of the universe after Daba breathed life into it. Once awakened by the breath of Daba, the elements of the universe began to throb. Hence, *kunun* applied not only to the world we could see and touch, but it also applied to the world we couldn't see. Therefore, all things had a cycle where they too woke up and went to sleep. From the dawn of time, the universe had never stopped waking up—never stopped pulsating. The truth was, even though we could not sense it, everything in the cosmos was vibrating at various pulsations we couldn't hear or see. Our elders said *where there was no vibration, there was no movement; and where there was no movement, there was no heat or energy. And where there was no heat or energy, there was no life.*

At the time of the teachings, I believed it was impossible to retain all these lessons, and for what purpose? If all things in the world woke up and went to sleep,—great! What was I supposed to do with that? With time and experience, the seed of knowledge that was planted in me back then, bore its fruit when decades later, walking on a breezy night in Manhattan—the city that never sleeps—I finally grasped the meaning of the old saying: *Regardless of the time, the moment you wake up is your morning, it is the start of a day, the beginning of a journey.* I didn't know what to make of the voice, but I was no longer oblivious to it. I had woken up to it and I could hear it.

I was overwhelmed with wistfulness: thoughts of Lalla, the elders, and the evenings spent avidly listening to them, not wanting their storytelling to end. The words of my elders were bringing me closer to uncovering the mystery and the purpose of the voice deep within. I didn't want to stop the past from coming back to me. My daily one-hour walk helped clear my mind and summon the memories of my evenings with the elders.

But not all those storytelling evenings were wonderful. There was one instance when a friend got in trouble for saying the wrong word to an elder. They regarded the retort as disrespectful and proceeded to scold all of us for his behavior, which in their opinion reflected how we all acted. We received a refresher course on how to be honorable human beings, specifically what behaviors were expected and acceptable in our families and in the community.

It didn't matter that we knew the fundamentals, which were woven in the lullabies, the tales, and the old songs we heard all through our childhood. Regardless, that evening, Lalla, and the elders were intent on telling us once more of the four primary principles that were to *help us navigate our individual boats in the waters of the river of life*:

- *Know yourself: Learn to understand, value, contain, and put up with all the things you are, for you are one and many.*
- *Be compassionate: The Creator made all beings the same way, but just like the ten fingers of your hands, Daba didn't make*

them equal. For what separated people—making some better than others—were the answers to the questions: What happened? And what did you do? Your words and your actions were testimonies of your decency and dignity. And never forget you cannot pick up a pebble with one finger.

- *Be driven: If you cannot accomplish more than your parents, make sure you don't do less than what they have done.*

- *Learn to be social: Society is only possible when everyone knows how to respect one another and comply with the established code of conduct. As neighbors and people of the community, we share our lives, spaces, and secrets with one another while maintaining and respecting the invisible low wall between us. This partition allows us to see each other's face while keeping our feet covered. The small invisible wall represents boundaries. The face is the part of our personal life we don't mind sharing, and the feet symbolize the things we want to keep to ourselves.*

You are one and many for you are made of you and all those who came before you. This portion of the lesson was left to the *griot*, Djéliba, to detail.

"The words are boiling inside me, rushing to come out. Where do I begin? What do I say and what do I keep away? The words are pushing, burning to come out," Djéliba told us.

Djéliba's life, as a *griot*, has been dedicated to learning and passing down the traditions and history of Mali through his oral history lessons.

At the sound of Djéliba's voice suddenly, all was forgotten—the reproach and the embarrassment. Our bodies tensed, our eyes, our ears, and all our senses turned to the man and his instrument—we were impatient and riveted by his every movement, his every word.

Djéliba concentrated on tuning his kora—the twenty-one stringed African lute-harp. It is said of these twenty-one strings that the first seven are played to recall the past, the middle seven are played to talk about the present, and the last seven are played to call the future. For *your yesterday, today, and tomorrow are the intertwined facets of your life.*

In our culture, music and spoken words complete and complement each other. Music gives weight to the words of the *griot.* It gives a rhythm to the spoken words that deepens the dramatic, cynical, or funny effect the words have on its audience. When the *griot* stops talking, music builds the suspense. You listen, wondering when and how the story will unfold. In the beginning there was the word…so says religious text and Djéliba's words held the beginning of our respective families.

The kora was ready. Djéliba stopped playing. The silence intensified our anticipation. Carefully, almost reverently, the *griot* began to play the most recognizable and popular of our traditional tunes called the *mother of all strings.* The music was tied to our history. It called up our past. And we listened, filled with deep pride.

"*N'diatiguiw*—my patrons, good evening. I am Djéliba Kouyaté, the great *griot.* I am a *djéli,* a master of the spoken words. We, the *griot,* are the memory of our people. We are the reporters, the archivists, the advisors, and the chroniclers of our times. History has no mystery for us and the art of speaking has no secret for us.

"From the time we begin to talk, we the *djéli* are taught how to weigh and tame words. We learn to respect and properly use words. For when people lend you their ear you cannot pour refuse inside of them. We are taught how to announce bad news and tell unpopular truths. But we also learn how to deliver beautiful words that bring joy and peace to the heart and soul. When disagreements or arguments occur, our tongues become the needle that patches things up, comforts and brings friends, families, and neighbors together.

"We are the link that brings the past to the present. Our words give life to the past. Without us, kings and heroes would be long forgotten. And who doesn't want to be remembered, I ask you? Our elders say: Death may eat the flesh, it may eat the bones, but death cannot eat your name and death cannot eat your actions.

"We take part in all the events from the most important to the least significant because our presence is the guarantee that the gathering will be recorded and remembered.

"I hold my knowledge from my fathers, who held theirs from their fathers. From our forefathers to us, we have told the history of our people during important events such as our gathering tonight. We sing, play the kora, and narrate centuries-old stories we have received from our elders and complete them with present events we have either lived or witnessed.

"Listen to my words—they are pure, they contain no lies. Listen to my words, oh you young and old who want to recall or learn the history of the Mandingo people."

Djéliba stopped talking but continued to play the kora. The interlude gave us time to digest everything he had said. Then: "My patrons," he began, "from the beginning of time, people have followed one another. Tonight, I'm going to talk about those who came before us and who, after finishing their field of actions, passed away living a legacy we still sing today.

212

"I will tell you the stories as I was told by my fathers. And then I want you, young people, tomorrow, in a month, or in a year, to go find books that recount what I will state from my memory tonight. I want you to go read the books to prove two things: one, attest the truthfulness of my stories; and, two, show you, oh believers of the written words only, that not knowing how to read or write doesn't make a person ignorant. As our fathers often said, 'There may be a lot of illiterate people in the Mandingo land, but there are no ignorant individuals, because the father and mother of each person have taught their child the knowledge they received from their elders along with the erudition they patiently acquired by observing, learning, and understanding humankind and Mother Nature's behavior.'"

Lalla and the elders proudly and loudly nodded in agreement as we pretended to ignore that his last jabs were intended for us.

While playing the kora, Djéliba recounted the legends of Lalla's clan as well as those of the founding families of Bamako, the capital of Mali. These were the stories of our lineages—the tribes of warriors, hunters, farmers, fishermen, shepherds, blacksmiths, and healers who communicated with and were assisted in their endeavors by the forces of the invisible world. That was why in each family there was a totem—an animal, a plant, or a tree that couldn't be hurt for it had provided guidance, solace, or protection to the first ancestor. We each belonged to a clan with this mythical, larger-than-life forefather whose valiant, fearless personality and actions were legendary. This first leader who had taken our family out of obscurity was followed by other heroes who had contributed to the fame of our individual families.

The stories of the *griot* reminded us of our roots. Regardless of whether we fit in or not, our life stories were imbedded in a clan, a community, and a country. We listened proudly, embracing the weight of worthily carrying the family name. Later in our conversations, we would boast about our illustrious lineage. We were going to be just like them—just as accomplished. Some vowed to be even more successful than those who came before them. Learning about their lives made me proud, but also set the expectations high for who or what I was supposed to be.

"You are not alone," Lalla and the elders often said. "You didn't arrive by yourself. Each of you is both *a beginning and a perpetuation in the never-ending cycle of Daba's creation.* Do you know what that means?"

We shook our heads as we replied, "No," even though we knew what was about to follow.

"It means you are one and many because there are many beings and things in you. The day you came into the world was both the beginning of your individual life and the continuation of a family through you. Each of you carry some of the characteristics of those in your family that came before you. You belong to a clan and a tradition. Inside each of you, there are many beings and forces you must learn to understand and live with so you can find your seat and be a true person.

"But remember," the elders warned, "these beings and forces are like you: They change. As you grow taller and become bigger, so will the powers inside of you. They will take on different shapes and forms and become stronger or weaker because of our teachings and your personal experiences—the good and bad things that will cross your individual path. You cannot know this now, but it is what we've been telling you for years now that will influence how you receive and react to the events of life."

And to reinforce the significance of what they had just said, one of the elders would unequivocally say, "Every person is an unknowable seed of the world—a miniature universe within the universe. You each are the guardian of all the beings and forces within you. Your purpose is to seek order and unity. We can only teach you what we know. You are responsible for using this knowledge to live with these beings and powers. And as long as you have not put in order the worlds and the forces within you, you will remain limited and incomplete—someone who doesn't know all that she or he is or can be. Therefore, *know yourself: learn to understand, value, contain, and put up with all the things you are.*"

They said that in the end what mattered was that even when they would no longer be here, they had provided us what we needed to go on and become adults who lived in accord with others while remaining true to who we were. We were part of the world community where all visible and invisible elements were interconnected. It was essential that we knew how to act, because with our deeds we could either uplift ourselves and the world around us when we were mindful people, or we could choose to become less human every time our actions hurt others. Our different relationships with our communities and the rest of the world were one of exchange—give-and-take, and balance. Hence, we could either mutually enhance or destroy each other. Thus, these words are found in many traditional songs:

Love the world, and the world will love you back.
Hate the world, and the world will hate you back.
Give up on the world, and the world will give up on you.

The lesson ended with the adage "*Every day the ear goes to school.*" It was both a plea and a recommendation to remain open—for provided you paid attention, you could learn something new about yourself and the world every day.

I was fortunate. I was educated about life by an extraordinary group of people who selflessly spent years offering a clan of children and teenagers the knowledge that had been imparted to them, along with lessons learned from their own experiences. They communicated their knowledge with such humility that I didn't recognize their words were invaluable. And when, at times, we questioned their insights because the proverbs and parables they used were either too obscure for us to understand or had nothing to do with what we were learning in school, Lalla and the elders would bluntly admonish and hush our objections: "The wind cannot break a tree that knows how to bend; an individual who had a solid upbringing would always know how to cope with life's challenges."

Then one of the elders would state for the hundredth time, "The world's competition is around chairs. Who sits where, higher or lower than whom? Schools will teach you what you need to know so you can sit in certain chairs. How you sit in them is taught at home by us." There was nothing to say after that.

It felt wonderful to recall the forgotten teachings, to marvel at the *old words*. I couldn't help but smile at my naiveté. I always wanted to believe I knew who I was and yet the wisdom of my elders told me otherwise. Their words confirmed I was more than what I had confined myself to be. Yes, I was the firstborn of a clan. I wasn't Lalla or Papa, even though I had some of their features, traits, and characteristics. I was a great-granddaughter, a granddaughter, a daughter, a niece, a sister, a cousin, a friend, a lover, a coworker, and a lover of books, food, and music. And so much more I was ready to uncover.

The stories of the *griot* reminded me that I belonged—the way Lalla had always told me. I belonged to a family, a community, and a country with its history and many cultures. I belonged to a civilization with traditions that shaped and influenced me in ways I was not always aware of. I belonged. What I did with my heritage—the knowledge passed on by my elders—was up to me. I belonged. And I knew where I came from.

I had solved the three riddles Lalla had asked me to reflect on. The first: When you don't know where you are going, go back to where you came from. If you don't understand where you came from, you will not know where you're going. The second: Why did I want the things that I wanted? What was the purpose of my pursuit? Finally, the last one: The thorns can only be pulled from where they penetrated. She asked me to uncover mine—pull them out so I can free myself and be me.

I discovered why I wanted the things that I wanted. And I realized *wounds do not heal with their festering thorns.* Understanding the whys of my unfulfilled life was like opening Pandora's box. Starting with my gut releasing the many wounds of my childhood—the angst of reliving, even years later and in new lights, my suppressed past; the shock that came with recognizing the damage lingering from each experience—to acknowledging that I was a worthy human being had been such a long consuming and rewarding process. Indeed, *every generation experiences the same cycle of having to define or redefine themselves—seeking the values and guiding principles that would help them find their seat.*

My quest had removed some of the ignorance I had about my own being. I was no longer a body, a mind, and an inner thing I could not define, but rather beings and powers that over the years had evolved with me. I was resilient, but the fighter, the fixer, and the problem solver had changed into something less consuming because the fear that fueled them, had lost its despotic power. I was many things—and some I didn't know yet, but I loved the fact that these discoveries made me more open to embracing and reflecting on the worlds I couldn't see and touch. I was a work in progress. I trusted and relied on the voice and the energies coming from my gut. Together they had helped me achieve what I couldn't have done listening to the outside world. I had a calmness that allowed me to follow Lalla's advice: Always try to *pull the bottom to the top*—go beyond the appearance of things. My heart overflowed with love and gratitude for my elders. I wanted to scream *you taught me well! You all taught me well*. It was an exhilarating, yet at the same time sad, moment. The things that for so long constituted my goals and ambitions for a successful and fulfilled life were no longer relevant or important. It was more essential than ever to understand what I was about. Our tradition said that from the beginning of time, the purpose of our being in the world had always been to seek to know ourselves. Who are you? What are you? Why are you here? Lalla and the elders added that all the things we were looking for were contained in our responses to these questions. And once we found our true answers, we would stop doubting ourselves.

That night, I meditated and prayed. I thanked Daba, Lalla, and all the elders for the love they gave me through their knowledge of life. I was reflective, vulnerable, and raw. This openness let in the rays of love and compassion for Anna. My newfound serenity, however, would be short-lived. A little nothing would cause mayhem within, pushing me to finally confront the many hushed and unresolved aches of my complex relationship with Maman. It all started with a phone call.

Chapter Fifteen

IF YOU SAY TO YOUR HABITS,
"THIS IS WHERE I LEAVE YOU"

Words are energy. Words are power.
Words can start or end everything.

"It doesn't matter—as long as you know you cannot come without it." Harshness was what she resorted to when she wanted things her way. Her words were bitter and made it clear I had no choice. I was to comply. Period. Besides, it was too late; the bulky package had already been delivered.

Almost two years after the rushed, unplanned trip, I was returning to Dakar to see Lalla and Maman. My elders had been through a lot—and I felt I needed to visit more often. I was annoyed because it wasn't nice to send a bulky package to my home without asking me first if I could add it to my luggage and bring it to her. I tried to be understanding but I was mad. Maman knew how to get under my skin. Her short and abrupt call had awakened deep-rooted anger, pain, frustration, and resentment that were too profound for me to make sense of. It was threatening to undo all I had worked so far for to reach a place of serenity.

"C'mon Anna. It's not that bad. It's just a package."

I fought to calm myself down. How could a simple phone call create so much internal turmoil? True, things were never simple when it came to Maman and me. Our relationship was made up of multiple layers of feelings, intricately woven one into another—love, pain, anger, fear, resentment, gratitude, guilt, and shame—repressed emotions I had never faced.

"Go back to where you came from," she once adamantly declared.

It didn't matter what Lalla had said to make me feel less sour and lost. Maman, the woman I idolized, had rejected me, the frightened teenager I had been on the night when I needed her the most. We didn't have a relationship before that, and after that fateful night, I had to work to prove myself worthy of her love. And somehow, as much as I tried, I seldom managed to rise high enough to meet her expectations.

But how could I acknowledge and understand my angst when everything I had been taught said I must respect and revere her? Loving her should have been natural and simple. After all, she was my Maman. She was responsible for giving me the most precious gift of all—life. And so, as I wrestled with myself, fighting to keep my emotions in check, all my poise, all my certainties and confidence vanished. I was once again enveloped in pain, resentment, and anger that ran much deeper than the simple annoyance caused by a few words.

It's just a big box. If you think about it, it's really not that deep! It really doesn't matter, I repeated, trying to reason myself. It did matter—because whenever I passed the package sitting near my bedroom door, I would recall the conversation with Maman and become angry all over again. *And it's not the first time*, the young girl inside of me stubbornly said. But here I was thrown back in the cauldron of overcompensating to be loved by the woman who gave me birth.

It wasn't the first time Maman expected me to do exactly what she wanted. And it wasn't the first time I was told to adhere to a decision that had been made without any regard for or input from me. Maman had always done things this way. She and my brother, her son from her mariage to his father, would talk about what needed to be done (a house repair, medication, household bills), then Maman would call to inform me of my expected contribution in the matter. I was an afterthought. I had always been able to brush off the sting that came with not being included in their conversations. For years I pretended it didn't bother me, yet here I was, fuming. I wanted to push down my anger and pain like I had done many times in the past. But, the resentment and the irritation were too strong and they refused to be dismissed or be labeled an overreaction.

There is no "I'm right, you are wrong" between you and your mother for no child could ever repay the burden of the woman who carried her for nine months—266 days—then endured the labor and pain of giving birth to you. Every traditional song, lullaby, and tale about the relationship between children and elders had the same moral at the end of the story: Good things happen to the submissive child and bad things happen to the one who rebels. Obedience is how you show respect to parents and elders. Children who show patience and submission to the elders—especially their mothers—would gain Daba's favor and the *baraka*, the good fortune indispensable to the realization of any project or ambition. To not have the Almighty's favor was to sentence yourself to a life of failure and misery—a life of unimaginable suffering, banned from the family, the community, and of course Daba. And *to add water to their words*—to prove the veracity of their statement—the elders would point to the person or the family whose misfortune everyone knew. That same fate awaited those children who dared to rebel against their parents or the seniors.

For all these reasons, the young girl I had regressed into with this phone call fought to suppress her anger. I told myself time after time I loved Maman, as I was sure she loved me too. I reluctantly began to mold myself into the compliant, eager-to-please daughter who did not contradict her mother. I clung to the words of a proverb that helped explain and justify why it was wise to choose to remain a docile child. *The cloth a mother uses to carry a child has two sides. The first side is used by the mother to carry her child, and the second side is used by the child to take care of her.* She had given birth to me, and now that I was an adult, it was my turn to take care of her.

If you say to your habits, "This is where I leave you," after a while if you don't come back to them, they will find you. I had been in a good place. I had freed myself from a life ruled by expectations, pressure, and fear of what others thought of me. But one conversation with Maman made my beliefs and certainties disappear.

But your heart is not a knee you can just bend at your will— you don't get to command and control your feelings. It was a *case of the impossible dance*—a situation where regardless of the step or direction you take, you end up losing an important part of you. I resented having to say yes to bringing the package to Maman. I resented forcing myself to remain silent. But if I chose to make my life about me and refuse to cater to Maman, could I live with myself? Could I face the disapproval of the entire family, and my own guilt for not doing the right thing? Would I be okay with being a disappointment once again? My turmoil was exhausting. I was afraid of what my forbidden anger would bring me to say or do if left uncontrolled.

And so, I restrained myself and settled with what I called a reasonable compromise: Going forward, I would cater to no one except Maman. In my interactions with her, I would be on my best behavior. I would continue to be the obedient and submissive daughter who didn't contradict her wishes. Though my decision made me feel uneasy, it was Maman. I couldn't go on harboring resentment toward the woman who gave me life. Something in me needed her approval. Something in me was desperate to be a good child.

Settling for the path of nonconfrontation at all costs broke something in me. The solution I found to our relationship meant I would never challenge and never disagree with Maman. I felt shortchanged, as if I were committing an unthinkable trespass—refusing to give myself permission to feel how I felt about Maman. My heart wrenched in the way it usually did before a good cry. But the tears that would have brought relief didn't materialize.

In the end, I traveled to Senegal and bought Maman the package I could not refuse to take with me. During my stay, things were tense between Maman and me. I wasn't happy with her, and so I deliberately chose to be distant. My love, my attention, my hugs were for Lalla and Lalla alone; and when Maman joined us, I became indifferent and withdrawn. It was payback. I was filled with a silent, bitter grudge: How dare you have demands, when I couldn't count on you?

How could you have expectations of me when I could have none from you?

How could you want to lean on me when you weren't supportive of me?

Maman seemed perplexed by my manners but didn't ask questions. Finally, on the last day of my stay, it was time to say goodbye to Lalla. We were holding hands, and my grandmother simply said, "I know things are difficult with your Mother, but don't worry about it. Anna, I like what I saw in you. Don't worry about anything. Stay the way you are. Stay on the path you are on. The path you are on is good. Don't be afraid because I will always pray for you. Even when I am no longer here, just call me, and know I will always pray for you even from the world beyond."

Fighting back tears, I knelt down, bowed my head on her lap and felt her loving hands on me as she blessed me. I hugged and kissed her, then rushed out of her room so she wouldn't see my tears. I hugged Maman and for a minute I regretted my behavior. Maman seemed lost, as if she didn't know how to reach me. I sensed vulnerability in her I had not felt before. Maybe she wanted to say something, ask me what was wrong, but she didn't; and I needed to leave for the airport. We were two hedgehogs who couldn't get too close because we each had experienced the pain of being rejected by the other. I walked out the door and by the time I arrived at the airport, regret had vanished.

It's what you have in your belly that will prevent you from sleeping. A few days after I returned from my trip, I was still distressed because I didn't know what to do with my feelings about Maman. I went to bed restless, and it was during that agitated sleep he appeared in front of me. I fretted, troubled and a little scared of what I saw: his face. But it was his eyes that were most clear. His gaze made me feel uneasy. He wasn't happy. He stared at me without blinking. I was uncomfortable, but I couldn't look away. My uncle Layes gazed at me intently, seeming frustrated.

Unlike the first dream where I was surrounded by other beings, this time it was just Uncle Layes and me. We were wrapped in a blurry mist that seemed to have taken the shape and color of my uncle's state of being. I was puzzled and I tried to smile. He didn't smile back. He shook his head in disapproval. Something in me said, "This is not good. This is not good at all." I didn't know how long we kept staring at each other in a gloomy silence. I got the sense my uncle wanted me to do something, yet I didn't know what message he had for me. Throughout the entire span of the dream, Uncle Layes didn't say a word. I can't say how long the dream lasted, I just recall that I suddenly woke up as if someone or something had brusquely interrupted my sleep, but I was alone in my room. I was troubled and a little afraid. Why was my uncle frustrated and angry? What did I do wrong?

The dream shook me so much it became urgent I discern its meaning. What was Uncle Layes trying to say from the world beyond? I called Syba, the man who could interpret the mystery of my disturbing vision. Syba was a mystic who had the gift of divination and the ability to decipher messages of those who had left the Earth.

"How was he?"

"Well, I could only see his face, and the rest was enveloped in a fog I can't really describe. All I can tell you is he wasn't happy, and that bothers me. I had never sensed this exasperated anger from him, and I couldn't tell you toward what."

"Did he talk to you?"

"No, he didn't say a word. What do you suppose that means?"

"I don't know, but he's trying to tell you something. I need to look into it at a deeper level late tonight. Call me tomorrow, and I will tell what is revealed to me."

I took a deep breath and exhaled, relieved to have been able to unburden this mystery on someone else.

I patiently waited for the twenty-four hours to pass. The next day, as soon as my eyes opened early in the morning, my head reminded me that I needed to call my spiritual guide late in the afternoon. The dream didn't want to go away. On the subway to work, I replayed it, trying to find something I could make sense of. Throughout the day, at every quiet moment, the memory of the dream came back to me with its lingering question: Why was Uncle Layes upset? Every hour seemed to drag forever. Finally, after lunch I could wait no longer. I dialed Syba's number. The phone rang once and he picked up.

"I knew it was you," he said laughing. His laughter was a good sign that maybe things were not so bad. I began to relax.

"Are you making fun of me?"

"No, I would never do that to you," he said, mocking me.

Then it was time to be serious.

"I saw him," he said.

"What's the problem? He's angry, right? But why?"

"You're right. He's upset…but not at you. Your uncle is unhappy that there are some things that he couldn't change before his departure. He is concerned with the way some things are still done in the family. He wants things to change, Anna. He's not mad at you, but he just wants things to change. He wants you to take your freedom. And don't be afraid—there is nothing wrong with you, and nothing bad will happen to you."

I was stunned and speechless.

"Anna, are you still there?"

"Yes, Syba, I'm here," I said, still in shock. "Thank you so much."

"This is nothing."

I was about to hang up when my spiritual counselor said very solemnly, "Anna, don't be afraid. Take your freedom. Nothing will happen to you."

"I understand."

For the rest of the day, I remained wistful and dumbfounded. The following day after a good night's sleep with no dreams, something within me started to shift. And then from my gut, the words rose, traveling through my entire being, leaving behind the strong feeling that something major was about to happen: "Take your freedom, Anna. There's nothing wrong with you. Nothing bad will happen to you."

I exhaled with relief. With these words, I finally had permission to acknowledge and accept my conflicted feelings about Maman.

"There is nothing wrong with you" meant I could stop suppressing my angst. "Nothing bad will happen to you" meant I could rebel and free myself from the grip of Maman's control.

Without questions, the truth would never be known, and without challenges there would be no transformation.

Lalla and the elders taught that transformation happens when you decide to go battle against your own self and your deeply rooted beliefs. Indeed, it was a difficult struggle. But it was one from which you would ultimately emerge transformed, for better or worse. Things had to change, and for that to happen, I needed to understand the intensity of my feelings toward Maman. For so long I had tried to be a good daughter. I had kept the pain, anger, and resentment I felt hidden. The dream said that I could now let these emotions invade me without feeling guilty because they were rooted in events and circumstances I needed to rediscover. It was time to surrender to them so they could take me to the past I needed to deal with. Once I did that, I could hopefully be in a space that would help create and foster a new—dare I dream—loving relationship with Maman.

"Take your freedom, Anna," my spiritual guide firmly said. That was what Uncle Layes wanted me to do. That was what my innermost being aspired to do. Free myself of the pain, anger, and resentment I had been carrying with me and that seemed to appear more and more frequently during every conversation with Maman. Lalla said *the thorns can only be pulled from where they entered*; why did Maman, and Maman alone, trigger so much internal turmoil? Sure, Papa's and Lala's harsh words of expectation had wounded me but over the years I had seen every side of them to understand deeper. Their expectations were motivated by history and love. My Maman on the other hand had left me as a mere baby. I didn't see her again until I was a teenager. Unlike Lalla who sat with her children under a tree for days, she seemed to have chosen to leave without me.

I was ready to face the most definitive relationship of my life—the history and dynamics of the complex, demanding, and thorny love between three generations of women—a grandmother, a mother, and a daughter—three women of their time who carried within themselves their own heavy load of hushed, buried hardship and painful pasts.

Chapter Sixteen

LIKE TWO HEDGEHOGS

*If you come into the world and leave without
challenging and disturbing yourself and the world,
then what was the purpose of coming?*

L ike the lines of a song that gets stuck in your mind, the
words kept playing in my head as if they were hitting,
trying to knock down an invisible wall—the last barrier holding
back a downpour of forgotten happenings.

"Your uncle wants change, Anna. He's not happy with the
way things are still done in the family." Syba had said.

And neither was I. The maternal chain of command started
with Lalla, our matriarch, then moved down to Maman, Uncle
Layes, me, my brother, and our cousin. The younger member
of the family was to cater to the elder. The implicit rule was
rigid, still I had managed to follow it for my entire life. The
dream had revealed that this way of doing things had put a
strain on my uncle's generation, as well as mine. He had always
been an authoritative figure I loved. He was shy and didn't talk
much about himself or his life, and he never complained. I was
so busy conforming and trying to be obedient that it didn't
occur to me he too must have had his challenges.

"He wants you to free yourself. Have no fear—there's nothing wrong with you, and nothing bad will happen to you."

I was both in awe and grateful that my uncle had found a way from the world beyond to give me permission to free myself of the conflicting emotions I had suppressed. I didn't have to hide them. I didn't have to fight them. I didn't have to blame myself for feeling the way I did. But where would I start?

Maman and me. Nothing was simple. Nothing was easy. When Maman and I first reconnected in my teen years, I was elated until she rejected me right before leaving Mali. I was devastated. Maman was not the image I had created in my head. She didn't love me unconditionally. And it was my fault. I was to blame for her hurtful remarks and actions. I wasn't good enough. I blamed myself for doing the things that made Maman react the way she did. Her criticism only fueled my need to try harder to mold myself into what I believed Maman wanted me to be.

In my young adult years, and while in Mali, I worked hard to model myself into the attentive, affectionate, and pleasing daughter, Maman could approve of. I kept a job I didn't particularly care about so I could hear her say she was happy to see I had turned into a responsible adult. I called often to say the things I knew would make her happy; asking her how she was doing, telling her I missed her. And then, there were the many gifts we exchanged to show our love and approval of each other. Yet, when I faced serious money problems, it was Lalla, my beloved grandmother, who helped pay my debts. Maman didn't want to know. She didn't want any disruption to her life.

After I emigrated to the U.S., the distance between the two continents—America and Africa—made it easy to keep the peace between us. Maman and I were careful with each other. *Like two hedgehogs who couldn't get near without poking one another*, I didn't know how to be close to Maman without ultimately being spindled by her.

For Maman, I think I was both a dilemma and a stigma. She didn't know how to explain me to herself or to her close friends and relatives with adult children who were all married and had children of their own. Her only daughter was still single and in no hurry to find a husband and start a family. Lalla, on the other hand, wasn't bothered by my unmarried status and would often say, "You don't need a husband to be happy," she often said. "Look how many miserable couples there are around us. Some wished they never got married. All I ask of you is that you be happy. Lean on Daba only, and you'll be fine."

After the stroke something broke inside of her. Maman was vulnerable. Then, there was the stroke's devastating effect. She needed her children. But by that time, and despite the weight of wanting to be a good daughter, I was too wary of her reactions to really open up to her. How would I confront this issue?

Here I was riddled with pain and anxiety—because a conversation about a silly package revived all the times Maman had, for one reason or another, berated me, making me feel small and ashamed. Not to talk about the disappointments I faced in the moments when she didn't live up to the image of the mother I wanted her to be. My thoughts made me feel uncomfortable. I admonished myself for judging her. Something in me shot right back: I wasn't judging her, I was just now seeing the concealed half of the picture. And I needed to look at it, examine it, and understand it to pull the thorn it had embedded in me out.

Yes, Maman and I shared very good moments, but we also had many bad ones, some terrible times I had refused to acknowledge because I was desperately seeking her love and approval. I grieved for the little girl who for so long held on to what wasn't: the fairytale story between a mother and a daughter who loved and supported each other unconditionally.

Without questions, the truth would never be found.

I paused and asked myself, "If I decided to stop being a good daughter now, could that result in me one day walking away from her?"

"No, of course not," was the clear answer that came from my gut. How could I even think that? I would never abandon Maman. But I also didn't want to be forced into the role of gradually becoming her caretaker, both emotionally and financially. I didn't want to be submissive and dutiful the same way I had seen Maman be with her mother—my beloved, larger-than-life, domineering Lalla. I could not and would not let Maman expect me to be what she had been or do what she had done for Lalla.

What kind of relationship could we have?

"I care about Maman," I repeated. But there were too many unsaid things we had refused to talk about. These silenced matters were our hidden wounds. It seemed easier to go on as if we were totally oblivious than to confront them. And so, Maman and I had built a relationship on avoidance of those wounds. But they did matter. The silence didn't make them go away. Instead, the invisible scars that covered the festering would emerge through her harsh, bitter words and my hushed resentment. We knew how to hurt each other—her, through her vindictive remarks, and me, through my "disappearing acts." It was easy to go a month without calling. I hadn't expected this angry cascade of memories and resentments of how Maman and I sometimes treated each other.

I shut them down and sat in silence. Soon, I was calm again. And then, I shook my head and smiled as the irony of the situation sank in. Could my Lalla, my beloved elder who had forever kept a powerful grip on her children, have known she was giving me the pathway that would free me from being under the control of her daughter, my mother?

Stay still. Let your gut give you the answers.

Did Lalla have any idea that once I followed her advice, I would not be able to control or stop the process? And that probing into the past would take me this far back to my childhood? Would she have told me to listen to my gut—this bottomless emptiness that held all the big and small stuff of my life—if she knew what I was going through right now? Once again, the answer came, clear, certain: "Yes, she would have."

"Anna, I love you more than my own children," Lalla sometimes said. It was true. We were Daba's gift to each other.

I didn't know where I was going with these reminiscences. Something was going on inside me and I was determined to stay the course, no matter how emotionally challenging it might be. I needed to get to the root of all that was difficult between Maman and me.

What do you want? I took time to think carefully, then, as if I were making an important point to Maman herself, said, "I don't want to not be in your life." I took a deep breath and exhaled. "And I don't want not to help, but you simply *cannot* dictate what I will do for you. You cannot decide what I will be for you. You cannot make demands and expect me to just eagerly obey."

Irritation was back. I stopped. I didn't want to be angry. I didn't want to react. I just wanted to walk myself through a process and find the best, most positive resolution for me. "I want to be there for you, but on my terms."

Anger flared again. "I mean, how can you demand I be present, supportive, and do things for you when…," I stopped. A lump rose in my throat and I choked as if I were about to cry. My entire being ached as the words tore my insides and spilled out: "You were never there for me." I repeated this, emphasizing every word, "You—were—never—there—for—me."

The most difficult thing is not to give birth, but rather to raise and nurture a child.

Nine months—266 days.

For 266 days you carried me.

For 266 days you fed and nurtured me while I developed into a small human being in your womb.

For 266 days you kept me safe.

For 266 days you gave me some of you.

The umbilical cord was the lifeline that joined together and connected our two lives.

Through the umbilical cord, you fed and tended to me.

Through the umbilical cord, I received and experienced your joy, sadness, anger, fear, and anxiety.

For 266 days we were two people in one. We were inseparable.

Then you endured the pain of labor, giving birth to me. The umbilical cord that symbolized our unbreakable bond was cut. We were released, thus becoming two distinct individuals. It seemed that not long after that—maybe within months or a year—you were gone. You left so soon that I had no memory of you.

When I was seven years old, I found an old photo album. Across the pink cover were gold words written in calligraphy: *Notre Enfant*, our child. The album was filled with baby pictures of me—most of them alone; some with Papa holding me, others with friends of the family I would never meet. There was one with a stranger holding me. I was told she was my Maman.

If you yourself do not raise your child, she stops being your child and becomes a stranger who comes to visit you.

You were not there and so I didn't learn to know you as my Maman.

You were not there and so I didn't learn to know in what ways I was like you—in what ways I resembled you.

You were not there, so Papa, Lalla, relatives, and many good people stepped in, filling the place you had left empty with their love and guidance. They gave me a place, a name, an identity, and a history. I belonged somewhere. I belonged to a group of people that did not include you. They helped mold the infant I was.

I learned to walk by following their footsteps and running into their open arms.

I learned to talk by listening to their voices and imitating the sounds they made with their mouths.

I learned the dos and don'ts of our family and of our community, hearing them patiently and tirelessly telling me over and over again:

"Anna, stop, don't do that…."

"Anna, stop, don't touch that…."

"Who did that? You? Well done, Anna…very good."

They picked me up when I fell and wiped away my tears.

They comforted me when I was scared.

They received my secrets.

And every small, good action I did was praised and complimented as if it were a big thing. You missed that. You missed all of that. You weren't there for the birthdays. And you were absent for the good grades. The prizes of excellence won in primary school where Papa, the single parent, stood with the other couples and proudly watched as I walked to the podium to receive the award for reading and writing.

You were not there.

You were absent for all the small and big things of my life.

You were not there.

This was too much....

I stopped to let the little girl within cry and mourn your absence.

I stopped to acknowledge and accept the depth of the void your absence had left in me.

Your long, unexplained absence made me angry and resent you.

It mattered that you were absent.

It mattered that we never talked about it.

It mattered that I never knew why you didn't fight or insist to be in my life.

It mattered. All these years, I never got over you not being there.

My grandmother made sure I remembered I had a mother. Lalla became the bridge that kept you and I connected by sharing her fond memories of you. Whenever I spent time with my grandmother, she made sure to talk about you. And during one of your visits, you shared with me that Lalla always told you about me—the things I said and did. Lalla said things that made you endearing and kept you alive in my head and in my heart. You were a hard-working woman—a good daughter who always took care of her mother. You were the good daughter who didn't disappoint her mother. Lalla proudly showed me pictures of you and we both agreed you were beautiful.

Lalla was our bridge, hence we never had to learn to talk one-on-one without "our mediator." Lalla and I never talked about why you were not there. We never discussed the deep hole of "the missing things" your very long absence made in me. Despite Lalla's unconditional love, despite the fact Papa and other members of the family and the community had always been present, the truth was no one had ever been able to completely fill the space left by your absence, Maman.

My grandmother became our go-to to resolve our differences. She kept the peace between us. She listened to you complain about my unsympathetic and short phone calls and found words to excuse my brusqueness. She held my hands and calmed my angst when I told her you were unfair to me.

Here I was in my early fifties sitting with a calculator to count the days I had actually spent together with my Maman: 457, one year and three months. I felt raw and at peace. I understood why Maman set off such conflicted feelings in me. I had to accept that she and I would forever remain strangers who would visit one another from time to time. I lay still on the sofa, I can't recall for how long, but at some point, I must have dozed off. When I woke up, it was late afternoon. I wasn't hungry, but I forced myself to eat and then lay down again. I was drained but that didn't stop my thoughts from picking up where they had left off.

"Your uncle is upset there are some things he wasn't able to change before his departure."

I wasn't the only one whose mother-daughter relationship was shaped and impacted by a painful past. Lalla, Maman, and I were three women of our respective times who had to create their own sets of expectations, pressure and fear, to survive and thrive in eras that were not kind to them.

We are more the people of our time than the sons and daughters of our elders. Lalla, Maman, and I—women of three generations who were each shaped by the choices of the one who came before her.

In the beginning, there was Lalla, our matriarch, the warrior, the trailblazer. My grandmother grew up in an era where it was not common for girls to go to school. And so, she never learned to read and write. In her early teens, she was forced to marry my grandfather—the father of her two children—a much older man she didn't love. But it was also during the years of that unhappy marriage that her life would be shaped by women much older than she was, who took her in as their "little sister" because she was still a child far away from home. Lalla talked with great pride about these sisters who had gone to school and studied to become teachers, social workers, and midwives. They were courageous, women who had to abruptly readjust their lives each time their husbands were arrested for being political activists. The husbands were often in hiding or in prison for weeks and sometimes months at a time. During their long absences, their wives became the heads of their households and the sole providers for the families.

Lalla was shaped and influenced by these strong women. My grandmother told me that when she left my grandfather and came back to her father's compound at Duba with her two small children, the family refused to give her a room or food, hoping that the need to feed and shelter her kids would force her to go back to her husband. They hadn't counted on my grandmother being a fighter.

The single mother spent three nights sleeping under a mango tree with her two small children tucked under each arm. She braided hair and used the money to buy food. After three days of living under a tree, my grandmother found a room to rent and made a living braiding hair. She became the sole provider as her earnings allowed her to pay rent, feed her small family, buy clothes, and send her children to school. Lalla's world revolved around her two children. She taught them to stay close together and to let no one come between them—and no one did. They learned to rely only on Daba and Lalla. It became the three of them against the world—Lalla, the lioness, and her cubs. *Like the threads of one cover, they always stuck together.*

Lalla had an unbreakable will. She bent over backwards to give her all to her children and later to me—*the babe of her family.* No one could touch us. But she was also impatient and wanted things her way. Still, no matter how set in her ways my grandmother was, I was the only one in the family who could make her change her mind. All I had to do was ask. And every time I said, "Lalla, I don't agree." She'd ask, "Why, how would you like us to solve this problem?" I would give her my point of view. Lalla paused, then, "If you really think so, then let's do it your way."

Uncle Layes found ways to rebel from time to time. He didn't argue with Lalla, he just didn't do what she wanted him to do. But not Maman. Maman was the good, amenable child. She rarely went against her mother's wishes or words. Maman never forgot that *the blanket used to hold and carry a child had two sides: one side for the mother to carry the babe, and the other side for the child to take care of their senior parents.* But I believe one of the consequences of repressing her own will to comply with the demands of her mother was her treatment of me. Maman didn't just get angry—she erupted and unleashed mean and vindictive words that stung and made me feel awful for my mistakes or for the way I carried myself.

Children carry the scars of their parents' wounds. I never got to know the full story of the little girl who later would become my mother. The stories both she and Lalla shared with me were only about the good times—how Maman loved to sing while cooking, washing clothes, or doing other chores; the fond memories of an auntie who loved her dearly; sneaking out to parties after the elders went to bed. Maman didn't talk about the difficult times. What was life like for the daughter of a woman whose rebellious choices turned them into outcasts? How did my grandmother's daring, socially unacceptable choices impact my mother who was then about five years old? How did being whisked away at such an early age from life as she knew it to a new, hostile environment affect her? What did Maman think about late at night when things were quiet?

Did she see Lalla's tears? Did she sense her mother's fears?

Did she vow to right every wrong for her mother and her younger brother?

Did she promise herself that she would never cause Lalla any pain in the way the family had? Were her accomplishments and successes revenge on the world that had shunned and stigmatized them? And later, I knew that she had loved Papa, but she was reluctant to tell what had happened between them – what had he done that hurt her?

I once tried to ask Maman questions about her past and she became stiff and curt. I understood there were things she didn't want to talk about. Some parts of her childhood were taboo, and so was her relationship with Papa. Maman never spoke ill of Papa in my presence. "You never belittle a parent in front of the child," she said. He had not been so gracious when it came to telling me exactly what he thought of her. There seemed to have been happy moments in their stormy time together, carefree times, when she would hold on to his waist tightly as they rode about on his scooter.

"Do you know how your father and I used to bathe you when you were born?"

"No, tell me."

"We used to wash you together in a bassinet. We were so afraid to drop you. Your father and I were so careful. Hold her. Don't let her slip. He made me nervous. You were so small… our first child."

They separated before my first birthday, and I never got to find out when or how things went sour between them. When I pressed Maman, she shook her head and said that life with Papa was not easy. He hadn't been a kind young man. She sighed, smiled, and said, "Anna, it is only when you want things to work that you have a challenge, because then you care. You don't want to hurt the other person, you look for compromises, you look for ways to make things good. But once you reach your limits, when life becomes hell, it really doesn't matter what the other person thinks or wants; you just want to save yourself."

After she and Papa separated, she returned to her mother's house. Lalla sold all her gold jewelry to pay for Maman's nursing school in Senegal. And after she graduated, Maman started to work and made her life there. One day, in a rare moment, Maman had confided in me. She said she'd chosen to let Papa raise me to avoid a confrontation with him. Lalla had sided with Papa because she wanted Maman to finish school and didn't know how she could do that while taking care of a child. Maman hated conflicts. She didn't want to go against her mother and Papa's will, so she chose to stay away. She'd stared at me. So much sadness was in her beautiful eyes. Maybe she wanted to say more. In the end, she'd forced a smile and said, "Anna, you were never mine." I didn't understand. And I didn't know how to ask what she meant. We remained in an awkward silence until Maman regained her composure. Her eyes were tough again. We talked about something else.

Lalla made sure that we remained a close-knit family with her as our central figure who shaped, and deeply impacted each of us. Lalla's unconditional, powerful, and overprotective love had molded our relationships and defined how things were seen and done in our family. Lalla was controlling and quick to lose her temper. But I could never stay mad at her long. Why? Because she was "my Maman" who poured herself into me. She had always been devoted to me. I also knew the little girl hiding inside of her who smiled with all her heart every time I hugged and kissed her. Every time I told her how much I adored her.

In the end, we were three women of our times who were much more alike than I realized.

I was like Maman in my need to do things in order to be loved and accepted.

I was like Maman when I was an outcast.

I was like Maman when I laughed.

I was like Maman in more ways than I knew.

Ultimately, Lalla, Maman, and I had each done the most with what we had inherited.

It took a while to process this *thorn that had been pulled out*. Pain, anger, and resentment had vanished and left me reflective. I wanted Maman to be in my life, but going forward, our relationship would be on my terms. To establish myself as someone she must respect, I used Maman's own methods against her. No harsh or angry words, but a firm tone. I refused to tell her what I thought she wanted to hear. Our phone calls became brief.

Me: "I'm just calling to check in. Everything okay?"

Maman: "Yes, everything is fine. What about you? How are you?"

Me: "Can't complain. What about my Lalla? How is she?"

Maman: "She's fine, and just being difficult as usual. But she's not here right now. You want to call later so you can speak with her?"

Me: "Yes, I will." Or if I didn't want to call back: "No, just tell her I said hello and will call on another day."

My new attitude left Maman perplexed. She chose not to react, not to confront me. Time passed. My tone didn't change, but eventually Maman's attitude did. We didn't clash with words. We didn't confront each other. Instead, Maman answered abruptly when I called, and I countered with shorter phone calls. The only reason I didn't stop calling was because of Lalla. As long as Lalla was alive, I would not cut off all communication.

After almost four months of these cold, short conversations, Maman changed once more. The tone of her voice said she accepted the place I was giving her in my life. Maman didn't want to argue. Maman was convinced I didn't love her. She'd said more than once that the only person I truly loved was Lalla.

I never stopped doing the things I considered to be my duties—sending money when I could to help with the household and medical expenses and always calling to see how she and Lalla were doing. Maman complained to Lalla, hoping my grandmother would intervene. She told her I was difficult and too sensitive. Lalla retorted that I was fine the way I was and refused to mediate.

Arguments in the family are inevitable sparks that create smoke but never ignite. For just as your teeth sometimes bite your tongue, they remain tied together in the same mouth.

Coming to terms with the aching side of our relationship had set me free. It gave me the confidence to set boundaries.

I let go of the image of the good daughter I had created to please Maman.

I let go of the "dream mother" I had in my head.

I didn't know if we would ever be close. But I would always respect her and be there for her on my terms because she was my mother.

While I was trying to figure out the kind of relationship I could eventually have with Maman, fate was working on its own plan: life-altering events that would help elucidate the mystery of the voice inside my gut, as well as change what I believed I knew about Maman. For beyond our complicated mother-daughter story, filled with muffled judgments, bottled-up sentiments, and unanswered questions, there was love.

Love I didn't know she had.

Love I didn't know I had.

Chapter Seventeen

AND LIFE IS CALLED LETTING GO

*If you do not face your fears, they will come to you
through unforeseen occurrences.*

This was nothing, a simple exam I had done many times.
I was not worried.

"One more," she said in a neutral voice. She had an automated smile, the kind I imagined she had for the many people who came to her lab for the same test.

"Okay," I replied with an indifferent smile of my own.

This is not comfortable, the voice in my head whispered.

"Take a deep breath and hold it."

I complied. The distinct noise of the X-ray click-clacked and then, "You can breathe now. Relax."

I moved away from the machine.

It's a little cold in here.

"Have a seat. I'm going to see the doctor, and I'll be right back."

I hoped the doctor would at last confirm this shot was clear enough to see the bump inside my breast. This was our third attempt.

I waited in the small, cold, white room for someone to come and tell me I could go home.

I waited, my head calm and empty because there was nothing for me to think about.

I waited, refusing to count the seconds…and then the minutes.

I sat still, determined not to think, assume, or suppose. And then too much time had passed for it not to be something. Yet I would not imagine or draw conclusions. I would wait calmly until someone came in. The technician returned.

"Is everything okay?"

She didn't answer. Instead, she explained, "I had to wait for the doctor…." There was no emotion on her face, and I heard nothing in her voice. "Something on your X-rays. The doctor will explain. Now I'm going to take you into another room for a breast ultrasound."

I nodded, got up, and followed the young lady, who was helping me carry some of my personal belongings.

This was not how I imagined things.

This was a simple procedure.

Do not weep because of what happened to you for you don't know what tomorrow will bring. This was not the time to overthink and worry. Not yet. I wanted facts, and reality said that I didn't know anything.

Three weeks earlier I had been in the hospital because of my arthritis. My left arm ached so much it felt numb. To make matters worse, I could hear my heartbeat in my chest getting faster and faster. *The first symptom of a heart-attack is a heart-attack,* the TV commercial warned before recommending the pills that would prevent such a tragic accident. I panicked. Maybe these were my first signs. I rushed to the emergency room. After they ran all the blood tests and X-rays, I was relieved to find out there was no problem with my heart. But a few days later, a voicemail from the hospital urged me to contact them as soon as possible. The X-rays had shown an abnormality in my right breast. I went to see my doctor and was relieved when she couldn't detect a lump. We both agreed that, just to be on the safe side, I would schedule my annual mammogram.

And here I was now, on a bed in a dark room with my right arm up around my head while four strangers spoke as if I weren't there. I couldn't see their faces. I just heard the clear voices of the technician operating the ultrasound, someone who I assumed was the doctor, and two interns, all deliberating on the image on the monitor.

"Do you see it?" the doctor asked pointing to the monitor.

"Yes," voices answered.

Did they realize I was in an uncomfortable position with my arm up? Did they know my right arm was slowly going numb?

"I've never seen something like this before. I don't know what to make of it."

"Wait, where is it? I can't see it."

"It moves," the technician said, pushing the small transducer harder against my breast.

"Now I see it."

Silence. Then the voice of the doctor. "Hmm...strange. We're going to need more tests to find out."

After those words, the doctor and the interns left the room the same way they'd come in—without acknowledging me. I got dressed and walked to the front desk where a lady with a slight apologetic smile told me to return in three days for a biopsy.

I went home. It was late afternoon and I hadn't eaten all day, but I wasn't hungry. I felt dazed. Biopsy. *A small word can weigh so much.* In a few days I would return to the hospital for a biopsy. Slowly, this unfamiliar word—which had never been used to describe anything related to me—began to have all sorts of meanings for me.

Biopsy meant there might be something wrong with me.

Biopsy meant that, all of a sudden, I was facing things I didn't know and there was nothing at this moment I could do about it.

Concern was quickly followed by uneasiness. However, my mind didn't go viral, creating worst-case scenarios. I had found my seat. The unknown made me feel uncomfortable, but I refused to worry—I would not feed the anxiety with assumptions about everything that could go wrong. I would stay in the present and only handle and manage what I knew. What did I know? A lump was found, and a biopsy was needed to determine its nature. In three days, I would return to the hospital for the biopsy. "You will use no deodorant and no body lotion," I reminded myself. Then I imagined that soon after the procedure I would get the results, and that's when I would know for sure if I should worry or not.

But what if, my mind whispered. I stopped the trajectory of those thoughts before they could even begin. I refused to speculate until I found out. It was the sensible, logical thing to do. I would remain calm. I went on with my life as if everything were normal, as if I had nothing to worry about.

Once more I was in a small room with a bed, a monitor, and a young woman who said words in a tone, I believed, was meant to show compassion, "Did you use any deodorant?"

"No, Miss."

"Very good. Please undress from the waist up. Take your time. I'll be back shortly."

She smiled as if to say, "I'm sorry you are here." Or maybe it was my imagination, wanting to find some kindness in this very lonely moment. I complied, and when she returned with another woman, I was lying on the bed, my eyes staring at the ceiling. The young woman who had asked if I had used any deodorant spoke. She was the technician who would be operating the ultrasound machine. She introduced the doctor who would perform the procedure.

Cold gel on my skin, then the transducer used to locate the moving thing in me. A long needle entered and expelled inside of me, one, two, three times, the slightly burning anesthetic that would erase pain. They wanted to make sure I would not feel the many trespasses they were about to make on my body.

First a tiny incision, then another long needle ventured in. I didn't feel pain, just pressure. I closed my eyes as a stranger's hand carefully chased the elusive lump. The doctor and the technician both had their eyes on the monitor as the transducer guided them toward the wandering lump. Finally, the needle found it. More pressure as one hand pressed to enter and retrieve the tissue samples for the lab to examine.

After the biopsy, I was asked to not lift anything heavy for the rest of the day to avoid hemorrhaging. I was also told I would have to wait four or five days before calling my doctor to get my results. Four to five days was an awfully long time to wait. As if she knew what was going on in my mind, the technician said, "The lab is very busy right now." What was I supposed to do during that time? *Endure is what you do when you are powerless?*

I took a taxi home, thinking it was really cruel to have to spend four or five days without knowing. I arrived home feeling heavy and gloomy. Just as I began to consider all the things that could be wrong, the phone rang. I didn't want to talk, but I couldn't refuse to pick-up.

"*Allo*, Papa?"

"Anna, what's wrong? I haven't heard from you in a while."

I didn't have the strength or the will to lie, "I just came back from the hospital."

"What?"

"No, no, don't worry. I just had a biopsy. I'll get the results in a few days."

"What's wrong?"

"Nothing yet. Listen, they found a lump and they wanted to take some tissue to test it. Let's not worry before it's time. And even if it's something, Papa, you know we have the best treatments here."

"That's true," he said, sounding unconvinced. "But you know a parent never stops worrying about their children, no matter how old they are. Moreover, you never complain, so I worry."

"Don't, Papa. I'm okay. I'll call you back as soon as I have my results."

"Okay, I'll let you get some rest."

I was a little taken aback. I had no intention of telling Papa or anyone in the family, but the words came out as if I needed to unburden myself. This was my Papa who as harsh as he had been at times, had never left my side. Ten minutes later, my adult siblings called, one after the other. Papa had sounded the alarm and the Dao family tribe made emergency calls from wherever they were: Senegal, Mali, and Cameroon.

Tita, the doctor, and Iba, the financial expert, both worked for international organizations—one in health, and the other in telecommunications. They wanted to know if I needed them to take a flight to come see me. My answer was no. Was there anything they could do? Not really. But I appreciated their love and concern, and I promised to let them know the results as soon as I got them.

Mimi, our second sister, was a high-ranking government officer. A wife and mother, she scolded me almost as she would have her own children, Why didn't you say something sooner? Why did they have to hear the news of my health problems from Papa?"

"Because I didn't want to alarm anyone, and Papa called minutes after I came back from the hospital."

Fifi, the accountant, and Yuma, the lawyer, were the babies of our family. They called together to reassure me, "Don't worry a lump is a common thing at our age."

We laughed.

"We're sure it doesn't mean anything."

"I know, my doctor said the same thing."

The same demand came at the end of each conversation: "Call as soon as you get your results."

"Will do."

Hearing from my siblings warmed my heart. They gave me the love and support I needed at that very moment. The effect of the local anesthesia was starting to dissipate, and I began to feel the soreness. The questions sneaked out of my head, *What if…?*

What if it was cancer?

What if it was a malign incurable cancer?

What if it was nothing? But could it be nothing when they made me do a biopsy?

What if they had to remove my breast?

What if...? I quickly shook my head and stopped myself. I didn't want to go there. The what ifs hid the one thing I had been running away from for the longest time. The one thing that was the unavoidable and inescapable. I didn't want to say it, even though I knew that *saying the word fire did not create blazes*. I refused to talk about it, as if acknowledging and recognizing it would hasten its approach. Because I feared it, it haunted me, and my supplications didn't make it less daunting. It shook me to the core by striking people I adored. It was the root of my panic attacks that over the years were too many to count.

But I wasn't the same person. I was at peace within, and so I was no longer willing to run away. I didn't want to hush and suppress my fear. It was futile to fight the inevitable. It was time to face it, to understand why it terrified me and come to terms with the unchangeable truth that Earth ultimately owned man.

And so, the conversation with myself began. *No, no more running from this. Let's go beyond that. Let's say this is the beginning of the end for me. Let's say that soon*—my heart raced quicker and harder in my chest, but strangely enough, I did not panic—*soon, this is the end for me...and I die.* I exhaled, shocked by my own words, my own deduction. For the first time in my life, I had expressed my mortality calmly, clearly, and without going into a panic. I paused. This was a solemn moment. *If I were to die today...?*

I closed my eyes and breathed deeply, letting go of all my resistance. All the dis-ease that might have caused a disease.

And something extraordinary began to take place. Suddenly, my whole being—all the cells in my body, all my energies—were filled with light, peacefulness, and contagious joy. Something happened at that very instant. I recognized the Life in me. It was brief, but it was enough to fill me up with unimaginable peace.

Lying deep within and at the heart of my being was LIFE.

I AM LIFE. This statement was a validation of the teachings of my elders, the religious sacred books, and those of the mystics, scholars, and theologians whose work I embraced.

Lalla and the elders taught that Daba's voice created the universe and His breath gave it Life. The scholars and the sacred books stated that the Creator breathed part of its divine Spirit into the hearts of all the elements of creation. Therefore, *there is something of the Creator that dwells inside all forms of creation.* Daba breathed Life into each of us deep in the heart of our individual being, where—depending on how much one wanted to trust it—it would have the space to blossom, filling our inner beings to become an integral part of us and a pillar on which we could rely for guidance through our respective journeys on Earth. Life within was the conduit that allowed us to experience Divinity. It was the common thread that united pulsating, breathing, and living entities throughout the universe and to its source.

I AM LIFE. The Life within was my connection to Daba. And like the Creator, it had always been there, present in every moment of my existence like a hidden double, waiting for me to acknowledge and embrace it. It transcended all the Anna's I had been, and all the Anna's I will be without ever changing who or what it was: divinity, eternity enveloped in a temporary shelter—my temple, my body. If I considered all the things I once believed defined me—my name, my family, my friends, my values, my job, my income, my possessions, my relationships—who was I when stripped of all that? What remained? The Life in me that spoke to me through the voice in my gut—its voice reminding me I AM THE I AM.

I AM LIFE. The life within also said that my tie to Daba was above all religions for the Creator was present in all things, regardless of their beliefs. It gave certainty to my faith. For even in the midst of my greatest doubts—after I had relentlessly pursued Daba to no avail, and nothing in my life seemed to be getting better or be right—still I had this "knowing" that for the life of me I could not explain, that the Creator was there and I would be alright. And now again, after calmly contemplating my own mortality, I was filled with this profound, serene, and unquestionable certainty that I would be just fine.

I had known for a while there was life after life—the dreams had made that clear. Yet this glimpse of clear joy and serenity was something I had never experienced. Could it be that things were really better on the other side? I didn't want to go. I didn't want to die, but I also had a vision that life didn't end with the demise of my mortal, disposable body.

When you recall the names of the people you used to know,
You know the world is not a place where you come to stay.
When you wonder without knowing where have they gone?
You know the world is not a place where you come to stay.
You come to taste the world.
But the world is not a place where you come to stay.

Death—this great mysterious thing that regardless of race, color, age, or wealth made everyone equal—was like a spoon that sooner or later landed on everyone's lip.

Yes, my time on Earth was limited but I didn't want to die now. Even so, I was acutely aware that I really had no say in how long I would be here. Tomorrow was no longer guaranteed for me. Death was no longer something I could try to delay with prayers. There was a lump inside of me that the doctors, my family, friends, and I were worried about because no one knew what it was. This bump could be nothing, or it could end up being something harmful that could lead me— whether I was ready or not—to walk into the long corridor to the afterlife. And there was nothing to do except wait for the results from the lab. For four days I woke up and went through my daily routine, knowing and accepting that I was powerless.

Illness and death don't always go together, otherwise the world would be as empty as the palm of your hand.

At last, the day came and I could call my doctor. He was not available. Several long hours later, I received a call back, but I was on the train. The next day, I called again during lunch time, and about half an hour later, we finally spoke. I held my breath.

"Anna, I have good news for you. All your results came back negative. You have a lump, which is not unusual for women your age, but it has no cancerous cells."

I burst out laughing.

"What does this mean? What do I do?"

"It's a lump. In a year we'll see on your next mammogram if or how it progresses. But for now, you're fine."

After the conversation, I stayed still. I didn't have cancer. I was fine. I was going to live. Then after work, I called my relatives and close friends and reassured everyone. There was a lot of laughter during those calls. To say I was relieved was an understatement. Life would go on for now.

Days later, I was in my coworker Melanie's office. She and I got along well. We sometimes had candid conversations about our personal lives. I was sharing with her how my health scare turned out to be a wake-up call to face and accept my own mortality. She listened intently as she always did and then said, "To me your experience asks the bigger question: What do you want to do with your life versus what are you doing with your life at the present. I mean, think about it, Anna. Your life is your currency."

I was speechless, so I nodded as I let the sentence sink in: Your life is your currency. Melanie continued, "You know you have a limited amount of it. You don't know when you will run out of it. So, my question to you is, what are you doing with it? Are you spending it wisely?"

It was then that Melanie told me she was moving on. She had resigned from a highly paid position in an office she no longer wanted to be part of. She wasn't sure where she wanted to be, but she wasn't doing the things she really wanted to do. It was time for her to go away and figure out what the next chapter of her journey would be. And no, she had no safety net—meaning she didn't have another job waiting for her. Frankly, I didn't have her courage. My work was not the most challenging or rewarding, but it offered security and benefits I was grateful for and colleagues I liked. I was in good health, and fear no longer ruled and controlled my life. As for my relationship with Maman, it wasn't great, but we had mutual respect, and that was good enough for me. Maybe with time we would find ways to grow closer, and maybe never. Either way, I would be fine.

All major events are preceded by warning signs.

It was seven in the morning and within thirty minutes I received five calls with alarming, almost identical messages: Maman had been taken to the hospital, and no one knew if she would make it. I had to come. I called my brother. He too had received the same calls from our stepfather, our cousin, and close relatives. Upon his arrival a few days before me, my brother had texted: "I'm not going to sugarcoat it. She is not well."

Maman, what was going on? Why did you reassure me every time I called when you knew you weren't doing well? I wasn't angry, just worried. Then the night before my trip to Dakar, I rushed home from work to pack a light suitcase. I let myself sink into the sofa. I dozed off. Maman was in front of me. I could see her serene face. She spoke softly, "Anna, I came to say goodbye. You will not find me there."

"I know," I said. "Go in peace. Don't worry about me."

"Forgive me."

"I do, Maman...and you too forgive me."

"I did," she smiled.

I woke up suddenly, shaken. It was a dream. It was just fear. Even if the recovery was long, Maman was going to pull through. She would be alright.

The next day, December 24, I was on a plane to Dakar. When I arrived late evening on Christmas night, I found

Maman resting in her room. She smiled when I walked in. I hugged her gently. She felt frail and her beautiful, vibrant voice had become low, almost like a murmur.

My brother and I spent a week at Maman's bedside. She slept a lot. But when she was awake, she spoke softly and chuckled. In spite of the heaviness in the room and in the family—for no one dared ask if this was the end—we forced ourselves to have playful conversations that made her laugh. Lalla joked that Maman's weight loss made her look younger, and our stepfather better be careful. We showered Maman with compliments and encouragement when she managed to eat a small piece of chicken or a few yam fries. One beautiful day, from early afternoon to very late at night, Maman's voice and strength were back. Maman made us all laugh. It was a good day. It was a day that gave us hope of a recovery.

For a week, my brother and I talked to her doctors, bought everything she would need after we were gone. We also agreed on taking turns to visit and check on her recovery progress. My brother would come see her during spring break, and I would come back during the fall. Watching Mother, I erased the dream I'd had in New York and I left focused instead on the hope for a road that led toward reclaiming her health—even if it would be very long.

And then there was Lalla. She cried for hours when she thought no one could hear her, then she would pull herself together and come sit by her daughter, watching over her while silently and desperately praying for her to get better. Fate was incomprehensible. Why was her only daughter bedridden with her health deteriorating? It should have been her in that bed, not Maman. Was Daba going to let the green fruit fall before the ripe fruit again? Would she bury her surviving child?

Maman wanted to talk, but I wasn't ready to hear what she wanted to say. I could only deal with the present—accept and cope with what I had in front of me—Maman in bed, and frail. One silent tear on the corner of her eye ran down her cheek. She quickly wiped it away, but not fast enough for me not to have noticed. I wanted to believe against all odds that she would recover. Right before our goodbye, I said, "Daba willing, I will be back in September."

She gently replied, "That will be a good thing. Your mother is getting old."

"Just get better."

The three of us were in that room, Maman and her two children. I left Dakar on December 30, 2016. Thirty-six days later, my brother left me a message asking me to call him back. The phone rang.

"*Allo*...."

"Hi, you. I see I missed your call. How are you?"

Silence.

"Are you there?"

"Yes."

"What's wrong?"

"It's what we were afraid of...."

I dropped the phone. Hours later I was on a plane on my way to Dakar. Maman was gone.

All arrivals lead to departures.

When my brother and I walked into her room, there was no laughter to welcome us—a deafening silence made her transition a reality. My eyes fixated on the empty hospital bed in the corner of her room.

We had lost our mother. Lalla had lost her surviving child. "I have no more children...."

My grandmother didn't cry. Instead, she shared stories of her daughter with us, her grandchildren, our relatives, friends, neighbors, and all who came to help us mourn and lay Maman to rest. Her daughter was her rock. All her life, Maman had taken care of Lalla. She did everything she could to make my grandmother happy.

You come into the world alone and with nothing and you leave the world the same way you came in, with nothing. A few days after the funeral, Lalla, my aunts, and I came together late one evening to go through and give away some of Maman's personal belongings—her clothes, her jewelry, the gifts my brother and I gave her, the pictures and souvenirs she had kept over the years. A lifetime of memories and things she loved and preciously saved would now be separated. It took us hours to get through Maman's things, and Lalla, our matriarch, witnessed and supervised the distribution of her daughter's personal belongings without breaking.

The living close the eyes of the dead. While those who are dead give the living the chance to open their eyes to life. Maman was no longer here. There were no words that could ease my Lalla's pain. Still my brother, my cousin, and sweet Mariam, the caretaker, who was more like a family member, all rallied around our grandmother, intent on being there in any way she would allow us to be. Later, when it was time to leave, some of Lalla's nephews and nieces came to take her back to Mali, back to Duba where she was going to stay with Mariam by her side; and the rest of our large family would take turns visiting her and making sure she was all right. The night before we left Dakar to go back to our lives, I was alone with

Lalla. She held my hands and said, "Anna, now that I have no more children, all I ask of you is that you do not forget me." Battling my tears, I squeezed her hands and replied, "How can you think or say that? You know you are the most important person to me."

"I know," she said with a faint smile. Her heart was not there.

Soon after, we drove to the airport. Lalla went back to Mali while my brother and I flew back to the States.

I was consumed with making sure everything was done to make my grandmother comfortable. I spoke with Mariam every other day, and together we managed to make Lalla eat because she was never hungry. Mariam made sure she took her medications, I spoke often with my grandmother to let her know we were still here. My heart was aching for Lalla. I didn't know how to process my pain for Maman so I wrote this to her:

Mourning
You were there at my very beginning.
I was there at your end.
And in between, a lifetime of missing things:
Your presence,
Being together,
Getting to know each other.
Still, you were there at my very beginning
And I was there at your end.
Years of absence had created a hole no one could fill.
Years of absence had created a divide we could never mend;
We were mother and daughter,
Loving sometimes,
Estranged most of the time,
Unwilling to cut the ties that bound us.

You were there at my very beginning
I was there at your end.
I am back in the life I created for myself.
I am back in all that is familiar to me.
I am back slowly breathing and absorbing that you are no longer here.
I am back, letting the reality of your passing sink in.
Here they call it mourning.
For me, it is not going through an entire day without thinking about you.

It is calling again and again family and close friends to talk about you, hoping it would lessen the never-ending ache inside of my chest.

It is your voice reassuring me, telling me to stop worrying… that you weren't going anywhere…that you loved good food so much.

It is saying a million times you are no longer here and not being able to grasp the scope of what that really means.

It is waves of love from my heart, thinking, and saying "I love you" knowing or hoping that surely deep down you must have known.

It is remembering your contagious laughter, and the things you said that had me in stiches.

It is saying that we didn't always get along—we didn't always agree—but oh, how unimportant our disagreements seem now that you are no longer here.

In the end, quietly, and without me noticing it at first, you gave me the most precious gift—you passed on to me the one thing I had always witnessed you practice peacefully, humbly, and without ever pushing your belief on anyone: Faith.

Your Faith gave you grace in the midst of what I believed must have been the unimaginable pain of your ailment.

Your Faith made you find words to reassure your children even when you knew you were not getting better.

Watching you, I witnessed and learned that no matter how difficult a situation might be, you, Maman, found something to be grateful for.

I watched you taking in illness and letting go of life until your transition to the afterlife without anger or bitterness. Until the end, I never heard you once say, "Why me?"

During my last visit, Maman, you knew you were dying. I was in your room with Lalla, and she wanted to reassure you about the afterlife, "Don't worry, Rokia. Hardship is only on this side of the world. In the other one, you will be just fine. Don't be afraid."

I was angry. Why would Lalla talk like that? You were here. You were not going anywhere. You must have seen the expression on my face. Because you said softly, "Let's not talk about this right now."

I know you wanted to talk. But I wasn't ready. I had this fear inside of me that refused to see what was happening. When you saw how much I was afraid to consider what I thought was unimaginable, you let go. You smiled lovingly and carried on conversations as if everything were going to be alright. Your pains and fears were known to you, and Lalla. They were your private conversations with Daba.

As the people who loved you gathered with your mother and children to bid you farewell, one uncle summed you up perfectly: You came simply, lived your life humbly, and left peacefully. Your name was Humility.

My inheritance is laughter—I have been told many times that I have the same laugh as you.

And your legacy is Faith—the pursuit of the One Indisputable Truth that makes all things here on Earth bearable and the afterlife, something to not fear, and maybe even to look forward to.

I don't know if you knew this, but I'll say it one more time for you and most of all for me:

I love you and thank Daba for the gift of you.

Your Daughter

The sun didn't forget to shine, and life went on. Months later, I went back to Mali to see for myself how Lalla was doing. My grandmother couldn't believe I made this trip just to be with her. It was a small comfort. Lalla didn't say much. Living had become a burden, and she was waiting on Daba to reunite her with her children. She watched me come and go, talking with Mariam and doing all we could to give her the simple things she didn't ask for, but we did them anyway, hoping to please her.

Life went on, and with time, I began to accept that Maman was no longer here. The fear, the hurt, and the barriers I had built to protect myself and keep my distance from her had vanished. Memories brought back all the things that were good about her—her biting sense of humor, her unyielding determination to try to live a quiet, peaceful life, her courage and resilience, and most of all her faith. I remembered us holding hands; and my head resting on her lap. Illness beat and ate her body, but it couldn't make her lose her trust in the Almighty. Maman had faced her ailing health with a courage and a dignity I rarely saw.

I embraced our mother-daughter relationship—the good and the not so good of our story. The good times, the rejections that created unforgiving wounds that ran too deep for me to move beyond them and see her—really see her with her vulnerabilities, her fear, and a love so deep for her estranged daughter that she silently agreed to let me go, knowing I would never get to see and know the strong and courageous woman she was.

The word that now comes to me when I think of you is love. Yes, Maman Love. Hidden under your expectations of me, your anger, your harsh attitude, and words, was love. And buried under my judgment and resentment of you, was also love. Suppressed under our mutual presumption of what we should be to one another and our hushed frustration, was love.

Of my fifty-plus years on Earth, we only got to spend 457 days—one year and three months—together. Still, you must have done some things right because you had a more lasting and positive influence on me than I imagined. At long last, I found you loved me and I loved you back tremendously—more than I wanted to. More than I dared show you. More than you knew—or maybe you did know.

The living close the eyes of the dead. While those who are dead give the living the chance to open their eyes to life. Our mother-daughter story was left unfinished. We didn't get to talk about your own past and the events and circumstances that had influenced and shaped the woman you became. We didn't get to smooth the bumps of our complicated relationship. Yet, I found myself being okay with that. As incomplete as it was, it was our story.

You were there at my very beginning...

And I was there at your end...
In the end, we both in our own way let go.

One day I found a picture of Maman from the time when I didn't know her. She was young. It looked like she was dancing. She smiled happily. I kept this picture because that was how I wanted to remember her. And when I looked in the mirror and smiled, in the reflection the mirror sent back I recognized the smile of my mother.

Chapter Eighteen

I HEAR FOOTSTEPS BUT DON'T
RECOGNIZE ANYONE

A familiar place filled with unknown faces.

My eyes opened and saw the "Fasten Your Seatbelt" sign had just lit up. Our plane started its descent to Bamako. I sighed. I wasn't looking forward to our flight landing.

Bamako without the excitement that I would soon see Lalla.

Bamako without my grandmother impatiently waiting for me to arrive at Duba.

Bamako without Lalla. How would that be?

Lalla, my grandmother, the last living child of my great-grandfather sixty-five accounted children had been laid to rest that morning.

It was late afternoon when the plane finally landed in Bamako. I mechanically followed the people in front of me down the aisle. We stepped off the plane to the long corridor that took us to customs. Outside, the big red setting sun, a small breeze, and my brother's driver greeted me. "Welcome home, Auntie Anna. May Allah grant our elder paradise."

"Amine. Thank you, Alpha."

The phone rang. The driver answered and handed it to me.

"Hey, young man, how are you?"

"I should be the one asking you that question."

"Iba, I'm doing okay. It was just a long flight. Where are you?"

"I'm still in the office. Tita and Fifi are both out of the country. But Mimi, Yuma, and I spent the day at Duba. We were hoping you would arrive sooner. They had to go home. But we will all be there tomorrow. My driver is going to take you to Duba. What time would you like me to come take you home?"

"Is 7:30 p.m. too late?"

"No, not at all. See you then, sis. Love you."

"Love you too, Iba."

It was almost dusk—the interlude when, before the last rays of sun disappeared letting total darkness take over, men and women rushed to their homes. On the streets of Bamako, traffic created impatience and irritation. The noise and smoke of running engines had turned the breeze into a warm stickiness. Bicycles, motorcycles, cars, and buses were engaged in their daily race of hazardous maneuvers to beat a red light or cut in front of another vehicle, only to stop a little bit farther along. By the time we safely reached Duba, the sun had set.

I walked inside the familiar place where I once was happy and carefree. I walked the same pathways that used to seem so big but were now ordinary passages. I arrived at the place where Lalla used to live. Mariam ran to me, "Anna is here!"

We held on to each other and wept. Relatives rushed from different households inside Duba.

"What's going on? Who's crying?" a woman's voice asked.

"Anna."

"Who?"

"Auntie Lalla's Anna."

"Oh! She made it. This is so sad."

They came to offer sympathy and support as we walked together into my grandmother's living room. They remained quiet until I regained some composure. I put my glasses back on, looked around, certain that I would recognize their familiar faces. But aside from Mariam, my cousin Mohammed, his wife, and his mother, I knew no one.

There must have been twenty people around me. My relatives introduced or reintroduced themselves: three aunties I didn't remember. Lalla's baby sister, my late grandma Fanta's daughters; uncles I didn't know but whose fathers' names I vaguely recalled were the offspring of Lalla's big brothers; some cousins I hadn't met. Mariam and Auntie Adjara were with Lalla until the end.

"Anna, she went peacefully," Mariam said, as she held my hand.

"What happened?"

"It was early morning. She called me. I went into her room. She asked me to give her some water. I held her head up as she took a few sips. Then she asked for her rosary. I gave it to her. She said, "Forgive me." I don't know how I got to Auntie Adjara's door. All I remember was that I was knocking on her door."

"When I saw Mariam, I knew," Auntie Adjara continued. "I came in and I closed her eyes. Auntie Lalla looked so at peace. I have no doubt that she went home to Allah's Paradise. Anna, we are all sad. But the way I saw her, I just know that she is truly in a better place."

"You know that everyone came," Mariam said.

"Of course, everyone had to be here," Auntie Adjara said. "Even those who are in other parts of the world called. She was our last auntie. She was the last living biological child of our patriarch."

Her nephews, nieces, grandchildren, great-grandchildren, all came to Duba to bid farewell to Lalla.

Iba walked in and we hugged.

"How are you doing?"

"I'm fine. Stop worrying. You know she prepared me for this."

My brother acquiesced, not sure what to say.

"Mariam, I'm leaving. But I will see you tomorrow. What time do you get up?"

"You can come as early as you want. We can have breakfast together before people start coming in."

Iba put his arm around my shoulders as we walked to the car. The ride was silent. Iba left me alone with my reminiscences of Lalla.

You prepared me for this—the day when you would no longer be here. Still, it was strange and difficult to walk in and not hear your jubilant laugh as you said: "Anna is that you?"

"Yes."

"Thank Allah, my lagaré is finally here."

And after we hugged, you looked at me. "You know, starting the day you said you were coming. I never stopped praying to Daba for your safe travel."

Tomorrow I will not wake up early so that you and I can have breakfast together in your room. I am in pain, and so grateful to you at the same time. You said: "I will not leave you. I will stay until I know that you have found your way."

You kept your promise. You guided me until I found my seat. You stayed until Daba reassured you that you could let go, leave in peace. The car stopped. Iba and I exchanged a knowing look:

"Are you ready for Papa?"

We laughed. My brother and I walked in holding hands. Papa and Mama Deep Water were in the living room watching TV. It was late but they hadn't had dinner because they were waiting for us. They were sorry for my loss. They were supportive. Mama Deep Water had one of the rooms prepared for me, and Papa had called the plumber to repair the shower so I could have hot water. This was February, the end of the cold season in Mali. Temperatures in the morning were cool, but for this tropical country, there were considered cold.

The next morning, I had coffee with Papa and Mama Deep Water, and right after, the driver took me to Duba where my Mariam was waiting for me. We used these precious moments together before the rest of the family and friends started coming in to talk about Lalla and Mariam's future.

"Mariam, you are like a daughter to me. You are part of the family. As long as I am here, Daba willing, I will be there for you. I don't want you to worry. After all of this is over, I want you to think about what you want to do. Do you want to go to an apprenticeship school? Bamako has many of those where young adults can learn to be seamstresses, mechanics, or make household goods such as soaps made with shea butter or peanut butter oil. I will talk to Mohammed my cousin, uncle Layes only child. We are going to figure something out."

She nodded. Her eyes watered. She didn't say a word. She just held on to my hand. Mohammed walked in, "I thought I would come early, so we could go to the cemetery."

My cousin Mohammed and I took a cab to the cemetery. We walked to the very place Lalla had been laid to rest the day before. Her name, her date of birth and day of transition had already been engraved on the plaque. Mohammed and I knelt down and prayed together. My eyes went to the plaque at the head of her tombstone. My mouth pleaded, "Lallaboo." I had never called her that. Lallaboo was the nickname her father lovingly called her when she was a little girl. Lallaboo was the name Maman and others called her, meaning "I love you." Lallaboo made my grandmother's heart melt.

When Mohammed and I returned from the cemetery, my grandmother's living room and terrace were full of mourners. I didn't know or recognize most of the people. Those who knew Lalla personally shared their fond memories of her. Others had never met her but came to pay their respects because we were family—all tied by our elders to the same patriarch, Umar, nicknamed Teacher.

"Auntie Lalla was something else," an uncle chuckled. Do you know that when I was a kid in elementary school, all the children had schoolbags except for me? My father could not afford it. At the time, we were still living at Duba. One day, Auntie Lalla saw me crying. She called me and asked what was wrong. I told her everyone in school had bags for their schoolbooks except me. I was carrying my stuff in a plastic bag. Do you know what auntie did?"

"What?" we all asked.

"She took down the beautiful drapes she had in this room and made me a schoolbag. She sewed all the pieces together."

We all laughed.

"I remember that sewing machine," one auntie said. "You know her eyes couldn't see the hole in the needle where the thread had to pass, so she always called one of us whenever she had to change the color of the yarn or when it broke."

"And Allah forbid if you weren't home by dusk."

Oh yes, dusk! The rare times Lalla ever spanked me when I was a little girl were when I played too late and came running home a little after sundown.

Dusk: an ambiguous, disturbing time. A period when all the nocturnal forces awaken. The jinn, the spirits of the dead and those of the ancestors free at last, wandered in search of a body to possess and to live in.

"Yes, but you know, she wasn't the only one who would give us a hard time for not being home by sundown. All the lionesses did." I had to ask, "Why were Lalla and her sisters called lionesses?"

"Because they were strong women who weren't afraid to fight. Anna, our fathers were afraid of their sisters. And it's not that our aunties all got along, no-no, but if you had the bad luck of picking a fight with one of them, all the sisters would come together to fight you. I don't know what their father told them, but your grandmothers were strong opiniated women."

I spent the day listening to relatives talk about their late parents and life at Duba. My uncles and aunts were now the elders of the family. They wondered out loud how did time pass so quickly? They were now the grandfathers and grandmothers of a next generation growing up…my nephews and nieces.

That night after dinner, I went early to bed. I wanted to be alone. Remembrances brought back a particular memory. I chuckled. *OMG! What a beautiful and amazing woman you were. And what an interesting life you led.*

Years ago, before Maman's illness and Uncle Layes's passing, the phone rang. It was early Saturday morning. I wanted to ignore it. Still, I opened one eye and glanced at the screen and saw it was Maman. I picked up.

"*Allo*, Anna," Maman said very cheerfully. "I hope we didn't wake you."

"No," I lied.

"It's your grandmother. She didn't want to wait…she said she had to talk to you."

I was wide awake.

"Here," I heard Maman say as she handed Lalla the phone. "Anna?"

Lalla was giddy. She could hardly contain herself.

"Lalla! What's going on?"

Suddenly, my grandmother became shy. The little girl in her reappeared. She didn't know quite how to tell me what she wanted to say. Would I judge her? My heart melted. With endless love, I said, "*Do di.*"

She giggled happily and in a low voice confided, "I'm in love."

We burst out laughing—a contagious happy roar.

"Lalla, tell me everything…."

"You are so nosy! I still can't believe it. He is so good-looking, educated, and he is younger than me."

"Who cares. If you love him, I'm with you. I support you."

Lalla couldn't stop talking about the new man in her life. Love had transformed my grandmother into a bubbly young woman who was in awe of her good fortune at this stage of her life. She was in her late seventies, had been married before, and was content being a mother and a grandmother. She wasn't looking for love. Yet love found her and turned her into a lively and vibrant young woman. Ultimately, the relationship ended, and they went their separate ways but she'd loved again and I was happy. I was in awe of my grandmother for unapologetically daring to be who she wanted to be.

My last day at Duba, Mariam, Mohammed, and I met early in the morning to talk about the future. Mariam agreed to stay with him and his family. She wanted to be a seamstress, and Mohammed was going to find a good apprenticeship school for her to attend. I promised I would take care of the financial part. After lunch, Mariam left to visit the neighbors because she didn't want to say goodbye—she didn't want to see me leave.

The dead are only truly dead when the living have forgotten them.

I was back in New York City. Life went on as I carried my grandmother's spirit in me. I spoke of her often to my friends, colleagues, and relatives. The sentences usually began with, "Lalla, my grandmother, would say…," followed by some wisdom that summed up the lessons you taught me. And then, the gift arrived that would forever keep your memory alive for all of us.

Four months exactly after her transition, I was in the office working on a report. My phone vibrated. I picked up and read, "A new guest has arrived in the family." I didn't know that Mohammed and his wife were expecting.

I immediately called him. "You said we have a new guest. Is it a boy or a girl?"

"A girl."

"Mohammed, I'm claiming her. This one is mine!" To "claim a child" means you become a guardian to that child, and when the parents accept, you get to choose the name of the newborn.

Mohammed laughed, "I knew you were going to say that."

"How are the mother and the baby?"

"They're both doing very well."

The baptism ceremony took place on the seventh day of her coming into the world. On that day, after the early morning prayer, the Imam whispered in her right ear, then in the left ear, "Your Name is Lalla. Your Name is Lalla."

Later that day, Mohammed, his wife, and Mariam sent me pictures of the ceremony. In the evening, I called and we joked that we hoped she wouldn't be as feisty as her namesake. I made plans to be there for her first birthday. I made plans to be there to check on my "daughter" Mariam. She was now living with Mohammed and his family and seemed happy.

The disease that must take you will not leave you alive. Three weeks after the naming of our little Lalla, my sister Fifi came to visit me. We were having brunch when my phone rang.

"Hey, Mohammed, what a surprise. How are you?"

"I'm fine."

"What's wrong? Your voice is strange."

"Nothing. You seem busy I can call you later."

He hung up. I went outside and called him.

"Now you've got me worried—what's going on?

"Anna, Mariam is dead."

"What? When? What happened?"

"These past few days, she complained she wasn't feeling well. She passed away thirty minutes ago."

I hung up. Mariam was gone. Grief came without warning. Death stole a young life I adored. I cried and mourned the young lady who ran out of Duba because she didn't want to see me leave. I cried as I recalled her love and devotion to our family. She was part of us. I considered her "my first daughter." Mimi and I called the family to make sure everything was taken care of for her funeral. Mohammed confirmed that everyone at

Duba came. We were all in shock, in disbelief. We never found out what caused her passing. I suspect she was secretive and hid her illness. Our uncles, aunts, and neighbors all recalled the hard-working young lady who loved Lalla so much and was so loyal and dedicated to her.

Month after month, the sun continued to shine, and we learned to go on despite missing Lalla and Mariam. But there were moments of joy every time I got pictures of Lalla's namesake. Time passed and in June little Lalla was going to celebrate her first birthday. I wanted to be there. I was preparing to make the trip, but in March 2020 the world came to a screeching halt.

Chapter Nineteen

I WILL STAY

You cannot pick up a pebble with one finger.
We're in this together

*T*he coronavirus disease (COVID-19) came and wiped out our daily, meticulously organized, routines. We couldn't go to work. We couldn't visit family and friends. There were no trains to catch. No deadlines to meet. No walks in the park. No restaurants. No movies. Like millions of people, I was confined and had nowhere to go except within my inner being and the surroundings of the place I called home.

As the virus spread ruthlessly and the number of new infections and deaths kept rising to incomprehensible heights, the health experts and political leaders struggled to provide reassuring answers about the pandemic and its consequences. The world was restless, pulsating to the beat of fear and uncertainty. The world was in the midst of another unique crisis. Our political authorities and celebrities alike took turns reminding us of the ties that bound us: our humanity. *Regardless of where and how we lived, we often faced the same problems.*

"We're in this together!" became the message TV networks played over and over, telling us we were not alone.

We're in this together as we checked on our families, our friends, and neighbors. My siblings and I called each other and laughed when Papa said he didn't want any visitors.

We're in this together when every night from different corners of the globe we clapped and banged with our kitchen utensils to cheer those we used to take for granted—the "invisible people" who refilled the shelves of all the countless stores and took care of our sick and elderly. With gratitude we now recognized them as our frontline workers.

We're in this together as grief struck from New York to Bamako without distinction. Here, friends and colleagues lost spouses and relatives in hospitals and nursing homes. In Mali, I lost an uncle I had known all my life and two family friends within days of each other.

We're in this together since, in life, there were no coincidences, we all agreed. The pandemic had our full attention. What did it want to tell us? What did it want to teach us? Was it that we are not in control and Mother Nature can stop mere mortals at any time?

For me, COVID-19 brought a time of reckoning and a time of discovery. A time of reckoning because no one knew when or how this pandemic would ever end. A time of discovery because I learned to accept and get comfortable with the lingering anxiety that was all around and inside of me. But I also never imagined it would be so easy to get used to working from home in my PJs. With days of nothing to do, I instinctively turned my attention inward and leaned on my faith to help me stay sane as I spent hours in front of the TV watching the devastation of the virus around the globe and in the United States. My emotions cycled through fear and doubts, with respites of hope and solace when I prayed.

Lalla once said, "Anna, you'll become your own compass when you understand why you believe in Allah—when you trust your faith enough to lean on it and let it anchor you to the Creator."

Faith and prayers did not end the pandemic. They did not bring the miracle of seeing all that was wrong with our world disappear, but they brought relief by driving away the relentless uneasiness the never-ending stream of bad news we humans had created.

Prayers, reading, staying still, turning off the TV and choosing silence, even when I was afraid, gave my mind the space to learn to become comfortable with not knowing. The uncertainties of all our tomorrows gave meaning to one particular teaching of Lalla and the elders: *Learn to understand, value, contain and put up with all the things you are. For you are one and many.* Indeed, as human beings we are and will always be so much more than we can fathom. The pandemic caused major disruptions in our lives. Yet, it made me realize my hectic life—the hustling and bustling in the city that never sleeps— didn't necessarily translate into a meaningful life. Before the pandemic, my days were busy, my weekend were busy, my life was busy. Great! My life was filled with things to do. How important were those things? Did they make me happy? "Your life is your currency. What are you doing with it?"

I liked my job and my colleagues, but the confinement made me discover a craving and a passion for the world of spirituality I didn't know were dormant in me. After the first few weeks spent glued to the TV, I wanted some time out. There was no good news. I created a space where I found peace reading religious and spiritual books by authors of various faiths and nationalities that resonated with the truths deep within. As

Lalla, the elders, and the mystics so often said, *There is only one Summit—One God—but the paths to reach the Creator are as many and as diverse as the whole human race.* The many paths are in response to our different natures. Thus, everyone can choose, or not, to find their own way to the Creator.

Prayer was, and is, my moment of silent meditation and conversation where, for a time, I separate myself from all the events and noises of the world to turn my attention to the Life inside me that connects me to Daba. I go inward to *pull the bottom to the top*—go beyond the appearance of things and the news headlines—to see and understand myself and the events of the world differently.

And during daily prayers—my "check-in and sacred time" with Daba—I expressed gratitude for my blessings—expected or unexpected, and I appealed to the Almighty's mercy for my troubles, those of my loved ones and of the world.

With faith and prayer, I got to experience all that I can explain—how it feels to be elated and content, to have inner peace and serenity. How does compassion manifest in my interactions with others? And then there are the things I can't find words to describe: faith—my unwavering trust in the unconditionally loving and comforting Divinity in my life.

I liked the calm and reflective person of faith who was not afraid of the unknown I had become—the Anna that Lalla had hoped I would be:

Unapologetically ME when I'm on top of a mountain, and

Unapologetically ME when I'm at the bottom of a wave.

I smiled as I recalled the famous words of Rumi:

This being human is a guest house.5

Every morning a new arrival.

A joy, a depression, a meanness,
Some momentary awareness comes

As an unexpected visitor.

Welcome and entertain them all!

Even if they are a crowd of sorrows,

Be grateful for whoever comes.

Because each has been sent,

As a guide from beyond.

I had changed so much. I wasn't the same person. And the words of an old song say,

The world is a place where you learn to know.

Uncountable are the values and benefits of knowledge.

Lalla and the elders would add:

To know yourself is no small endeavor.

To know yourself is a big thing.

---

5 Excerpts from website: https://gratefulness.org/resource/guest-house-rumi/2 Copyright 1997 by Coleman Barks.

It is not given to everyone to know thy self.

It is not given to everyone to be a true person.

It took some time, but these are some of the truths I have learned to know.

It took some time, but here are the truths I now understand.

Spring 2021 arrived. As the numbers of infections and deaths from the virus steadily declined to new lows, our office reopened. I was grateful to still have a job, but not so happy to have to get dressed to go to work.

The pandemic and the new way of life it created for the people of the world taught me two important lessons: how vital it is to turn my attention inward to listen to the voice of Life within; and how to live my life with detachment—the distance needed to get the larger picture—not indifference.

Indeed, the voice inside my gut was instrumental in helping me find my seat—be grounded and settled within. It is the voice of Life that Daba breathed into each of us deep in the heart of our individual being. I like to think of the voice of Life within as our individual hidden spring. In all of us, there is a divine source we are supposed to tap into in our time of need. For example, when happenings turn your life upside down, inward is where you go, it's what you lean on to anchor yourself so the outside chaos doesn't create a mayhem within. But that internal source is available to us only after we dig and remove all the shields and buffers we have accumulated through the years, in my case through decades.

Silent meditation created detachment.

Detachment is the breath I take, the space I create, or the distance I walk so I don't get engulfed and consumed by people's demands, events and circumstances, or my own problems.

Detachment is the pause that allows me to put things in perspective—so that I don't surrender to merciless anxiety when the world comes to a screeching halt as disasters strike across the globe.

I had become what Lalla and the elders hoped all my contemporaries would ultimately turn out to be at the end of our initiation to the *good path*: true human beings who had learned to know and live in agreement with the different facets of their beings. The lessons of our elders showed that the material and immaterial worlds weren't incompatible. They completed each other. And it was our responsibility to use the tools they provided us to harmonize the different dimensions of our being.

Today, faith, prayer, and my relationship with Daba the Creator are the central pillars of my life. I have a list of things I am passionate about and would like to achieve before the end of my time on Earth. For each, I have created achievable work plans I can follow. As I work on my projects, I leave it to the Creator to approve, edit, and/or transform my trajectory and the final outcome of all my proposals. For if I were to define what I could or could not accomplish on my own, my life would have been very limited. It would have been a narrow straight line to the top—but what top, and for what purpose? I don't know. I would have disregarded the very things that have shaped and influenced me—the diverse group of people who raised me; the cities and the cultures I discovered; the books I read and the eclectic music I listen to. And I wouldn't have paid much attention to the complexities and the spectrum of the human emotions, including those within my own being. That's why it is only fitting that the Almighty, who is beyond what I can fathom, should be the power that guides me on a journey that is so much more than what I can envision.

And as an observer of how the events of my life keep unfolding, I would say that Daba accepted my invitation to make me sense the Divine Presence in my life. And the mystic books state that the Almighty said:, "My Earth cannot contain Me, nor can My Heaven, but the Heart of my believing servant can contain me."

In June, Lalla's namesake turned two. I was sick and couldn't travel. Three months later, Papa fell ill. By the time I arrived in Bamako, he had been released from the hospital and was resting at home. Every morning after breakfast Papa and I had one our two hours together where it was just the two of us in the family room. Papa complained about all the things he could no longer do. It took too much time to get out of bed and get dressed. Too many medications he had to take. Other mornings, we commented on the shows he liked to watch. This particular morning, my father kept to himself.

"Papa, are you okay?"

"Yes," he smiled. "Why?"

"You're so quiet, I was starting to worry."

"You worry too much. I was just thinking."

He didn't finish his thought. I stayed quiet, my eyes glued to the TV program I really didn't care about.

"Do you know why I was named Zana, and what it means in our dialect?"

"No."

Our family spoke Bambara, the national language, but Papa never taught us the dialect from his village.

"It means rain."

He smiled. The profound love he had for the place where he was born was obvious in the way he talked about it.

"It was pouring rain the day I came into the world. Your grandfather came from the field. The midwife stopped him at the door, 'Your guest has arrived. It's a boy.' Your grandfather went back out and brought a rooster that he handed to the midwife. The chicken was both a gift to welcome the newborn, and to make soup for my mother."

He paused. He hesitated. Then, "Your grandmother left when I was young."

He didn't say it. The pain in his voice and his eyes did. She didn't come back for him. He was left behind. And he was still hurting. That thorn had never been pulled out. Papa struggled to find words to talk about what I could only imagine must have been the painful episodes of his childhood. He didn't. He sighed, and we watched TV. In that moment, I felt for him. Finally, after he regained his composure, he turned to me and smiled. I smiled back. We heard footsteps. Soon, someone would walk in and end our moment. Papa leaned close to me and whispered, "You know, my dear daughter, I never told you this, but your mother was a good woman. You have her kind compassion."

The world stopped turning. *Did I hear right? Maman was...?*

"Good morning."

"Hello, young brother, how are you?"

"I'm good, thank you. I didn't know you had a visitor. Anna, when did you arrive?"

I got up to hug Uncle Madou, as Papa answered: "She arrived a few days ago to see her Papa. She worries too much."

He was proud to brag that his daughter, who lived in the United States, had dropped everything to come home when he fell ill.

"You're a good daughter," Uncle Madou said. "You make us proud."

"Thank you."

As Uncle Madou and Papa started a new conversation, my mind was still stuck on his words. *Did Papa say my mother was a good woman? What do I do with that?* I looked down at my feet. Papa was wearing sandals. *Oh! I have your toes.*

"Good morning, Auntie Anna. Ready when you are." It was the driver. He was going to take me to Mohammed's home.

"That's right. You're having lunch with Mohammed and his family," Papa said.

I kissed Papa loudly on the cheek. His body trembled. He couldn't help it. It happened every time something touched him deeply.

And Daba created nothing that can be compared to love.

Love will make you find the good in people. I loved my father. Love didn't erase our tumultuous past. Love didn't make me forget how cruel he had been. Still, love allowed me to accept and coexist with all that was good and all that was terrible about Papa.

I didn't want to play the blame game and vilify him for our past. Our lives were complex. He was Papa—a man filled with ambitions, love, anger, insecurities, and contradictions. Not everything he said was gospel. But I wanted to be kind. Maman would have said, "It's when you're in a position of power that you choose graciousness by showing restraint and compassion."

Family! Dolly Parton's song, Family, she wrote with Carl Perkins summed it up best: saying,

"*When it's family, They're a mirror of the worst and best in you.*"

Lalla, Papa, Maman, and Uncle Layes's, love and wrath influenced and shaped who I have become. In retrospect, nothing in my life happened the way I thought it would. But I wouldn't change my past. Everything I have experienced contributed to making me the person I am today. My life has been difficult, and incomprehensible at times, yet it gave me so much more than I could have imagined. I have no regrets. I was, and am, happy with where the events and circumstances of my life have led me. I carry the loving and guiding spirits of Lalla, Maman and Uncle Layes in me. I have no interest in dwelling on what might have been if Papa had said what he said about mother decades before. I have let go and let the past stay in the past. I have someplace else I need to be.

The day you came into the world was both the beginning of your individual life and the continuation of a family through you.

Finally, I made it to Mohammed's home.

"Hi, sis, we were waiting for you! Come in."

"I'm sorry. I wanted to be here earlier."

"Don't worry, you're here just in time. I just finished cooking. I hope you like what we prepared for you," his wife Sira said.

"You're a great cook, and I'm very hungry."

We sat together on the terrace. My three nieces came to say hello, but there was no sign of little Lalla.

"She's probably in their room playing with her dolls, Mohammed said. "She doesn't like it when it's hot outside."

We laughed.

"Are you serious?"

"Yes. She may be only two, but this little girl already knows what she likes and doesn't like. I'll go get her."

I was excited and nervous at the same time. Will she cry when I try to hold her? Will she run away?

Little Lalla appeared. She was wearing a red dress with matching sandals. My heart melted.

"Come say hello to your auntie," Mohammed said as they walked to me. "She claimed you the day you were born."

Mohammed let go of her hand. I opened my arms to the precious little girl who already had my heart. She walked to me, holding my gaze.

"Hi Lalla, how are you, babe?"

She held her arms up, waiting for me to pick her up. I held her tight and sat her on my lap. She rested her head on my chest. As my hand patted her cheek, I thought *one day, when it's just you and me, I will tell you with endless love and gratitude why I chose to name you Lalla. I will tell you about your namesake, the other Lalla—my mother, grandmother, and confidante who didn't hide herself from me.*

Lalla lifted her head up and my eyes met her big, beautiful, trusting eyes. She looked at me as if she had always known me. I sighed, relieved and happy. I pulled her closer and whispered in her ear, "My love, you are Lalla. Anna's Lalla. And Daba willing, I promise you, I will stay until I know you have found your way."

Lalla held my fingers. We smiled at each other. It was the beginning of our story—Anna's Lalla. But that tale will be for her to tell when and if, she ever decides to. As for me, I had become Lalla's Anna.

ACKNOWLEDGMENTS

$\mathcal{F}$irst and foremost, Daba, the Creator. I am grateful for where my life journey has taken me thus far. And Daba created nothing that can be compared to Love. I love my family. I am grateful to them, and all the events and circumstances that shaped me and made me the person I am today.

Thank you, Professor Cherif Keita.

Gratitude to Marva Allen, Patrice Samara, and the editorial team at Wordeee for your patience and all the work you did to make this labor of love a reality.

Love and gratitude to my Meaningful Conversations Community. I look forward to our every gathering. Thank you for your kind support, and for listening to my stories and laughing at my jokes.

Love and special gratitude to Maria and Jeremy Owens-Fajardo; Christian Jones; Tamara "Myra" Alicia; Marcus G. Monroe; Behzad D. Panah.

This book was a labor of love. Thank you to all who have offered words of encouragement when I needed it throughout the years. And special thanks to Lillian Harris, Millie Ortiz-Powell; Lee Rada and Paul Gates.

9 781959 811404